fall in love with

The Book of Mormon

LEARN HOW TO SLOW DOWN AND
FIND INSPIRATION ON EVERY SINGLE PAGE

THIS BOOK BELONGS TO

____

FOUNDER / AUTHOR
Shannon Foster

ARTIST
Heidi Carter

CREATIVE DESIGNER
Kelsie Monsen

EDITOR
Barbara Saylor

DESIGN EDITOR
Katie Lewis

PROJECT ASSISTANT
Allison McGrew

PRODUCTION MANAGER
Tyson Foster

THE RED HEADED HOSTESS

www.TheRedHeadedHostess.com

The Book of Mormon

a guidebook for learning

LEARNING TO SLOW DOWN AND FIND INSPIRATION
ON EVERY PAGE IN THE BOOK OF MORMON

www.TheRedHeadedHostess.com

@redheadedhostess

Table of Contents

If you would like to study the Book of Mormon in one year, follow the weekly schedule.

Hello,

I have spent over 20 years trying to help people fall in love with, and understand, the scriptures. When I am trying to help someone, I almost always ask this question:

"What are your obstacles to having consistent and impactful scripture study?"

The answers I receive are always the same: "I don't understand them," "I forget," "I start a habit and then stop," "I don't have time," etc.

*And this is always what I teach: **Slow down.***

It is so easy to read too fast, and if we do, we will miss a lot. When we slow down in our study, we give the Spirit time to instruct us, reveal to us, and increase our understanding. We can pause to consider what more might have happened in each story. We might then have time to consider what it might have been like for Lehi to walk away from his home for the last time, or wonder how Sariah chose what to take and what to leave, or to imagine what their last day at the synagogue might have been like.

As we slow down, those previous obstacles will begin to slip away.

This book is designed to help you slow down and record what you are learning. This book is a tool, but the real magic will come as you fill the pages.

Shannon Foster

FOUNDER OF THE RED HEADED HOSTESS

This Guidebook

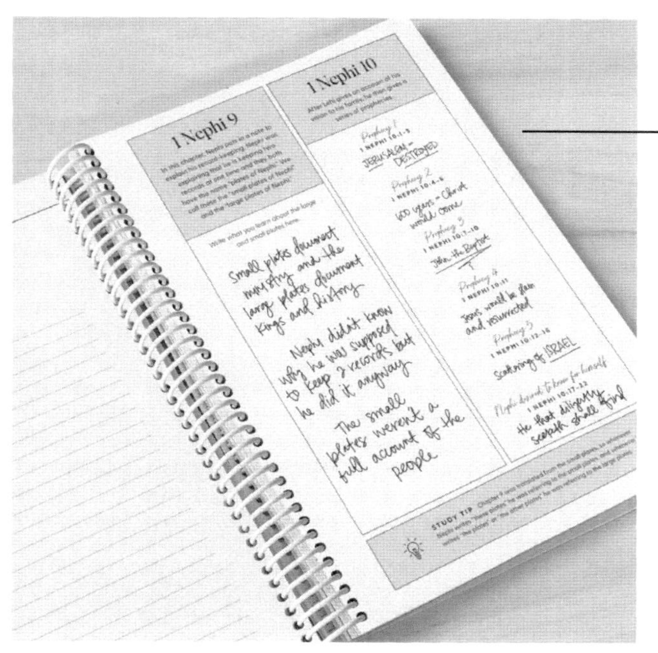

There is no right way to use this guidebook. Here are some ideas:

As you study each group of verses, just write an overview of what is happening. This will help you follow the storyline.

Or you can write a favorite phrase.

Or you can record your own thoughts, lessons you are learning, or things the Spirit is teaching you.

You can also draw pictures of what you are learning.

You can fill your pages with drawings or a mix of drawing and writing.

HOW TO USE THIS GUIDEBOOK

(continued)...

You can also use the book to make teaching notes for your family or class.

- *What are things you want to discuss?*

- *What are questions you can ask?*

Make notes of your ideas right in your book.

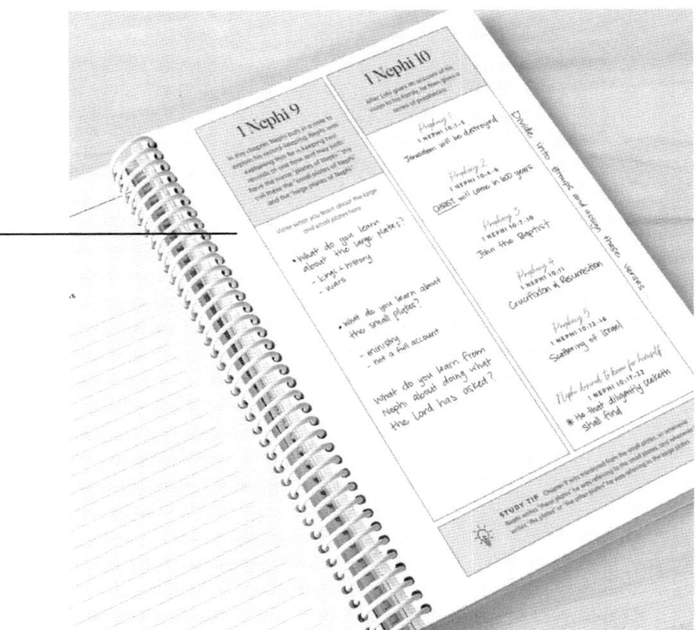

Whatever you do, do not try to be perfect.

It is okay if you write outside of the lines.

It is okay if your handwriting is messy.

Recording what you are learning is far more important than how the page looks.

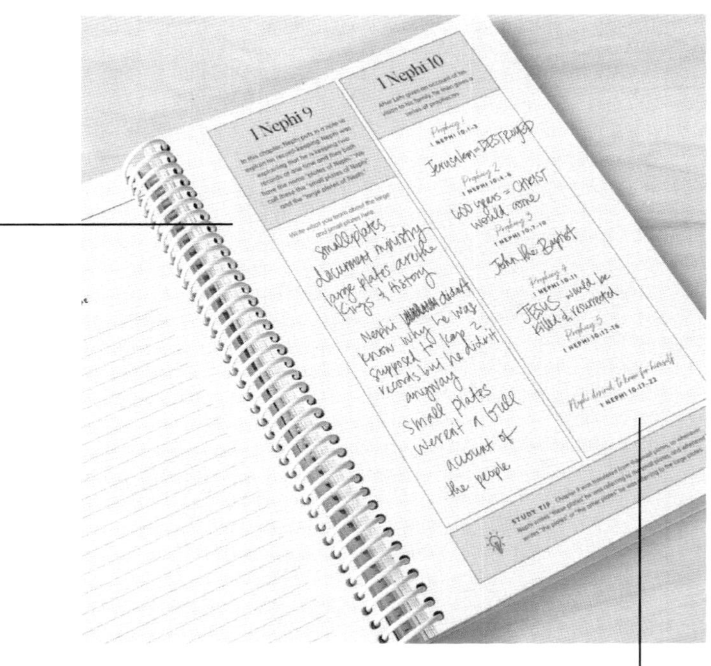

It is also okay to have empty boxes or pages.

Think of every note you make like a deposit in a bank. Every deposit matters.

Don't let a blank page stop you from making more deposits and receiving (and recording) more wisdom.

Page Titles

Page titles are quick statements you can write on the top of each page in your scriptures. It is a simple overview of what is happening on that page. These page titles can help you understand what is happening, find scriptures you may be searching for, and easily review a storyline.

Here are some examples of what your page titles can look like:

| 3 | *Lehi warns the people* | 1 NEPHI 1:17–2:4 |

unto his children, of which I shall not make a full account.

17 But I shall make an account of my proceedings in my days. Behold, I make an ᵃabridgment of the record of my ᵇfather, upon ᶜplates which I have made with mine own hands; wherefore, after I have abridged the record of my ᵈfather then will I

those whom he hath chosen, because of their faith, to make them mighty even unto the power of ᵈdeliverance.

CHAPTER 2

Lehi takes his family into the wilderness by the Red Sea—They leave their

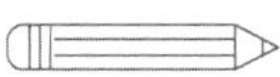

| 199 | *Alma the Younger and Sons of Mosiah persecute the Church* | MOSIAH 27:1–10 |

brethren; and they were also ᵃadmonished, every one by the word of God, according to his sins, or to the sins which he had committed, being commanded of God to ᵇpray without ceasing, and to give ᶜthanks in all things.

CHAPTER 27

ᶜneighbor as himself, ᵈlaboring with their own hands for their support.

5 Yea, and all their priests and teachers ᵃshould ᵇlabor with their own hands for their support, in all cases save it were in sickness, or in much want; and doing these things, they did abound in the ᶜgrace of God.

6 And there began to be much

Book of Mormon Page Titles

Study Tips

① Slow Down

You will understand more if you slow down as you study. Slowing down will give the Spirit more time to reveal truths to you and increase your understanding. This book is designed to help you slow down and record what you are learning.

② Pray Before

Before you study, pray for the Spirit to be with you as you study. The scriptures were written by inspiration so that is the best way to read them.

③ Have a Study Station

Do you have a special place to study? Having everything visible and easy to reach can help you consistently study. Set out some favorite pens, your scriptures, some sticky notes, a dictionary, and whatever else you might use as you study.

④ Set a Reminder

If you have a phone or digital watch, consider setting a reminder every day to study your scriptures. You could even come up with a fun phrase that will motivate you to prioritize making time for the Lord.

⑤ Share

You will regularly have incredible insights as you study. Consider sharing those with your family, a friend, or on social media. The Holy Ghost might even inspire you with a thought that some-one else needs to hear and prompt you to share what you have learned.

Introductory Pages

TITLE PAGE OF THE BOOK OF MORMON

The Title Page of the Book of Mormon is a translation from the last leaf of the plates. This is what Moroni wanted future readers to know about the purpose of the Book of Mormon. This Title Page is part of the sacred text of the Book of Mormon.

INTRODUCTION

The Introduction to the Book of Mormon was added to the Book of Mormon in 1981. It introduces the Book of Mormon to today's reader by describing the book and giving background information.

THE TESTIMONY OF THREE AND EIGHT WITNESSES

While Joseph Smith was in possession of the gold plates, the Lord appointed others to become witnesses of the plates. These are their testimonies of what they saw, heard, and touched.

THE TESTIMONY OF THE PROPHET JOSEPH SMITH

This is an excerpt from Joseph Smith History 1:29-60 and are Joseph Smith's own words about how the Book of Mormon came forth. He tells us of the angel Moroni directing him to the plates and instructing him. He also tells how he obtained the plates, the warnings he received, and the bitter persecution he endured.

A BRIEF EXPLANATION ABOUT THE BOOK OF MORMON

This offers a breakdown and explanation of the Book of Mormon, including:

· the four different plates used in the Book of Mormon

· the 15 books in the Book of Mormon

· what Mormon and Moroni abridged

· Moroni's role in bringing forth the Book of Mormon in the last days

· information about this edition of the Book of Mormon

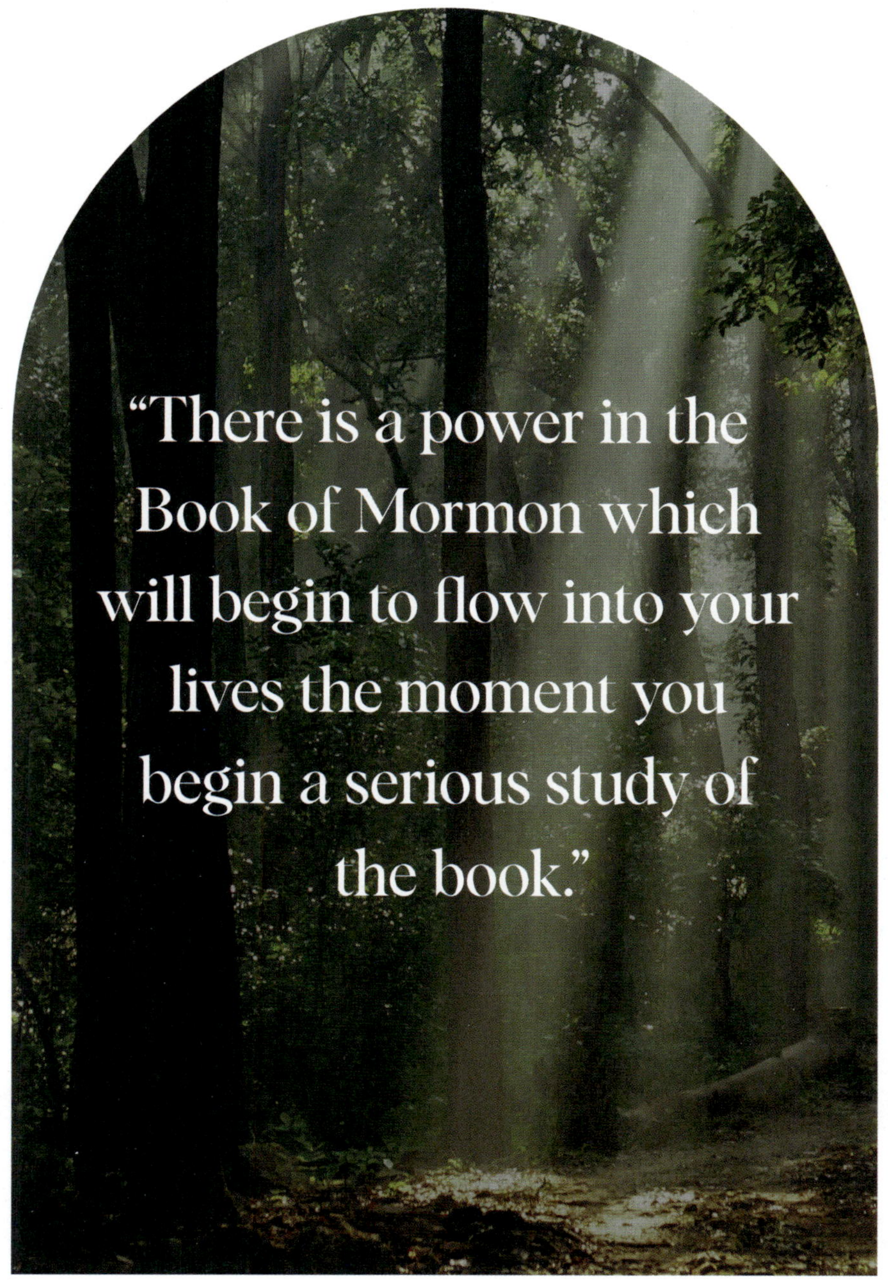

President Ezra Taft Benson

TEACHINGS OF THE PRESIDENTS OF THE CHURCH: EZRA TAFT BENSON, 141

The Title Page

"You can invite a friend to read the Book of Mormon. Explain that it is not a novel or a history book. It is another testament of Jesus Christ. Its very purpose is "to the convincing of the Jew and Gentile that Jesus is the Christ, the Eternal God, manifesting himself unto all nations."

PRESIDENT RUSSELL M. NELSON
October 2010 General Conference

Personal Insights

The Title Page of the Book of Mormon was written by Moroni. Therefore, these words are a direct translation from the last leaf of the plates.

What did Moroni want the world to know about the Book of Mormon? In the space below, write down some things that stand out to you.

The Introduction

OF THE BOOK OF MORMON

This is not an original part of the plates. This was added to the Book of Mormon in 1981 when President Spencer W. Kimball was prophet. What valuable information is given in this introduction? Write or doodle what you find below.

the testimony of the
Three Witnesses

the testimony of the
Eight Witnesses

Are there some things in the testimonies of the witnesses that someone could say without seeing and feeling the plates? Are there some things you could say? Put some of those phrases here:

The Prophet Joseph Smith

*Make notes, doodles, drawings, or timelines
in the space above as you read the
"Testimony of the Prophet Joseph Smith."*

A Brief Explanation
ABOUT THE BOOK OF MORMON

*As you learn about the plates that make
up the Book of Mormon, make notes,
doodles, or drawings around the diagram.*

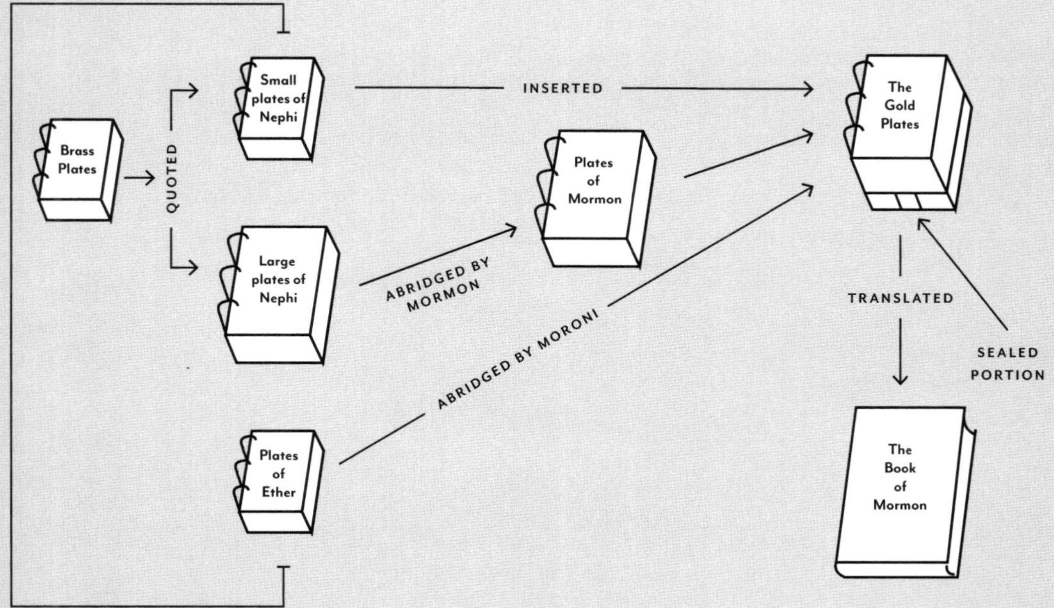

1 Nephi

- Nephi wrote his records in order to persuade men to come unto Jesus Christ (see 1 Nephi 6:4) and be saved.

- Nephi wrote these words after he arrived in the land of Nephi. Consider that in these first chapters, Nephi was looking back and recording things he felt were of most worth for us to know.

- Nephi had three audiences in his mind when he wrote his records.
    1. His father's descendants (2 Nephi 33:3).
    2. The covenant people in the last days (2 Nephi 33:13).
    3. All the people of the world (2 Nephi 33:13).

And it came to pass that after we had sailed for
the space of many days we did arrive at the
promised land; and we went forth upon the land,
and did pitch our tents; and we did call it the
promised land.

1 Nephi 18:23

1 NEPHI

Timeline

Here is 1 Nephi at-a-glance. The main stories are found in the timeline below. If you ever want to find a story in your scriptures, you can look at this page for help. You can add your own notes to this page as well.

1 NEPHI 1

- Lehi sees a vision
- Lehi prophesies to Jews about the destruction of Jerusalem
- Lehi mocked by the people and they seek his life

1 NEPHI 2

- Lehi and his family depart into the wilderness

1 NEPHI 3–4

- Nephi and brothers return to Jerusalem and get plates of brass from Laban

1 NEPHI 11–14

- Nephi sees a vision of tree of life, the life of Jesus Christ, the land of promise, the Apostasy, the Restoration, the Book of Mormon, and the building of Zion

1 NEPHI 8

- Lehi sees vision of tree of life

1 NEPHI 7

- Nephi and brothers again go to Jerusalem to invite Ishmael and his family into the wilderness
- Laman and Lemuel bind Nephi with cords in the wilderness, Nephi breaks bands

1 NEPHI 18

- Nephi and brethren build and finish ship
- Lehi and Ishmael's family sail towards promised land
- Nephi bound on ship and freed
- Arrival to promised land

1 NEPHI 16

- Laman, Lemuel, Sam, Nephi, and Zoram marry the daughters of Ishmael
- Lehi receives the Liahona
- Ishmael dies in the wilderness

1 NEPHI 19

- Nephi makes plates of ore and records history

People to Know

If you need a reminder of who is who, return to this page.

Lehi

Lehi was called to prophesy to the Jews. The Lord commanded him to take his family and depart to the wilderness where they were led to a new promised land.

Sariah

Sariah was Lehi's wife and mother to Laman, Lemuel, Sam, Nephi, Joseph, Jacob, and at least two daughters. Her testimony was strengthened in the wilderness (1 Nephi 5:8).

Laman

Laman was the oldest son to Lehi and Sariah. He planned to kill Nephi after Lehi's death. After arrival in the promised land, he became the leader of those who did not follow Nephi.

Lemuel

Lemuel was the second eldest son to Lehi and Sariah. He was like Laman in his rebellion against Lehi, Nephi, and the Lord.

Sam

Sam was the third son to Lehi and Sariah. After arrival to the promised land, he and his family followed Nephi.

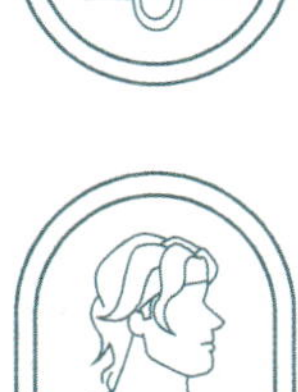

Nephi

Nephi was the fourth son to Lehi and Sariah. He had faith in whatever commandment the Lord gave him. He obtained the brass plates, built a ship, made a record, and led his people.

Laban

Laban was wicked. His fore-fathers had kept a record on plates of brass. Laban possessed these plates and kept them in his treasury.

Zoram

Zoram was a servant to Laban and had access to the brass plates in Laban's treasury. Zoram followed Nephi and Nephi's brothers into the wilderness. He followed Nephi when they arrived in the Promised Land. Zoramites descended from him.

Ishmael & Family

Ishmael was persuaded to follow Lehi's family into the wilderness along with his wife, two sons, and five daughters. The eldest daughter married Zoram and the other four married Lehi's sons.

Lehi's Daughters

Lehi and Sariah had at least two daughters (see 2 Nephi 5:6).

Jacob

Jacob was the son of Lehi and Sariah and he was born in the wilderness. He became a priest and teacher to his people and wrote the book of Jacob.

Joseph

Joseph was the youngest son of Lehi and Sariah. He was born in the wilderness and was named after a past prophet and a future prophet: Joseph of Egypt and Joseph Smith. Joseph became a priest and teacher.

1 Nephi 1-5

In these chapters

Lehi receives a vision // Lehi prophesies about the destruction of Jerusalem // Lehi takes his family into the wilderness // Laman, Lemuel, Sam, and Nephi return to Jerusalem for the plates of brass // The Lord guides Nephi in receiving plates of brass // Nephi, his brothers, and Zoram return to wilderness // Lehi searches plates of brass

What Was Happening in Lehi's Day

Lehi and his family lived in a time of extreme danger, turmoil, wickedness, and uncertainty. The Lord sent many prophets to warn the people that they needed to repent or else Jerusalem would be destroyed.

HERE ARE A FEW THINGS YOU MIGHT WANT TO KNOW ABOUT LEHI'S DAY.

Under the leadership of King Nebuchadnezzar, Babylon was the world power. Babylon had taken control of the kingdom of Judah before the events in 1 Nephi 1.

The Lord had sent many prophets to warn the Jews that if they did not repent then the city of Jerusalem would be destroyed. Jeremiah, Obadiah, Nahum, Habakkuk, and Zephaniah were all prophets during this time. This was also the time of Daniel, Shadrach, Meshach, Abed-Nego, and Ezekiel.

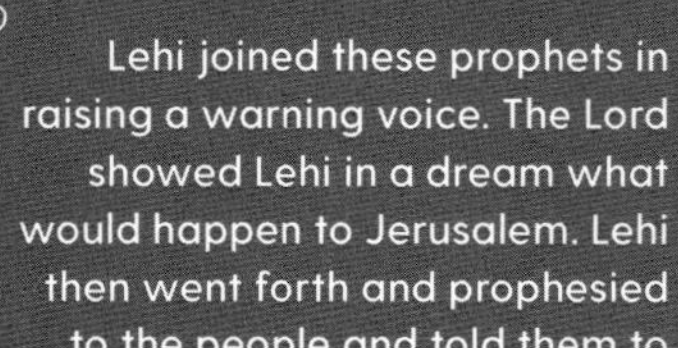

Lehi joined these prophets in raising a warning voice. The Lord showed Lehi in a dream what would happen to Jerusalem. Lehi then went forth and prophesied to the people and told them to repent.

Soon after Lehi and his family left Jerusalem for a new promised land, Babylon destroyed Jerusalem—just as the prophets had warned. The surviving Jews were carried off to Babylon. This would have been the fate of Lehi's family (or worse) if they had not followed the Lord's direction to leave Jerusalem.

1 Nephi 1

Draw or write what is happening and what the Spirit is teaching you.

1 NEPHI 1:1–3

1 NEPHI 1:4–6

1 NEPHI 1:7–15

1 NEPHI 1:16–17

1 NEPHI 1:18–20

STUDY TIP

In verse 20, Nephi gives the overarching theme that runs throughout the Book of Mormon and can be a theme in your own life. Even though Lehi was experiencing severe persecution,and even though his family was soon to be asked to do some really hard things, it was all to "make them mighty even unto the power of deliverance." All these things will be for their good. The Lord will make them mighty and deliver them.

What does your family need to be delivered from?

1 Nephi 2

Lehi's family had a choice to make: to stay or to go. Staying would be much easier, convenient, and familiar. They were landowners in Jerusalem. They had riches, gold, silver, and other precious things. How could they leave all of that? What would become of them if they left? What would become of them if they stayed?

1 NEPHI 2:1–7	1 NEPHI 2:8–15	1 NEPHI 2:16–24
Lehi's family leaves Jerusalem	*Laman and Lemuel murmur*	*Nephi receives a witness*

Nephi and the Brass Plates

Study 1 Nephi 3–5 and (starting at number 1) fill this story map with your notes. You could write what is happening, draw more pictures, and add your own thoughts and insights.

Watch This

After you study these chapters, watch this video and see what additional lessons you can learn.

Nephi Is Led by the Spirit to Obtain the Plates of Brass | 1 Nephi 3–5 | 25:45 minutes

1 NEPHI 3:23-26
7

Laban's Treasury
1 NEPHI 4:20-24
10

House of Laban
1 NEPHI 3:11-13
4

1 NEPHI 4:5-19
9

1 NEPHI 4:25-37
11

1 NEPHI 3:14-21
5

1 NEPHI 3:27-4:4
8

1 NEPHI 3:10
3

House of Lehi
1 NEPHI 3:22
6

1 NEPHI 4:38
12

1 NEPHI 3:9
2

1 NEPHI 5:1-9
13

The Red Sea

1 NEPHI 3:1-8
1

START HERE

As you study each scripture, draw a line connecting the dots in numerical order

The Brass Plates
1 NEPHI 5:10-22

What was upon these plates that was so important? List what you find here.

"And it came to pass that I, Nephi, said unto my father: I will go and do the things which the Lord hath commanded, for I know that the Lord giveth no commandments unto the children of men, save he shall prepare a way for them that they may accomplish the thing which he commandeth them."

Keep your own record side-by-side with these great prophets testifying of these important doctrines and principles.

TIMES I HAVE MOVED FORWARD WITH FAITH AND THE LORD STRENGTHENED ME...

1 Nephi 6–10

In these chapters

Nephi explains his purpose in writing   //   Laman, Lemuel, Sam, and Nephi return to Jerusalem to invite Ishmael and his family to join them in the wilderness   //   Nephi bound with cords   //   Lehi's vision of the tree of life   //   Nephi explains his two sets of records   //   Lehi prophesies

Lehi and his family lived at the same place in the wilderness by the Red Sea until chapter 16, which is when they received the Liahona to guide them further into the wilderness and towards their promised land.

Until then, the Lord directed, tutored, and guided them in ways that would prepare them for what was yet coming.

As Lehi's and Ishmael's families prepared to travel further toward the promised land, the Lord gave Lehi a vision or a dream. Lehi showed the heart of a father in 1 Nephi 8:3-4. He had seen a vision with angels, trees, rivers, and buildings in the air. But he did not merely say, "I saw a building in the air and this tree with the most delicious fruit ..." Instead, he shared that this vision gave him joy for Nephi and Sam and fear for Laman and Lemuel. His focus was on his sons and what he learned about them in this dream.

600 B.C. – 592 B.C.

There is no clear way to determine how long Lehi and the others were in the wilderness, but the footnotes give us an approximate 8-year period of being sometime between 600 B.C. and 592 B.C. Babylon will carry out the destruction of Jerusalem in 589 B.C., so this tragic event was very close. They were leaving just in time. Imagine the wickedness in Jerusalem at this point.

1 Nephi 6

📖 Overview + Question

Nephi inserted his own words about the plates of brass and the record he was keeping. What does he teach you about what he was writing and why he was doing so?

1 Nephi 7

Draw or write what was happening and what the Spirit is teaching you.

1–5 | **The next command**	
6–7 | **The rebellion**	
8–15 | **Nephi's testimony**	
16–18 | **Nephi bursts bands**	
19–22 | **Nephi forgives**	

Further Learning

Elder Bednar gave a devotional at BYU Idaho on October 23, 2001. In this devotional, he used this example of Nephi breaking free from these bands. This may become one of your favorite talks. To hear his story of Nephi, start listening at 13:10.

Lehi's Dream

*Draw or write what was happening and
what the Spirit is teaching you.*

1 NEPHI 8:1

Life in the wilderness

1 NEPHI 8:2-4

Lehi had seen a vision

1 NEPHI 8:5-9

The beginning of the dream

Visualizing Lehi's Dream

Look up the scriptures and write notes all over this page as you learn about Lehi's dream / vision.

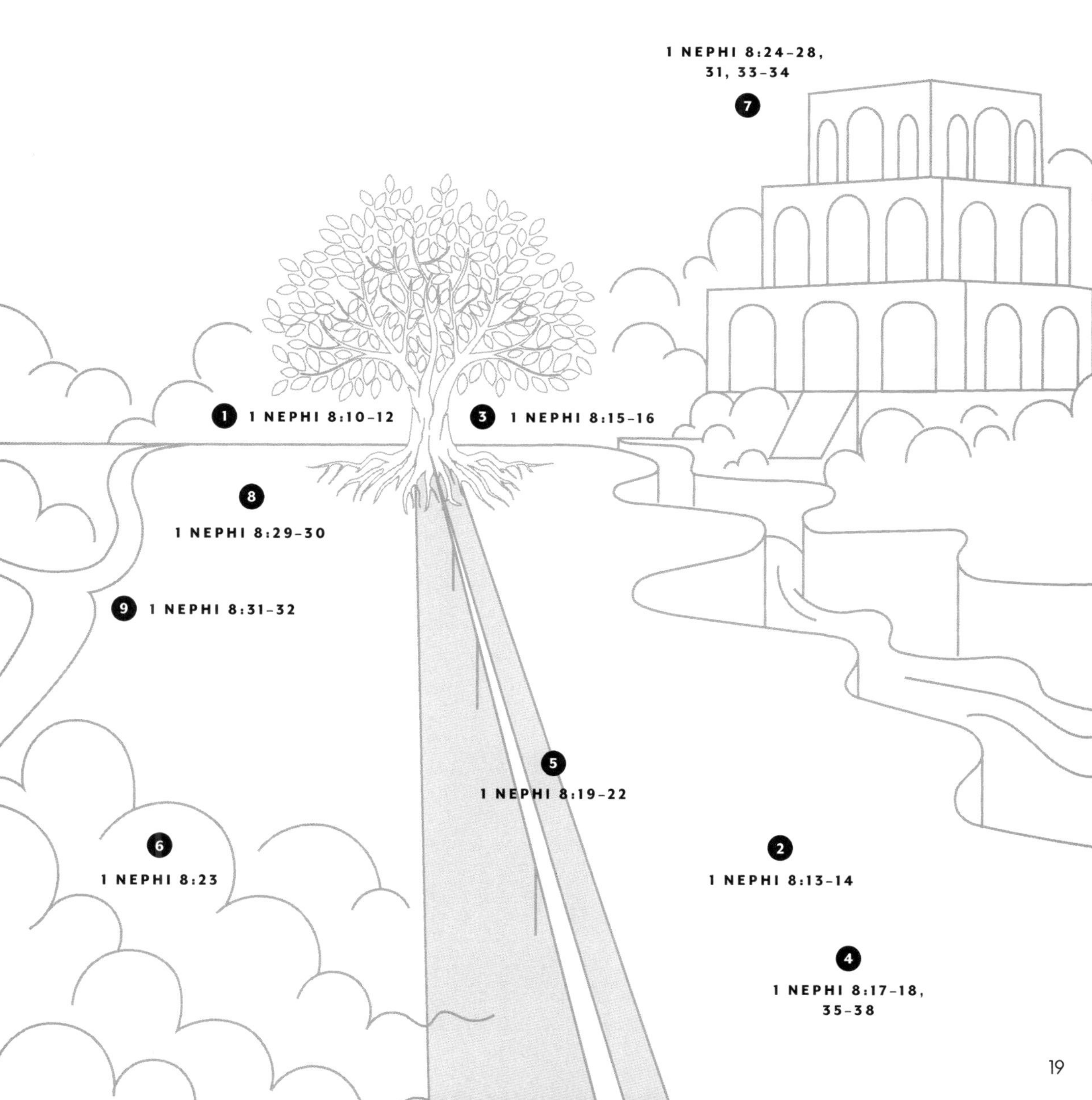

Keep your own record side-by-side with these great prophets
testifying of these important doctrines and principles.

TRUTHS FROM THE TREE OF LIFE VISION I HOPE MY CHILDREN RECOGNIZE...

1 Nephi 9

In this chapter, Nephi puts in a note to explain his record-keeping. Nephi was explaining that he is keeping two records at one time and they both have the name "plates of Nephi." We call these the "small plates of Nephi" and the "large plates of Nephi."

Write what you learn about the large and small plates here.

1 Nephi 10

After Lehi gives an account of his vision to his family, he then gives a series of prophecies.

Prophecy 1
1 NEPHI 10:1–3

Prophecy 2
1 NEPHI 10:4–6

Prophecy 3
1 NEPHI 10:7–10

Prophecy 4
1 NEPHI 10:11

Prophecy 5
1 NEPHI 10:12–16

Nephi desired to know for himself
1 NEPHI 10:17–22

STUDY TIP Chapter 9 was translated from the small plates, so whenever Nephi writes "these plates" he was referring to the small plates, and whenever he writes "the plates" or "the other plates" he was referring to the large plates.

1 Nephi 11-15

In these chapters

Nephi receives vision   //   Nephi sees tree of life   //   Nephi sees Jesus' birth, ministry, and Crucifixion   //   Nephi sees his descendants and their downfall   //   Nephi sees the Apostasy, Restoration, and last days

a glimpse at

Nephi's Vision

1 NEPHI 11:1-6

Nephi ponders and sees the Spirit of the Lord

1 NEPHI 11:7-12

Nephi sees the tree and desires to know what it means

1 NEPHI 11:13-36

Nephi sees Jesus' birth, ministry, and Crucifixion

1 NEPHI 12:1-23

Nephi sees his descendants. He sees the history of Nephites and Lamanites

1 NEPHI 13-14

Nephi sees the last days

The Book of Mormon begins with a boy (Nephi) who desires to know truth for himself. As he acts on that desire, mysteries are unfolded to him and he accomplishes such great things that we are still talking about him.

At the end of the Book of Mormon, we are promised that we can know the truth for ourselves (see Moroni 10:5). Then the Book of Mormon was given to and translated by Joseph Smith, who as a boy desired to know the truth for himself. It is the same teaching and the same promises, by different men living hundreds of years apart.

1 Nephi 11

Nephi's Vision

Nephi sees Jesus' birth, ministry, and Crucifixion. Draw or write what was happening and what the Spirit is teaching you.

1 NEPHI 11:1–6
Nephi Sees the Spirit of the Lord

1 NEPHI 11:7–12
Nephi Sees the Tree of Life

1 NEPHI 11:13–20
Birth of Jesus Christ

1 NEPHI 11:21–23
Meaning of the Fruit on the Tree of Life

1 NEPHI 11:24–31
Jesus' Ministry

1 NEPHI 11:32–33
Jesus Is Slain

1 NEPHI 11:34–36
Apostles Persecuted | Meaning of the Great and Spacious Building

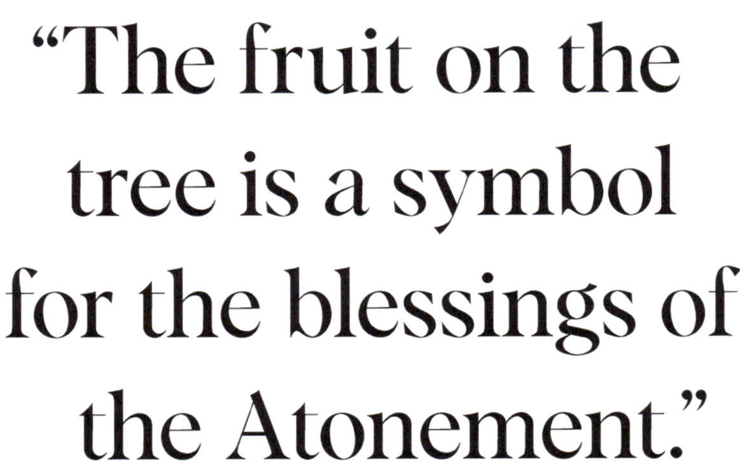

"The fruit on the tree is a symbol for the blessings of the Atonement."

Elder David A. Bednar

OCTOBER 2011 GENERAL CONFERENCE

1 Nephi 8:30 says that those who continually held fast to the rod of iron "came forth and fell down and partook of the fruit of the tree."

HOW ARE YOU PARTAKING OF THE BLESSINGS OF THE ATONEMENT?

Nephi's Vision

After Nephi saw the ministry of Jesus Christ, he was then shown the future of his descendants. He sees the promised land and the multitude of people that will inhabit it, the wars that will occur, and the cities that will be built up until the time period of 3 Nephi. He was seeing how the symbols in Lehi's vision will apply to his future people.

1 NEPHI 12:1–5	**1 NEPHI 12:6–10**	**1 NEPHI 12:11–14**
Nephi's sees his future descendants upon the land of promise	*Nephi sees Jesus come to his descendants*	*Nephi sees Zion among his descendants*

1 NEPHI 12:15–17	**1 NEPHI 12:18**	**1 NEPHI 12:19–21**
The meaning of the mists of darkness and the river	*The meaning of the great gulf and the great and spacious building*	*Nephites are destroyed*

1 NEPHI 12:22–23

Lamanites dwindle in unbelief

Nephi saw how the symbols from Lehi's dream would apply to his descendants. How do the symbols in Lehi's dream apply to your generation, your family, and your life?

Nephi's Vision

The vision continues on after the Nephites have been destroyed and the Lamanites live in apostasy in the promised land. Nephi then sees "many nations and kingdoms" and among them he sees a great church. Nephi sees the Apostasy, Restoration, and last days.

Draw, doodle, or write what was happening and what the Spirit is teaching you.

1 Nephi 13:1-3

Nephi sees kingdoms of the world

1 Nephi 13:4–9

Nephi sees a great church form

1 Nephi 13:10–12

Nephi sees Columbus discovering America

1 Nephi 13:13

Many come to America seeking freedom

1 Nephi 13:14–15

Lamanites scattered

1 Nephi 13:16–19

Wars seeking independence

1 Nephi 13:20–34

Plain and precious truths removed from the Bible

1 Nephi 13:35–42

The Gentiles will receive Bible and Book of Mormon in last days

1 Nephi 14:1–6

Promises and warning to Gentiles in last days

1 Nephi 14:7

A marvelous work in the last days

1 Nephi 14:8–17

Latter-day conflict between the Lord's Church and the church of the devil

1 Nephi 14:18–30

The Apostle John will write about the rest of the vision Nephi saw

Nephi Teaches His Brothers

After the vision was complete, Nephi went back to his family and found that his brothers were arguing about what Lehi saw in his dream. Nephi had asked God for understanding, and what he received was a vision of God's works upon the earth.

Laman and Lemuel, on the other hand, were still in the same confused state as they were before. Nephi now knew that the stubbornness of his brothers will be more far-reaching than just their family. Nephi's distress is shown in verses 4–5 where Nephi writes that he was overcome and had to receive strength before he could talk with his brothers.

1–3
What Nephi discovered happening after his vision

4–5
How Nephi felt

6–7
Why Nephi's brothers were arguing

8–9
What Nephi asked and how they responded

10–11
How to receive personal revelation

12–18
The gathering of Israel in the last days is like an olive tree

19–20
The Jews will be restored in the last days

21–25
Nephi explains the meaning of the iron rod

26–30
Nephi explains the river of water

31–36
Nephi explains the justice of God/Hell

1 Nephi 16–22

In these chapters

Lehi's sons marry Ishmael's daughters // Lehi receives the Liahona // Nephi's broken bow // Arrival to the land Bountiful // Nephi commanded to build a ship // Nephi filled with God's power // Ship is complete // Sailing towards the promised land // Nephi bound on ship // Arrival to promised land // Nephi makes plates

In 1 Nephi 16, Lehi received direction from the Lord that it was time to move on. They would have set up living quarters and would have discovered how to best live in that part of the wilderness, so moving on would be difficult for them; but doing the easy thing is not how we make it to our promised lands.

So the Lord gave them a new command and then will give them a new tool to help them keep that command.

Lehi's and Ishmael's families were still by the River Laman (see verse 12). This is the original place they had come to in 1 Nephi 2. They had come to this place, and here they were to accomplish certain commandments of the Lord (including getting the brass plates and getting married). Then once those things were accomplished, it was time to move on to the next new place and the next new commands.

"Just as Lehi was blessed in ancient times, each of us in this day has been given a spiritual compass that can direct and instruct us during our mortal journey. The Holy Ghost was conferred upon you and me as we came out of the world and into the Savior's Church through baptism and confirmation ... what ye should do' (2 Nephi 32:5)."

ELDER DAVID A. BEDNAR
April 2006 General Conference

1 Nephi 16-17

Draw or write what is happening and what the Spirit is teaching you.

Watch This

After you study these chapters, watch this video and see what additional lessons you can learn.

The Lord Commands Nephi to Build a Ship
1 Nephi 17-18 | 15:18 minutes

1 NEPHI 16:1-6	1 NEPHI 16:7-10	1 NEPHI 16:11-17
Nephi pleads with brothers	The Lord tells them to continue traveling	Following the Liahona in the wilderness

1 NEPHI 16:18-25	1 NEPHI 16:26-32	1 NEPHI 16:33-39
Nephi breaks his bow	The Liahona	Ishmael dies

1 NEPHI 17:1-3	1 NEPHI 17:4-6	1 NEPHI 17:7-16
What truths and principles can you find in these verses?	Write or doodle about where the Lord led them next.	Write about the next command the Lord gave Nephi.

1 NEPHI 17:17-22	1 NEPHI 17:23-55
Laman and Lemuel's beliefs	Nephi's response

1 Nephi 18–19

Draw or write what is happening and what the Spirit is teaching you.

Watch This

After you study these chapters, watch this video and see what additional lessons you can learn.

Lehi's Family Sails to the Promised Land
1 Nephi 18 | 12:48 minutes

---

1 Nephi 18:1–4

How Nephi knew how to build the ship

1 Nephi 18:5–8

Time to sail towards new promised land

1 Nephi 18:9–13

Laman and Lemuel bind Nephi

1 Nephi 18:14–16

Nephi praises the Lord

1 Nephi 18:17–21

Nephi freed

1 Nephi 18:22–25

Arrival to promised land

1 Nephi 19:1–6

Nephi makes plates

1 Nephi 19:7–9

Jesus will come in 600 years

1 Nephi 19:10–12

Jesus will be crucified

1 Nephi 19:13–17

Future of Jews/Gathering of Israel

1 Nephi 19:18–24

Nephi teaches brothers

What is the house of Israel?

"Because of their faith and obedience in the premortal life, thousands upon thousands of the sons and daughters of God were foreordained to be members of the house of Israel in mortality. This foreordination carries with it nobility as well as great responsibility. As members of the house of Israel, we are princes and princesses, members of a royal covenant family commissioned to be the 'salt of the earth' (Matthew 5:13) and the 'light of the world' (Matthew 5:14) to take the fulness of the gospel of Jesus Christ 'to every nation, kindred, tongue, and people' (D&C 77:8)."

Doctrines of the Gospel Student Manual, Chapter 21

Read This

12 Facts about the Gathering of Israel
July 2019 New Era

1 Nephi 20

Isaiah teaches how Israel has treated the Lord. Nephi knew this because he witnessed it in Jerusalem before his family left.

Isaiah writes poetically. It's OK if you don't understand everything you read. Start by writing a phrase or teaching next to each group of verses that teaches you something about the house of Israel in the past.

1 Nephi 21

In the last chapter, Isaiah was speaking to the Jews of his day. Now in this chapter, he emphasizes that Christ will not forget His covenant people.

Continue writing a phrase or teaching next to each group of verses that teaches you something about the house of Israel in the future.

1 Nephi 22

Nephi then teaches his brothers what Isaiah's prophecies mean.

Fill this space with things you learn about Israel and events in the last days.

2 Nephi

- Nephi's purpose was to invite us to come unto Christ, so Nephi included many things that will help us learn of Christ and come unto Him. As Nephi compiled his record, he included many teachings from other wise men. Notice how much of 2 Nephi is not actually Nephi's own words:

2 Nephi 1–3 . . . . Lehi's last teachings

2 Nephi 6–10 . . . . Jacob's teachings

2 Nephi 12–24 . . . . Nephi quotes Isaiah

2 Nephi 27 . . . . Nephi quotes Isaiah

Wherefore, men are free according to the flesh;
and all things are given them which are expedient
unto man. And they are free to choose liberty and
eternal life, through the great Mediator of all men,
or to choose captivity and death, according to the
captivity and power of the devil; for he seeketh
that all men might be miserable like unto himself.

2 Nephi 2:27

2 NEPHI 1–33

Timeline

Here is 2 Nephi at-a-glance. The main stories are found in the timeline below. If you ever want to find a story in your scriptures, you can look at this page for help. You can add your own notes to this page as well.

2 NEPHI 1–4

- Lehi prophesies and teaches his posterity
- Lehi dies

2 NEPHI 5

- Nephi's brothers plan to slay him
- The Nephites separate themselves from the Lamanites

2 NEPHI 11–24

- Nephi quotes Isaiah's prophecies about the scattering and gathering of Israel, Jesus Christ, and the Second Coming

2 NEPHI 6–10

- Jacob teaches about the Jews
- Jacob quotes Isaiah's teachings about Jesus Christ and the gathering of Israel in the last days
- Jacob teaches about the Atonement of Jesus Christ

2 NEPHI 25–30

- Nephi prophesies of the Savior's death and visit to the Nephites following His Resurrection
- Nephi prophesies about the Book of Mormon

2 NEPHI 31–33

- Nephi invites us to follow Christ and feast upon His words

People and Places to Know

If you need a reminder of who is who, return to this page.

Nephi

Nephi became a great prophet. He guided the Nephites as they separated from the Lamanites. He loved the writings of Isaiah and bore powerful testimony of Jesus Christ.

Land of Nephi

This is the land where the Nephites went when they separated from the Lamanites (2 Nephi 5:5-8). It was later inhabited by the Lamanites.

Promised Land

When the Lord promises a land as an inheritance to His people, that is called a promised land. In the Book of Mormon, the Lord promised a land to Lehi and his descendants. That promised land is upon the Americas.

Jacob

Jacob was a younger brother to Nephi. Jacob never knew Jerusalem because he was born in the wilderness. He became a priest and a teacher to the people and some of his sermons are recorded in 2 Nephi 6-10.

Nephites

The Nephites were the group that separated themselves from the Lamanites. Many of them were descendants of Nephi.

Isaiah

Isaiah is an Old Testament prophet whose prophecies were recorded on the brass plates. Nephi and Jacob read Isaiah's prophecies and quoted him extensively.

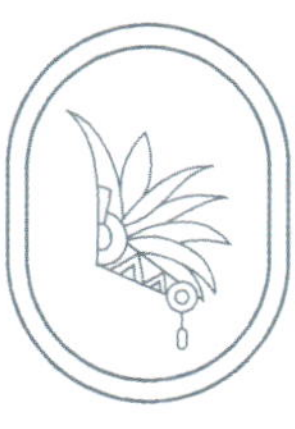

Lamanites

The Lamanites were a group who rejected the gospel and felt they had been wronged by Nephi and his descendants. Many were descendants of Laman.

2 Nephi 1-2

In these chapters

Lehi counsels Laman, Lemuel, Sam, and sons of Ishmael   //
Lehi counsels Zoram   //   Lehi teaches Jacob

Lehi is now close to death. In 1 Nephi 1, Lehi speaks to Laman, Lemuel, Sam, and the sons of Ishmael. In these verses, we can see a father trying to help his sons see the Lord's hand in their lives. We learn that Lehi has had a vision and knows that Jerusalem was now destroyed. Not only has the Lord spared their lives, but he has led them to a special land that has a very specific purpose.

Before they ever built the ship and traveled to the land, Laman and Lemuel called their father a visionary man and doubted that the land he spoke of existed, and they just wanted to go back to Jerusalem. But now they have built a ship, crossed the ocean, and were living upon this land. Now Lehi will teach them about the land they have been guided to, and Lehi will help them understand that this land requires certain things of its inhabitants.

"This America is no ordinary country. It is a choice land, 'choice above all other lands' (1 Nephi 2:20). It has a tragic and bloody past, but a glorious and peaceful future if its inhabitants really learn to serve their God.

"If we would but believe the prophets! For they have warned that if the 'inhabitants of this land are ever brought down into captivity and enslaved, it shall be because of iniquity; for if iniquity shall abound cursed shall be the land' (See 2 Ne 1:7)."

PRESIDENT SPENCER W. KIMBALL
October 1961 Conference Report

2 Nephi 1

Write or draw what you learn in each group of verses.

2 NEPHI 1:1–4

Lehi speaks to Laman, Lemuel, Sam, and the sons of Ishmael

2 NEPHI 1:5–12

What the Lord requires of this promised land

2 NEPHI 1:13–15

Lehi seeks to help his sons see what they could have

2 NEPHI 1:16–23

Lehi warns his sons of the eternal consequences of their choices

2 NEPHI 1:24–29

Lehi speaks of Nephi's righteous leadership

2 NEPHI 1:30–32

Lehi speaks to Zoram

Lehi Talks to Jacob

In 2 Nephi 2, Lehi speaks to his son Jacob and this will be a very different teaching moment. Jacob was the fifth son of Lehi and Sariah and the oldest of the two sons born after they left Jerusalem; therefore, he has only known a nomadic life.

2 Nephi 2:1–4

What you learn about Jacob

2 Nephi 2:5–10

Jesus is the only way

2 Nephi 2:11–13

Why is opposition necessary?

2 Nephi 2:14–16

Adam was to act

2 Nephi 2:17–18

Who is Satan and what did he do?

2 Nephi 2:19–21

A state of probation (trial, examination)

2 Nephi 2:22–25

The Fall was part of God's plan

2 Nephi 2:26

Why we need the Atonement of Jesus Christ

2 Nephi 2:27–30

We are free to choose

The Fall is an integral part of Heavenly Father's plan of salvation (see 2 Nephi 2:15–16; 9:6). It has a twofold direction—downward yet forward. In addition to introducing physical and spiritual death, it gave us the opportunity to be born on the earth and to learn and progress.

GOSPEL TOPICS: FALL OF ADAM AND EVE

"Wherefore, men are free according to the flesh; and all things are given them which are expedient unto man. And they are free to choose liberty and eternal life, through the great Mediator of all men, or to choose captivity and death, according to the captivity and power of the devil; for he seeketh that all men might be miserable like unto himself."

Keep your own record side-by-side with these great prophets testifying of these important doctrines and principles.

WHAT ARE SOME CHOICES IN YOUR LIFE YOU ARE GRATEFUL YOU MADE? WHY?

2 Nephi 3–5

In these chapters

Lehi teaches Joseph about Joseph of Egypt and Joseph Smith // Lehi dies // Nephi trusts in the Lord // Laman and Lemuel plan to slay Nephi // Nephites separate from the Lamanites

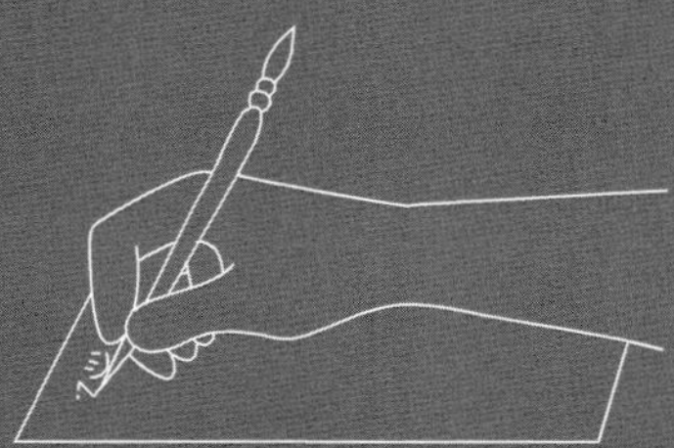

One constant message throughout 1 Nephi is how hard Nephi tried to reach his brothers. As he wrote upon the small plates, Nephi included many of the times he tried to help them return to the Lord. For many years, Laman and Lemuel were reachable. But by 2 Nephi 5, Lehi was no longer there and Nephi was officially the leader among them. This was the final straw.

Before Lehi died, he spoke to his youngest son, Joseph. Lehi taught Joseph about two other Josephs: Joseph of Egypt (who was their ancestor), and a future Joseph, Joseph Smith (whom God had a great work for).

After Nephi led those who would follow him away, they built a new home. There they "lived after the manner of happiness" (2 Nephi 5:27).

"Since first making my personal discovery about living after the "manner of happiness," I have thought deeply about the principles involved and about how timeless and universal they are. The same patterns and elements of daily life that enabled Nephi and his people to be happy 560 years before Christ work equally well today."

ELDER MARLIN K. JENSEN

Ensign, December 2002, 61

2 Nephi 3

Lehi taught Joseph about two other Josephs: Joseph of Egypt (who were their ancestor) and a future Joseph, Joseph Smith. Beginning in verse 5, Lehi quotes Joseph of Egypt as he prophesied of Joseph Smith.

In the boxes below, write or draw what you learn about each of the Josephs in 2 Nephi 3.

JOSEPH (LEHI'S SON)

JOSEPH OF EGYPT

JOSEPH SMITH

Watch this!

After you study these chapters, watch this video and see what additional lessons you can learn.

Lehi Blesses Joseph | 2 Nephi 3:3–15 | 1:54 minutes

Lehi's Last Words

This chapter contains Lehi's last words.

Write or draw what he taught or what happened in the spaces below.

2 NEPHI 4:1–7

Lehi to the children of Laman

2 NEPHI 4:8–10

Lehi to the children of Lemuel

2 NEPHI 4:11

Lehi to Sam

2 NEPHI 4:12–14

Lehi's death

Nephi's Psalm

2 NEPHI 4:15-35

After Lehi's death, Nephi put his trust in the Lord and gloried in God. Many people call these verses "Nephi's Psalm" or "The Psalm of Nephi."

Write or draw some of your favorite phrases from this psalm. You could also write your own phrases.

The Nephites and Lamanites Separate

Follow the numbers and write or draw what you learn in each group of verses.

Watch This

After you study these chapters, watch this video and see what additional lessons you can learn.

The Nephites Separate from the Lamanites | 2 Nephi 5 | 25:42 minutes

❶ 2 Nephi 5:1–4

What was the situation now among Nephi, Laman, and Lemuel?

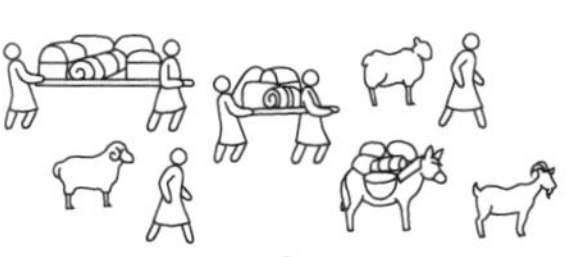

❷ 2 Nephi 5:5–8

What did the Lord direct Nephi to do? Who went with him?

❸ 2 Nephi 5:9–19, 26–28

Where did the Nephites go? What kind of a city and civilization did they build and create?

❹ 2 Nephi 5:20–25

What do you learn about the Lamanites?

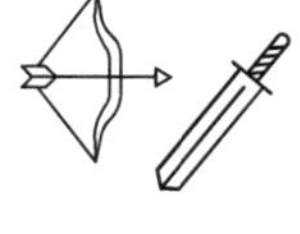

❺ 2 Nephi 5:29–34

What do you learn about the plates Nephi made and the state of the Nephites and Lamanites?

2 Nephi 6–10

In these chapters

Jacob teaches the Nephites

In 2 Nephi 5, we learned that both Jacob and Joseph were set apart as priests and teachers over the land, and in these chapters we see how diligently Jacob fulfilled this calling.

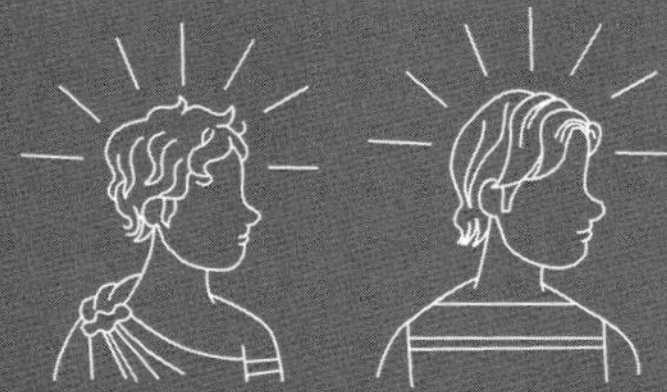

Jacob's sermon to the people is recorded in 2 Nephi 6-10. In chapters 6-8, he quoted Isaiah and taught about how Christ will save/restore the house of Israel. Then in chapter 9, Jacob gives a not-to-be-missed sermon about why we need the Atonement of Jesus Christ and why we need to be saved.

Jacob loved the prophecies of Isaiah, and he will quote these prophecies to the Nephites so they "may learn and glorify the name of [their] God."

So all of these chapters together teach how Jesus saves. He will save the house of Israel, and He will save you.

Isaiah was not an ancient prophet to Nephi and Jacob. Isaiah was a prophet until around 700 B.C., which was just 100 years before Nephi left Jerusalem. Therefore, Isaiah's prophecies were very relevant to the Nephites including Isaiah's prophecies of the scattering of Israel (which they were a part of), the coming of the Messiah, and the eventual gathering of Israel (which you are a part of).

2 Nephi 6

Write or draw what you learn in each group of verses.

In verses 6 and 7, Jacob quotes what we know as Isaiah 49:22-23. Isaiah wrote of a future time when the Lord will use the Gentiles to raise up His standard which is the restored Gospel of Jesus Christ. These Gentiles will gather Israel, and the visual is so beautiful, for they will bring them in their arms and upon their shoulders.

2 NEPHI 6:1-3

What were Jacob's desires?

2 NEPHI 6:4-5

Why does Jacob want to read to them the words of Isaiah?

2 NEPHI 6:6-7

What does Isaiah teach about the gathering of Israel?

2 NEPHI 6:8-11

What does Jacob teach about what had happened to the Jews in Jerusalem?

2 NEPHI 6:12-18

Jacob teaches that the gathering of Israel in the last days will be unstoppable. What do you learn?

What is a Gentile?

THE WORD "GENTILE" CAN MEAN DIFFERENT THINGS.

It can mean someone who is not of the lineage of Israel (Jacob).

However, in the last days, "Gentiles" can be people who are of the house of Israel but they do not descend directly from the Jews. For example, Joseph Smith was considered a Gentile because he was not a Jew. Yet he was of the house of Israel through the lineage of Joseph of Egypt.

2 Nephi 7

In this chapter, Jacob quotes Isaiah 50 and this is a Messianic chapter which means that it teaches of the coming Messiah.

HELPFUL TIPS	WHAT I LEARNED
2 Nephi 7:1 There are several questions in verse 1 that are directed toward the house of Israel. They are estranged from the Lord and He is asking them, "Who left?" He is pointing out that they left Him.	
2 Nephi 7:2–3 This imagery shows Christ coming to His people but they are not there; they are not waiting for Him. They are busy with other things and other Gods.	
2 Nephi 7:4–11 These are Messianic verses, meaning that they prophesy about Jesus Christ.	

2 Nephi 8

In this chapter, Jacob quotes Isaiah 51 and the beginning of Isaiah 52. These prophecies are about the gathering of Israel and Zion in the last days.

HELPFUL TIPS	WHAT I LEARNED
2 Nephi 8:1–5 In verses 1-2, the Lord asks Israel to remember the covenant Abraham and Sarah made (Israel is a part of that covenant). Then verses 3-5 explain what Zion will be like. And verses 6-8 teach that the only thing that is sure is Christ's salvation.	
2 Nephi 8:6–16 "Rahab" can represent any enemy that comes against Israel. These verses teach that Israel should not be afraid of what man can do for he is merely "made like unto grass," which is fragile.	
2 Nephi 8:17–25 Jerusalem has suffered greatly during earth's history, but the Lord will come and fight the battles for the Jews. He will take the cup they have had to drink (symbolic of their suffering), and make their enemies drink it.	

Why the Atonement of Jesus Christ Is Necessary

The Bible teaches us when and where the Atonement of Jesus Christ took place, but here in 2 Nephi 9, Jacob explained WHY the Atonement was necessary, and what would happen if there had been no Atonement.

Write or draw what you learn.

Watch This

After you study these chapters, watch this video and see what additional lessons you can learn.

Jacob Teaches of the Atonement of Jesus Christ | 2 Nephi 6–10
7:52 minutes

2 NEPHI 9:1–3	2 NEPHI 9:4–6	2 NEPHI 9:7
The Jews will be gathered back into the house of Israel	*Jacob's testimony that Jesus will fulfill the Atonement*	*What would happen to our bodies if there were no Atonement* *"Corruption = bodies*

2 NEPHI 9:8–9	2 NEPHI 9:10–15	2 NEPHI 9:16–26
What would happen to our spirits if there were no Atonement	*But there was an Atonement, so we will be delivered*	*The eternal nature of our choices*

2 NEPHI 9:27–38	2 NEPHI 9:39–44	2 NEPHI 9:45–54
Warnings	*What to remember* *"Jacob says "remember" 5 times.*	*Jacob's invitation*

Israel Will Be Gathered

Jacob, no longer quoting Isaiah, addresses the redemption of their future children. He knows what will ultimately become of the Nephites but that there is a future day when they will be part of the restoration of the house of Israel.

2 Nephi 10:1–2

Their future children

2 Nephi 10:3–6

No other nation would have crucified Christ

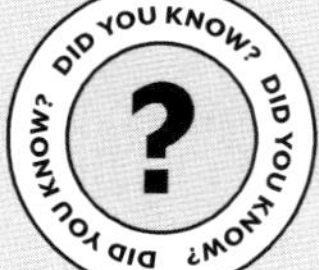

In verse 3, Jacob names "Christ" as a title for the Redeemer. Up to this point, Jesus has been called things like "Holy One of Israel" and "Redeemer." But after Jacob reveals the name of "Christ," it will be used over and over again by other prophets in the Book of Mormon.

2 Nephi 10:7–9

But for all they have done, the Lord has not given up on them. He has a plan.

2 Nephi 10:10–15

Their promised land (the Americas) is a land set aside for the gathering and for Zion.

2 Nephi 10:16–19

The Lord WILL gather Israel.

2 Nephi 10:20–22

The Lord remembers those who are scattered.

2 Nephi 10:23–25

Ye are free to act for yourselves.

Gathering of Israel

With the Hebraic definition of Israel in mind, we find that the gathering of Israel takes on added meaning. The Lord is gathering those who are willing to let God prevail in their lives. The Lord is gathering those who will choose to let God be the most important influence in their lives.

PRESIDENT RUSSELL M. NELSON
October 2020 General Conference

"You—my dear extraordinary youth—were sent to earth at this precise time, this most crucial time in the history of the earth, to help gather Israel," the prophet said. "There is nothing happening on this earth right now that is more important than that. There is nothing of greater consequence. Absolutely nothing. This gathering should mean everything to you. This is the mission for which you were sent to earth."

PRESIDENT RUSSELL M. NELSON
Worldwide Youth Devotional, June 3, 2018

When we speak of gathering Israel on both sides of the veil, we are referring, of course, to missionary, temple, and family history work. We are also referring to building faith and testimony in the hearts of those with whom we live, work, and serve. Anytime we do anything that helps anyone—on either side of the veil—to make and keep their covenants with God, we are helping to gather Israel.

PRESIDENT RUSSELL M. NELSON
October 2020 General Conference

For centuries, prophets have foretold this gathering, and it is happening right now! As an essential prelude to the Second Coming of the Lord, it is the most important work in the world!

PRESIDENT RUSSELL M. NELSON
October 2020 General Conference

WHAT DOES THE GATHERING OF ISRAEL MEAN TO YOU? WHAT ARE YOU DOING TO HELP GATHER ISRAEL?

2 Nephi 11-19

In these chapters

Nephi delights in Isaiah // Nephi quotes Isaiah about the scattering and gathering of Israel, the Millennial day, the Second Coming, the birth of Christ, and more.

After Jacob's words, Nephi continues teaching and writes that he is going to write more of the words of Isaiah just like Jacob had. Nephi is using Isaiah's words as an additional special witness of Jesus Christ. In 2 Nephi 11:2-3, Nephi explains that he, Jacob, and Isaiah had all seen the Savior; therefore, together they make three witnesses of Jesus Christ.

Nephi said that he is going to send all three of their testimonies forth together to prove to his children that his testimony is true. They had all seen, they all know, and they are all bearing witness. And now, today, they have born witness to billions of people.

Isaiah witnessed the time when Northern Israel was captured by Assyria. Ten tribes were scattered to the world at this time as they were carried off and lost their identity as being Israelites. Isaiah saw the scattering and he saw how devastating that was. Isaiah's prophecies were full of hope that the day would come when the Lord will restore Israel—a day when they would be gathered again and be the Lord's covenant people.

We live in the day Isaiah spoke of. We are the gatherers Isaiah was speaking of. It is our responsibility to bring Israel back together.

📖 Overview

After Jacob's writings, Nephi quoted 13 chapters from Isaiah, but first he explained why he was doing this. Look for some of his reasons in this chapter.

2 NEPHI 11:1–2	**2 NEPHI 11:3**
2 NEPHI 11:4	**2 NEPHI 11:5**
2 NEPHI 11:6–7	**2 NEPHI 11:8**

What was Nephi's connection to Isaiah?

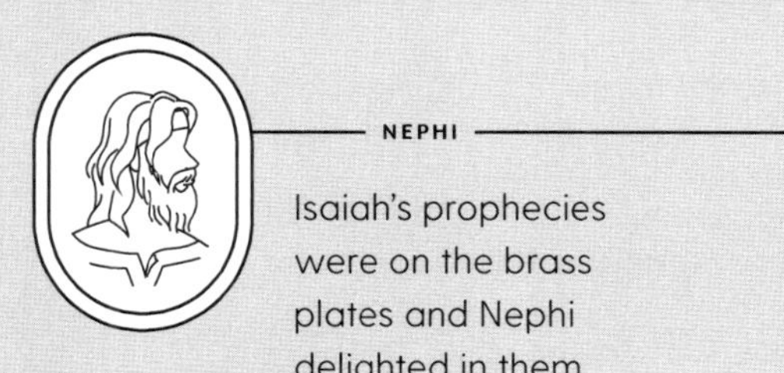

NEPHI

Isaiah's prophecies were on the brass plates and Nephi delighted in them.

ISAIAH

Isaiah was not an ancient prophet to Nephi. Nephi was born less than 100 years after Isaiah finished prophesying.

2 Nephi 12

This chapter has a lot to do with you. Isaiah was writing about a temple in the last days, the gathering of Israel, the Millennium, and the Second Coming of Jesus Christ.

HELPFUL TIPS	WHAT I LEARNED
2 Nephi 12:1–3 When the Lord's people have been on the earth and have not had a temple, mountains have been used as sacred places to approach the Lord. In the last days, when temples will again be upon the earth, is the day that Israel will be gathered.	
2 Nephi 12:4–5 Isaiah prophesied about the Millennium when peace will prevail and there will be no need for weapons. "house of Jacob" means "house of Israel," meaning God's covenant people.	
2 Nephi 12:6–9 Anciently, east was a sacred direction. Isaiah is saying that the Israelites had looked to other sources for spiritual guidance. These verses show Israel's current state.	
2 Nephi 12:10–13 The day will come when all the things that Israel has put their trust in will become worthless. Cedars of Lebanon were towering trees, and Isaiah used them to represent prideful people who elevated themselves above others.	
2 Nephi 12:14–18 Isaiah lists "all" and "every" prideful thing or place that will be destroyed. The destruction will be complete and total.	
2 Nephi 12: 19–22 These things that man has put his trust in will instead be thrown into caves. Isaiah's plea is to stop putting their faith in the frailty of man who is always a breath away from death.	

Despite the lack of righteousness in the world today, we live in a sacred, holy time. Prophets, with loving and longing hearts, have described our day for centuries.

ELDER QUENTIN L. COOK

April 2016 General Conference

2 Nephi 13

Isaiah describes the covenant daughters of Zion. What does Isaiah teach you about what worldliness ultimately brings?

HELPFUL TIPS	WHAT I LEARNED
2 Nephi 13:1–5 "Stay and staff" refer to their supply of bread and water, or the things they need. Here Isaiah was warning the prideful and wicked that they will be punished.	
2 Nephi 13:6–10 Judah, who was once great and powerful, will become a shadow of what it once was. Isaiah paints a picture to show Judah's future. Typically, the oldest brother would take over a family estate and lead the rest of the family. But all of these traditions will be in upheaval, and an older brother will ask his younger brother to lead - not because he is the better leader but because he is not as destitute as the older brother. But the younger brother will reject this because he only has supplies enough for himself.	
2 Nephi 13:11–15 Isaiah continues to warn Judah. They have had bad rulers and the poor have suffered. If Jerusalem were a vineyard, then the Jews have destroyed it, and they have taken away from the poor.	
2 Nephi 13:16–17 Isaiah then speaks to the daughters of Zion who had become like the world (his words apply to both men and women). Isaiah was speaking of his own day and of a future day when vanity and appearance were of utmost importance.	
2 Nephi 13:18–23 Many of the beauty accessories have changed over time and have different names, but the principles can still be understood.	
2 Nephi 13:24 The days of wearing all of these ornaments will come to an end; and instead of putting on the fancy clothing, they will be putting on sackcloth, which was an unrefined fabric.	
2 Nephi 13:25–26 Instead of mincing and tinkling along, these daughters will be sitting upon the ground, in grief, mourning at the gates—a completely different life than they previously had.	

2 Nephi 14   Daughters of Zion will be redeemed

HELPFUL TIPS	WHAT I LEARNED
2 Nephi 14:1–6 Chapter 13 taught about the widespread wickedness, pride, and despair among Israel. Chapter 14 prophesies of the redemption and cleansing of Israel, even in the midst of a wicked world. The day of redemption will come for these daughters! The day will come when these daughters will abandon the ways of the world (see verse 4).	

2 Nephi 15   Israel will be scattered and then gathered

HELPFUL TIPS	WHAT I LEARNED
2 Nephi 15:1–2 Grapevines were capable of producing a lot of fruit if cared for, otherwise they will die or only produce a small amount of grapes. These characteristics made the grapevine a good comparison to the house of Israel.	
2 Nephi 15:3–7 Because the vineyard has failed to produce, these verses explain what will happen to it. What once was protected and cared for, instead, will become desolate and just like all the land surrounding it.	
2 Nephi 15:8–17 Isaiah gives six "woes" in this chapter. These are things that bring grief and misery. The first two woes are in these verses.	
2 Nephi 15:18–23 Isaiah gives woes 3, 4, 5, and 6 in these verses. Pay special attention to the woe in verse 20.	
2 Nephi 15:24–25 When a farmer has gathered his grain, he would then "winnow" his grain to separate the seeds from the "chaff" and the "stubble." He would gather it and toss it in the air. The wind would then blow the lighter chaff and stubble away while the seed would fall back to the ground. Once the farmer gathered his seed, he would burn the chaff and stubble with a fire that would grow extremely fast. Isaiah is likening the fate of the chaff and stubble to those who fall within the six woes.	
2 Nephi 15:26–30 An "ensign" is a flag or standard raised during times of battle. If you see the flag, that means it is time to come together to fight. Or if you hear a whistle ("hiss"), that holds the same meaning. It is a call to gather. Isaiah is describing the speed and haste in which the people will gather.	

2 Nephi 16

Isaiah sees the Lord and is called to prophesy

HELPFUL TIPS	WHAT I LEARNED
2 Nephi 16:1–4 Isaiah describes the vision he received as he was called to prophesy. Isaiah sees the Lord on His throne and seeks to describe indescribable things. Isaiah sees "seraphim" which is plural for "seraph." Seraphim are "fiery beings" or angelic beings (see Bible Dictionary). Wings are symbols of power.	
2 Nephi 16:5–7 Isaiah looked around and realized that he was not worthy. One of the seraphs then took a live (or hot) coal from the altar, a symbol of the Atonement of Jesus Christ. So this coal is laid upon Isaiah's mouth and then burned (or cleansed) Isaiah's sins away.	
2 Nephi 16:8–10 Now Isaiah was ready and he responds to the Lord's question, "Whom shall I send?" Isaiah replies, "Here am I; send me." Then Isaiah receives the call to go preach to the people.	
2 Nephi 16:11–13 Isaiah asked the Lord how long the Israelites will reject the Lord, and the answer is that they will continue to reject until they are scattered or removed far away.	

2 Nephi 17

Inside this chapter of prophecies of Isaiah's day is the prophecy of the birth of Christ.

HELPFUL TIPS	WHAT I LEARNED
2 Nephi 17:1–2 In Isaiah's day, the great Assyrian Empire was threatening smaller countries like Israel, Syria, and Judah. Israel and Syria wanted Judah to join them in an alliance. King Ahaz was the king of Judah. The Lord tells King Ahaz not to join in the alliance (see v. 4).	
2 Nephi 17:3–9 Isaiah knew the plans of Syria and Israel. Their plan was to replace King Ahaz with a king of their choosing who would form the alliance with them.	
2 Nephi 17:10–16 The Lord will give Ahaz a sign. The sign is that a virgin will bear a son and call his name "Immanuel," which means "with us is God." In verse 15, butter and honey were foods that children liked.	
2 Nephi 17:17–19 This is the warning to Ahaz to listen to Isaiah. If he doesn't listen, he will bring upon Judah consequences that have not yet been seen there. Verse 18 compares the soldiers that will come upon them to bees and flies - they will be everywhere.	
2 Nephi 17:20–25 This is the nature of the land of Judah when the people are carried off. The land will be full of briers, and only hunters will venture into the thorns seeking meat for food. These hills, which were once so cared for, will be only left for their few grazing cattle rather than for crops.	

HELPFUL TIPS	WHAT I LEARNED
2 Nephi 18:1–4 Ahaz did not heed Isaiah's counsel to trust in the Lord. Instead, Ahaz asked the Assyrians (the enemy) for protection. Isaiah will now turn to the people and warn them, and he tells them a prophecy. A child will be born, and before that child will grow very old, destruction will come.	
2 Nephi 18:5–8 The waters of Shiloah were gentle, flowing waters that provided life-sustaining water to the inhabitants of Jerusalem. In this context, the water symbolized the Lord's guidance and the spiritual source for the people. Since the people are rejecting the source, another river (the Assyrians) will flood or attack their land.	
2 Nephi 18:9–12 Isaiah is warning the people against making any alliance with any world power. If they do, they will regret it. They need strength, but it is not found in other countries.	
2 Nephi 18:13–15 The Lord will give them the strength they need. He will be their protective rock of offense and a sanctuary for the righteous. But to the wicked, He is a stone of stumbling, or something that gets in their way.	
2 Nephi 18:16–18 These prophecies, now recorded, are a witness to the people.	
2 Nephi 18:19–22 These verses warn of seeking after other sources for spiritual guidance. If they do so, they will be led astray. The law and the testimony are the right source. Any other forms of spiritualism will bring trouble and darkness.	

Isaiah's day // Jesus will be born and will be a Prince of Peace // Evils that will bring destruction

HELPFUL TIPS	WHAT I LEARNED
2 Nephi 19:1 The Land of Israel was divided as an inheritance for the descendants of the 12 tribes of Israel. Zebulun and Naphtali were given land in the northern part of Israel which bordered other nations. Their lands were known as the "Galilee of Nations" because there were many mixed nationalities. These lands were the first to be captured by the Assyrians.	
2 Nephi 19:2–5 These lands will see hard days but will yet experience greatness and will still fulfill its destiny. The day will come when this land will be redeemed, and it will come through the Savior, the Prince of Peace. He won't gain that peace through the typical battles with confused noise and soldiers fighting one another, but it will come through the cleansing of the earth.	
2 Nephi 19:6–7 "Because of the wickedness of the people, Isaiah and others often spoke in figures, using types and shadows to illustrate their points.... "For instance, the virgin birth prophecy is dropped into the midst of a recitation of local historical occurrences so that to the spiritually untutored it could be interpreted as some ancient and unknown happening that had no relationship to the birth of the Lord Jehovah into mortality some 700 years later." Elder Bruce R. McConkie | October 1973 Ensign	
2 Nephi 19:8–12 Verses 8-20 mention evils that will be destroyed and ultimately bring destruction to the people. These are dual prophecies. They are speaking of the destruction in Isaiah's day as well as those preceding the Second Coming. **EVIL #1: PRIDE** The people thought that they were strong enough and could replace everything that was destroyed with better things.	
2 Nephi 19:13–17 **EVIL #2: WICKED LEADERS** These verses are referencing the wicked leadership. The head is government leaders and the tail is false prophets.	
2 Nephi 19:18–21 **EVIL #3: WICKEDNESS** Wickedness is compared to a forest fire that spreads everywhere using the people as fuel and causing the land to be darkened.	

2 Nephi 20-25

In these chapters

Nephi quotes Isaiah concerning the Second Coming, the gathering of Israel, the Millennium, and more // Nephi teaches that Jesus will come 600 years after his family left Jerusalem.

A Key to Understanding Isaiah

Nephi chose to couch his prophetic utterances in plain and simple declarations. But among his fellow Hebrew prophets it was not always appropriate so to do. Because of the wickedness of the people, Isaiah and others often spoke in figures, using types and shadows to illustrate their points. Their messages were, in effect, hidden in parables. (2 Ne. 25:1–8.)

For instance, the virgin birth prophecy is dropped into the midst of a recitation of local historical occurrences so that to the spiritually untutored it could be interpreted as some ancient and unknown happening that had no relationship to the birth of the Lord Jehovah into mortality some 700 years later. (Isa. 7.)

Similarly, many chapters dealing with latter-day apostasy and the second coming of Christ are written relative to ancient nations whose destruction was but a symbol, a type, and a shadow, of that which would fall upon all nations when the great and dreadful day of the Lord finally came. Chapters 13 and 14 are an example of this.

ELDER BRUCE R. MCCONKIE
October 1973 Ensign

The Lord Will Be in the Midst of Zion

I mention all these things in order that the Latter-day Saints may be re-refreshed in regard to the great events that must take place in the latter times, and that strangers who are in our midst may have a more full understanding of the views of the Latter-day Saints in regard to the ancient prophecies. You see we are looking for the building up of Zion on the earth, for the lifting up of the standard of the Lord, an ensign for the nations; or in other words, as I read at the commencement of my remarks: "For behold Zion shall go forth and become the joy of the whole earth, (Ps. 48:2) and the glory of God shall be upon her; (Ps. 102:16) and the day shall come when the nations of the earth shall fear and tremble because of her, and shall fear because of her terrible ones." (D&C 45:67 D&C 64:41-43) Why? Because the Lord himself will be in the midst of Zion, (Isa. 12:6) before he comes on the Mount of Olives.

ORSON PRATT
Journal of Discourses 14:343

HELPFUL TIPS	WHAT I LEARNED
2 Nephi 20:1–4 The fourth evil from the previous chapter is found in the first four verses. **EVIL #4: TURNING AWAY THOSE IN NEED** Will those who turn away those in need then turn to God and ask for help when destruction comes?	
2 Nephi 20:5–7 These verses prophesy of the destruction of Assyria, the nation who thought themselves to be all powerful.	
2 Nephi 20:8–11 "Are not my princes altogether kings?" Assyria is boasting that even their army commanders are as powerful as kings. The king of Assyria looks over his conquered cities and says, "Should I not also do this to Jerusalem?"	
2 Nephi 20:12–15 Assyria will conquer Israel, but only because the Lord was allowing it. The ax in verse 15 is Assyria and the person holding the ax is the Lord. But the ax is the one taking all of the credit.	
2 Nephi 20:16–19 Assyria will ultimately be destroyed like a forest fire that destroys a forest in a single day. The fire will be so complete that a child can count the trees that remain standing.	
2 Nephi 20:20–23 These verses prophesy of the gathering of Israel in the last days. A remnant of Israel will return.	
2 Nephi 20:24–26 "My people that dwellest in Zion" is a plea for the Lord's people to rely on Him. Although they may be temporarily under the rule of a nation such as the Assyrians, He will ultimately deliver them.	
2 Nephi 20:27–32 Isaiah is giving a graphic description of the Assyrians' advancing armies (which is representative of wicked nations in the last days). They are getting closer and closer to Jerusalem as they pass through city after city.	
2 Nephi 20:33–34 Assyria is compared to a forest of trees and the Lord will come and lop the bough. A bough refers to the branch on the tree, and the Lord will come in with His power and suddenly destroy the great and feared Assyrian army.	

2 Nephi 21 — Prophecy of Jesus Christ, the Millennium, Gathering of Israel

HELPFUL TIPS	WHAT I LEARNED
2 Nephi 21:1 In the previous chapter, the Lord has hewn down Assyrian trees. Now there will come a new tree. Out of the "stem of Jesse" will come the mortal Messiah. Jesse was King David's father, and the Messiah was prophesied to come through that kingly line, which was known as the Davidic line.	
2 Nephi 21:2–9 Verses 2-5 teach about Christ's ability to judge righteously. Verses 6-9 describe life during the Millennium and the peace and knowledge that will be upon the earth.	
2 Nephi 21:10–16 Just like Egypt was unable to stop Moses from leading Israel across the Red Sea, nations in the last days will be unable to stop people from gathering His people (see v. 16).	

2 Nephi 22 — The Millennium

HELPFUL TIPS	WHAT I LEARNED
2 Nephi 22:1–3 These verses contain two short psalms. The first psalm is in verses 1-3, and the second psalm is in verses 4-6. These psalms each portray how during the Millennium all men will praise the Lord. The imagery in verse 3 is so beautiful. Like one might draw water from a well for their physical needs, let us likewise turn to Christ for our spiritual salvation. Imagine someone who is spiritually parched and finally finds the living water of peace, hope, and salvation.	
2 Nephi 22:4–6 This is a song for Zion and the excellent things that the Lord has done for them. Notice in verse 6 the mention that Christ is in the midst of them, because He will be dwelling with them.	

2 Nephi 23 The destruction at the Second Coming

HELPFUL TIPS	WHAT I LEARNED
2 Nephi 23:1 Babylon was a symbol of the wickedness of the world. This chapter contains a dual prophecy (the destruction of Babylon which is like the destruction of the world at the Second Coming of Jesus Christ).	
2 Nephi 23:2–5 Here the Lord is gathering His forces. A banner (or ensign) is raised in verse 2, which is what armies would follow and then gather to. Who is the army? Verse 3! The sanctified ones, or those who have been made holy through Christ.	
2 Nephi 23:6–9 The wicked will not be able to stand up to the power of the Lord, for He is the "Almighty" (verse 6). The description of the wicked, as their fate becomes clear, is truly sad (see verses 7-8).	
2 Nephi 23:10–16 So great will be the destruction that those who survive will be precious as gold. A "roe" is likely a gazelle. Picture a gazelle that is being chased or a lost sheep with no shepherd - this is how man will be as the destruction is occurring.	
2 Nephi 23:17–22 Babylon, who was once a great city, will be completely desolate. Instead of a bustling city, animals will inhabit the empty houses.	

2 Nephi 24 Gathering of Israel , the Millennium, Lucifer will be cast out

HELPFUL TIPS	WHAT I LEARNED
2 Nephi 24:1–3 Israel will be restored. "Strangers shall be joined with them" refers to the uniting of the house of Israel and Gentiles in holiness.	
2 Nephi 24:4–20 This is a song meant to be sung to the king of Babylon who represents the head of wickedness of the world, so this is a dual prophecy since he represents Satan here. Read this as a song that is sung when Satan is revealed and cast out.	
2 Nephi 24:21–27 This is the harsh sentence put upon those who follow Satan (or "children of Satan"). They will be cut down. The bittern (possibly a water fowl like a pelican), and pools of water will replace where they once were.	
2 Nephi 24:28–32 What should we look to in order to be protected from our enemies? Zion.	

My Soul Delighteth in Plainness

Nephi explains that he has not caused his people to learn the ways of the Jews because, ultimately, he does not want them to be like the Jews; so his people and those who receive his plates might have a hard time understanding Isaiah. And Nephi himself does not teach like Isaiah does; instead, he delights in teaching in plain terms so that they may learn.

2 Nephi 25:1–8

What do you think it means to teach with "plainness"? (v. 4)

2 Nephi 25:9–11

What will happen to the Jews

2 Nephi 25:12–14

When Jesus comes to the Jews

2 Nephi 25:15–17

Scattering and gathering

2 Nephi 25:18–20

Who the Messiah is

2 Nephi 25:21–22

What will come of Nephi's writings

2 Nephi 25:23

Why Nephi writes

2 Nephi 25:24–25

The law of Moses

2 Nephi 25:26

Why Nephi writes

2 Nephi 25:27

The law of Moses

2 Nephi 25:28–30

The right way

Why did Nephi quote Isaiah?

Nephi knew that Isaiah's prophecies were going to be of great worth unto us in the last days, and we will understand them. This is why he has inscribed Isaiah's prophecies, word for word, line after line, onto his plates. **For us** (v. 8). Even though we do not teach like the Jews did, we will understand Isaiah because we will have the gift.

Nephi wrote his record to help bring others to Christ. What can you do to also bring others to Christ?

"And we talk of Christ, we rejoice in Christ, we preach of Christ, we prophesy of Christ, and we write according to our prophecies, that our children may know to what source they may look for a remission of their sins."

Keep your own record side-by-side with these great prophets testifying of these important doctrines and principles.

NEPHI WROTE HIS RECORD TO HELP BRING OTHERS TO CHRIST. WHAT HAVE YOU DONE? WHAT CAN YOU DO?

2 Nephi 26–30

In these chapters

The Nephites will be destroyed and their voice will speak forth from the dust   //
The coming forth of the Book of Mormon   //   The last days   //   The Lord will do a
marvelous work and a wonder   //   Israel will be restored

---

2 Nephi 26–30 is full of prophecies that will happen to Nephi's
descendants and prophecies concerning those in the last days.

THESE PROPHECIES ARE ABOUT YOU.

> Prophecy is but history in reverse—a divine disclosure of future events.
>
> **PRESIDENT EZRA TAFT BENSON**
> 1974 Ensign

Nephi prophesies of the the coming forth of the Book of Mormon.

SCRIPTURES	WRITE OR DRAW WHAT YOU LEARN:
2 Nephi 26:1	*Prophecy:*
2 Nephi 26:2	*Prophecy:*
2 Nephi 26:3–7	*Prophecy:*
2 Nephi 26:8–9	*Prophecy:*
2 Nephi 26:10–13	*Prophecy:*
2 Nephi 26:14–17	*The coming forth of the Book of Mormon*
2 Nephi 26:18–21	*The world when the Book of Mormon comes forth*
2 Nephi 26:22	*How Satan works*
2 Nephi 26:23–28	*How the Lord works*
2 Nephi 26:29	*What priestcraft is*
2 Nephi 26:30–31	*What charity is*
2 Nephi 26:32	*What the Lord commands*
2 Nephi 26:33	*Who the Lord invites to come to Him*

Prophecies about the Last Days

If you notice the chapter heading in your scriptures, this chapter can be compared to Isaiah 29, but Nephi is not quoting Isaiah word for word; he is reflecting on Isaiah's prophecies and adding his own testimony to it. Nephi and Isaiah are prophesying of the great amount of iniquity that will exist in the last days. The iniquity is so great that it is like they are "drunken with iniquity" (v. 1).

2 NEPHI 27:1	**2 NEPHI 27:2–3**	**2 NEPHI 27:4–5**
The earth will be covered with iniquity.	*Those who fight against Zion*	*The spiritually blind*

2 NEPHI 27:6–11	**2 NEPHI 27:12–14**	**2 NEPHI 27:15–18**
The Book of Mormon	*Witnesses of the Book of Mormon*	*A learned man will view the translation (Martin Harris and Charles Anthon)*

2 NEPHI 27:19–23	**2 NEPHI 27:24–27**	**2 NEPHI 27:28–35**
An unlearned man (Joseph Smith) will translate the plates	*A marvelous work will come to bring truth to the earth*	*Why this is a marvelous work*

The Lord described the work of this dispensation as "a marvelous work and a wonder." He spoke of a "covenant [that would] be fulfilled in the latter days," allowing "all … the earth [to] be blessed."

ELDER NEIL L. ANDERSEN
October 2021 General Conference

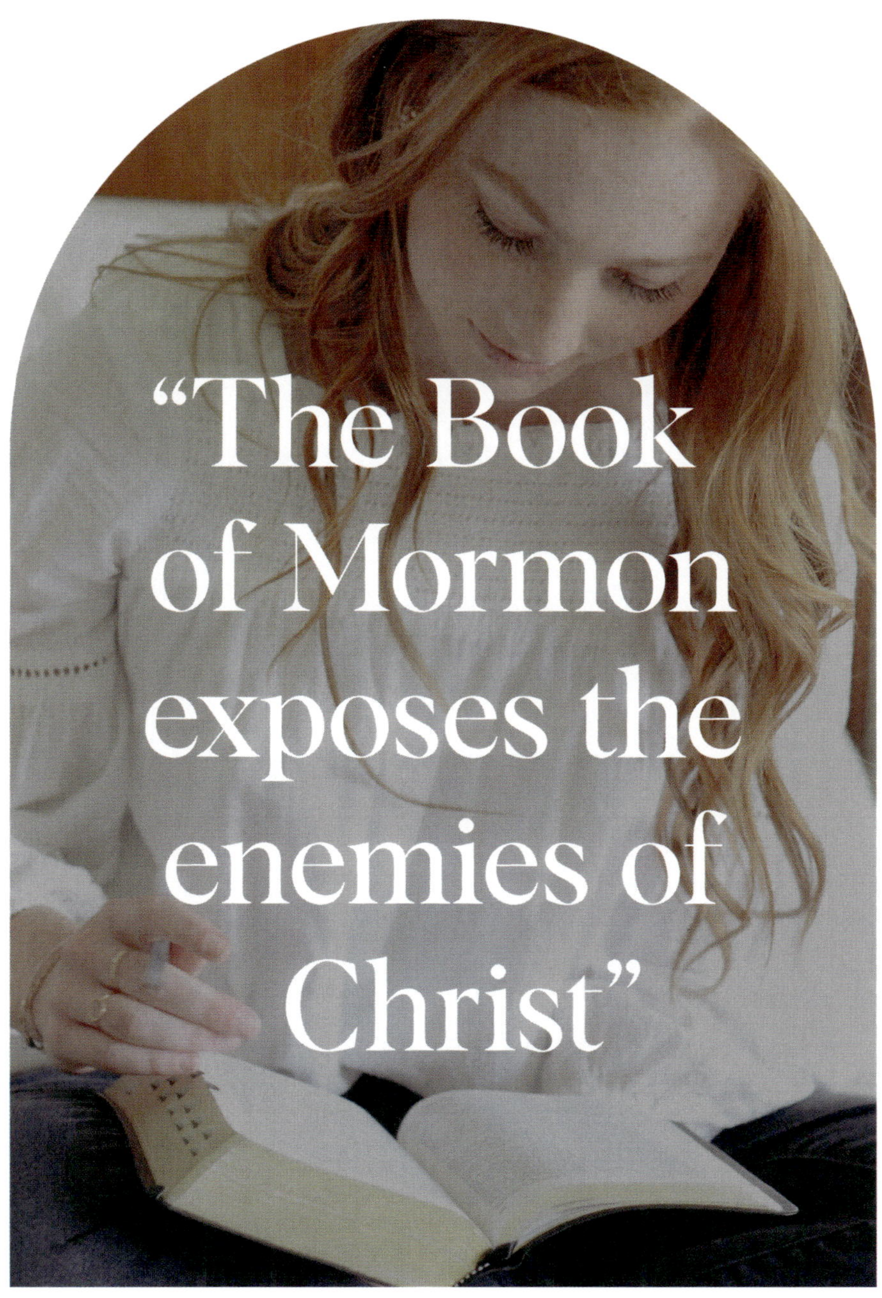

President Ezra Taft Benson

APRIL 1975 CONFERENCE REPORT

See how 2 Nephi 28 shows Satan's tricks and lies. →

Satan's Tactics
to Bring People into Bondage

Do you know what game film is? It is when you watch a video of your team or an opposing team's game. For example, a basketball player might prepare to play a team by watching hours and hours of game film of that team playing other teams. Why? To see how they work. To see what plays they use. Then that player can strategize a plan on how to play that exact team. This chapter is like watching Satan's game film and seeing how he will fool many into thinking they are choosing God, but he is really grasping them and leading them away.

Write or draw what these scriptures teach you.

2 NEPHI 28:1 *The certainty of prophecy*	**2 NEPHI 28:2** *The Book of Mormon*	**2 NEPHI 28:3–4** *Churches in the last days*
2 NEPHI 28:5–6 *False doctrines taught*	**2 NEPHI 28:7–8** *False doctrines taught*	**2 NEPHI 28:9–11** *Foolish doctrines*
2 NEPHI 28:12–15 *Because of pride*	**2 NEPHI 28:16–17** *Warning*	**2 NEPHI 28:18–20** *Satan's Tactic:* *Stir hearts to anger*
2 NEPHI 28:21 *Another tactic:* *Pacify them*	**2 NEPHI 28:22** *Another tactic:* *Flatter them away*	**2 NEPHI 28:23** *The reality*
2 NEPHI 28:24–29 *Warnings*	**2 NEPHI 28:30** *The Lord does not trick us;* *He teaches us.*	**2 NEPHI 28:31–32** *Warning*

2 Nephi 29-30

Can the Lord decide that He wants more scripture upon the earth? When He does bring more scripture to the earth, how does He want us to receive it?

<table>
<tr>
<td colspan="3" align="center">TIPS TO KEEP IN MIND AS YOU STUDY THESE SCRIPTURES:</td>
</tr>
<tr>
<td align="center">"Hiss forth"
means to go forth
with intensity.</td>
<td align="center">The Book of Mormon will
come forth in the day that
the Lord will gather Israel.</td>
<td align="center">A "standard" (or
ensign) is a flag
raised during battle.</td>
</tr>
</table>

2 NEPHI 29:1-2

When will the Book of Mormon come forth?

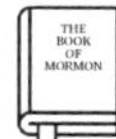

2 NEPHI 29:3-6

How will many act when the Book of Mormon comes forth?

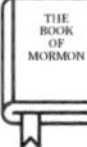

2 NEPHI 29:7-14

What reasons does the Lord give for bringing forth the Book of Mormon?

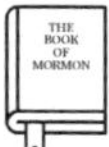

2 NEPHI 30:1-8

What will happen when the Book of Mormon comes forth?

RIGHTEOUS | WICKED

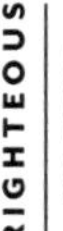

2 NEPHI 30:9-10

What will the Lord cause to happen?

2 NEPHI 30:11-18

What will it be like during the Millennium?

"As Latter-day Saints, we need not look like the world. We need not entertain like the world. Our personal habits should be different. Our recreation should be different."

ELDER ROBERT D. HALES

February 2002 Ensign

2 Nephi 31–33

In these chapters

Nephi's last words   //   Nephi teaches the doctrine of Christ

These are Nephi's last chapters (2 Nephi 31–33), and then Nephi will pass the records on to his brother Jacob. Nephi will die shortly after. So now as a seasoned prophet who has seen and learned many, many things, he can look back and see what he has included in the plates. In 2 Nephi 31:2 he writes, "the things which I have written sufficeth me, save it be a few words …"

What is it that he wants to be sure to still include? What does he want to plainly teach us that he feels he has not yet put in his record?

The doctrine of Christ.

Doctrines are unchanging, eternal truths. Here Nephi will teach plainly how to gain eternal life. So if someone were to ask the question about what God wants them to do in this life, this chapter answers it in very plain and simple terms.

"More so than in any other time in our history, there is an urgency in today's society for men and women to step forward and teach the gospel of Jesus Christ in the power of plainness. God delights when His truths are taught clearly and understandably with no conspicuous ornamentation. …When the plainness of Christian teaching and living is lost, apostasy and suffering result."

ELDER MARVIN J. ASHTON
April 1977 General Conference

Write or draw what these scriptures teach you.

VERSES 1-3 | The doctrine of Christ

VERSES 4-11 | The importance of baptism

VERSES 12-14 | Receiving the Holy Ghost

VERSES 15-16 | Enduring to the end

VERSES 17-18 | This is the way onto the strait & narrow path

VERSES 19-21 | Continue to press forward

"The ordinance of confirming a new member of the Church and bestowing the gift of the Holy Ghost is both simple and profound. Worthy Melchizedek Priesthood holders place their hands upon the head of an individual and call him or her by name. Then, by the authority of the holy priesthood and in the name of the Savior, the individual is confirmed a member of The Church of Jesus Christ of Latter-day Saints, and this important phrase is uttered: 'Receive the Holy Ghost.'

"The simplicity of this ordinance may cause us to overlook its significance. These four words—'Receive the Holy Ghost'—are not a passive pronouncement; rather, they constitute a priesthood injunction—an authoritative admonition to act and not simply to be acted upon (see 2 Nephi 2:26). The Holy Ghost does not become operative in our lives merely because hands are placed upon our heads and those four important words are spoken. As we receive this ordinance, each of us accepts a sacred and ongoing responsibility to desire, to seek, to work, and to so live that we indeed 'receive the Holy Ghost' and its attendant spiritual gifts.

-ELDER DAVID A. BEDNAR
October 2010 General Conference

2 Nephi 32

*"... feast upon the words of Christ; for behold, the words of
Christ will tell you all things what ye should do."*

2 NEPHI 32:3

① 2 NEPHI 32:1–2

What happens when you have the gift of the Holy Ghost

② 2 NEPHI 32:3

Feast upon the words of Christ

③ 2 NEPHI 32:4–7

Why people might not understand the doctrine

④ 2 NEPHI 32:8–9

Pray always

WHAT DOES IT MEAN TO YOU TO FEAST UPON THE WORDS OF CHRIST?

Nephi's Last Words

Nephi points out that he is not as mighty in writing as he is in speaking. After studying his words, would you say that he is not mighty in writing? Has he written words that have touched your heart and impacted your life? But he prefers to speak because there is power in teaching and testifying person-to-person. This is a good principle to remember in your life as you seek to bring others to Christ.

> *Why just unto the heart? Individual agency is so sacred that Heavenly Father will never force the human heart, even with all His infinite power. Man may try to do so, but God does not. To put it another way, God allows us to be the guardians, or the gatekeepers, of our own hearts. We must, of our own free will, open our hearts to the Spirit, for He will not force Himself upon us.*
>
> **ELDER GERALD N. LUND**
> April 2008 General Conference

---

2 Nephi 33:1

The power of the Holy Ghost

STUDY TIP
Notice in verse 1 that Nephi says that the Holy Ghost will carry truth "unto" our hearts and not "into" them. What is the difference?

---

2 Nephi 33:2–4

Nephi's words are of great worth

2 Nephi 33:5

Speaking harshly against sin

2 Nephi 33:6

What Nephi glories in

---

2 Nephi 33:7–9

Who Nephi has charity for

2 Nephi 33:10–11

Nephi wrote for all people

2 Nephi 33:12–15

Nephi's final plea

Jacob

DID YOU KNOW?

- Jacob, the son of Lehi and Sariah, wrote this book.

- Jacob was born in the wilderness. He never knew Jerusalem.

- Jacob was a priest and teacher to the Nephites. He faithfully and diligently labored to teach the Nephites to believe in Christ.

- Jacob saw his Redeemer (2 Nephi 11:3).

- Nephi passed the plates to Jacob, and then Jacob passed the plates to his son, Enos.

Hearken, O ye house of Israel, and hear the words
of me, a prophet of the Lord.

For behold, thus saith the Lord, I will liken thee,
O house of Israel, like unto a tame olive tree,
which a man took and nourished in his vineyard ...

Jacob 5:2–3

Timeline

Here is the book of Jacob at-a-glance. The main stories are found in the timeline below. If you ever want to find a story in your scriptures, you can look at this page for help. You can add your own notes to this page as well.

JACOB 1

- Nephi tells Jacob to write upon the small plates
- King appointed
- Nephi dies
- Nephites begin to grow hard in hearts and lifted up in pride
- Jacob and Joseph labor to teach people

JACOB 2

- Jacob denounces pride and the love of riches
- Jacob teaches about chastity

JACOB 4

- Jacob hopes his words written upon the plates will be received with thankful hearts
- Be reconciled unto Christ through the Atonement
- The Jews will reject Christ

JACOB 5

- Jacob quotes the prophet Zenos to teach of the scattering and gathering of Israel
- The allegory of the olive trees

JACOB 3

- Jacob teaches those who are pure in heart

JACOB 7

- Sherem preaches that there will be no Christ
- The Lord pours His spirit into Jacob
- Jacob responds to Sherem
- Sherem falls to the earth
- Sherem tells people he was deceived by the devil
- Jacob passes plates to his son Enos

JACOB 6

- Israel will be restored in the last days
- What will you do after you hear these words?

People to Know

If you need a reminder of who is who, return to this page.

Jacob

Jacob was a younger brother to Nephi and was made a priest and a teacher to the Nephites. He wrote the book of Jacob.

Joseph

Joseph was the youngest son of Lehi, was a priest and teacher among the Nephites, and labored with his might to teach the people.

Nephi

Nephi was leader to the Nephites. He died in Jacob 1:12.

Enos

Enos was Jacob's son. Jacob passed the plates to him.

Sherem

Sherem was a Nephite who persuaded many Nephites that there would be no Christ. Jacob taught him and he fell to the earth. He then told the people he had been deceived.

Jacob 1–4

In these chapters

Nephi passes plates to Jacob   //   Nephi dies   //   Nephites turn to riches and become prideful   //
Jacob teaches Nephites at temple   //   How to gain unshakable faith

Nephi

As Nephi neared the end of
his life, he passed the plates
into the very capable hands
of his brother Jacob.

Jacob

Jacob had a firm
testimony of Jesus Christ
and a deep knowledge of
Jesus' Atonement.

In Jacob 7, a Nephite named Sherem tried to convince Jacob that there was no
Christ, but Jacob's faith could not be shaken. As you study Jacob's words, look for
what Jacob did to develop such unshakable faith and consider how you and your
family can develop that kind of faith. Then as you face similar situations in life,
you (like Jacob) can say "I could not be shaken" (Jacob 7:5).

Jacob 1

Write or draw what you learn in each group of verses.

① JACOB 1:1–4
What Jacob should include on the plates

② JACOB 1:5–6
What Jacob knew

③ JACOB 1:7–8
What Jacob labored to do

④ JACOB 1:9–12
King appointed; Nephi dies

⑤ JACOB 1:13–14
The people

⑥ JACOB 1:15–16
The state of the Nephites

⑦ JACOB 1:17–19
Jacob and Joseph

JACOB "LABORED DILIGENTLY" (V. 7) TO HELP THE NEPHITES COME UNTO CHRIST. WHAT HAVE YOU DONE TO BRING OTHERS TO CHRIST?

Jacob's Words to the Nephites Spoken at the Temple

The Nephites gather to the temple to hear Jacob teach, and we can see in Jacob 2:8 that many of them come expecting to be taught "the pleasing word of God." But Jacob's errand was different this time.

Jacob teaches about Pride and Chastity | Jacob 2-3 | 10:30 minutes

Jacob 2

1–3	**4–7**	**8–11**	**12–16**
Jacob speaks to the Nephites	*They are beginning to sin*	*Why Jacob was teaching them*	*Pride and riches*
17–21	**22–24**	**25–30**	**31–35**
The solution	*Immorality*	*The command*	*Warning*

Jacob 3

1–2	**3–8**	**9–10**	**11–14**
To those who are pure in heart	*To those who are not pure in heart*	*What they should remember*	*Shake yourselves awake*

Jacob 4

This is a faith-building chapter. Jacob, who was a man of great unshakable faith, teaches us how we can also obtain this great faith.

<table>
<tr><td>1-3 | Why Jacob engraves upon the plates</td><td>4-5 | The true intent of the law of Moses</td></tr>
<tr><td>6-7 | How Jacob's faith became unshaken</td><td>8 | How to find out mysteries of God</td></tr>
<tr><td>9-10 | Why we should never seek to counsel the Lord</td><td>11-12 | Be reconciled to Christ through His Atonement</td></tr>
<tr><td>13 | What TRUTH is</td><td>14-18 | The Jews will reject Christ</td></tr>
</table>

Wherefore, we search the prophets, and we have many revelations and the spirit of prophecy; and having all these witnesses we obtain a hope, and our faith becometh unshaken, insomuch that we truly can command in the name of Jesus and the very trees obey us, or the mountains, or the waves of the sea.

UNSHA'KEN, adjective

Not shaken; not agitated; not moved; firm; fixed.

Not moved in resolution; firm; steady.

WEBSTER'S 1828 DICTIONARY

Keep your own record side-by-side with these great prophets testifying of these important doctrines and principles.

MAKE A LIST OF THINGS, EXPERIENCES, PEOPLE, AND RESOURCES THAT HAVE HELPED YOU GROW YOUR FAITH.

Jacob 5–7

In these chapters

The Allegory of the Olive Trees   //   Israel will be restored in the last days   //
Sherem the Antichrist   //   Jacob passes the plates to his son Enos

What is an allegory?

An allegory is a story that uses objects and people to teach a truth. The elements in the story (like the olive tree) represent something else.

Who was Zenos?

Zenos was an Old Testament prophet. His prophecies were on the brass plates but are not in our Bible today. Jacob copied this allegory from Zenos onto the plates.

House of Israel

Because olive trees could easily turn wild, they are a good symbol of the house of Israel. God expected good fruits from the house of Israel, but Israel easily became corrupted.

Things to Know about Olive Trees

In order to produce good olives, olive trees require a great amount of care. When left uncared for, the tree gradually becomes wild. Wild trees have strong roots but do not produce fruit as valuable as the cultivated olive tree does.

"Grafting" was a common practice in ancient times where one would take a branch from one tree and insert it into a different tree.

One purpose of doing this might be to help an olive tree which was no longer bearing fruit. One would take a branch from a healthy tree and "graft" it into the wild tree in hopes that it would strengthen the tree.

Jacob 5

📖 The Allegory of the Olive Trees

In this allegory, the master of the vineyard will find a dying olive tree in his vineyard. The master then does all he can to save it, which will take planning, effort, and time. He will then visit his vineyard four times, each time observing his tree(s) and doing all he can to save them. Study this allegory to see what happened during each visit.

Visit 01

Write or draw what you learn in each box.

JACOB 5:1–3 *The dying tree*	**JACOB 5:4–6** *Trying to save the tree*	**JACOB 5:7** *Dying branches burned*
JACOB 5:8–9 *The Master's plan*	**JACOB 5:10–12** *Wild branches grafted*	**JACOB 5:13–14** *Branches from the tree grafted into other trees*

> *"The parable of Zenos, recorded by Jacob in chapter five of his book, is one of the greatest parables ever recorded. This parable in and of itself stamps the Book of Mormon with convincing truth. No mortal man, without the inspiration of the Lord, could have written such a parable.*

JOSEPH FIELDING SMITH
Answers to Gospel Questions, 4:141

Visit 02

Make notes about what was happening in the vineyard.

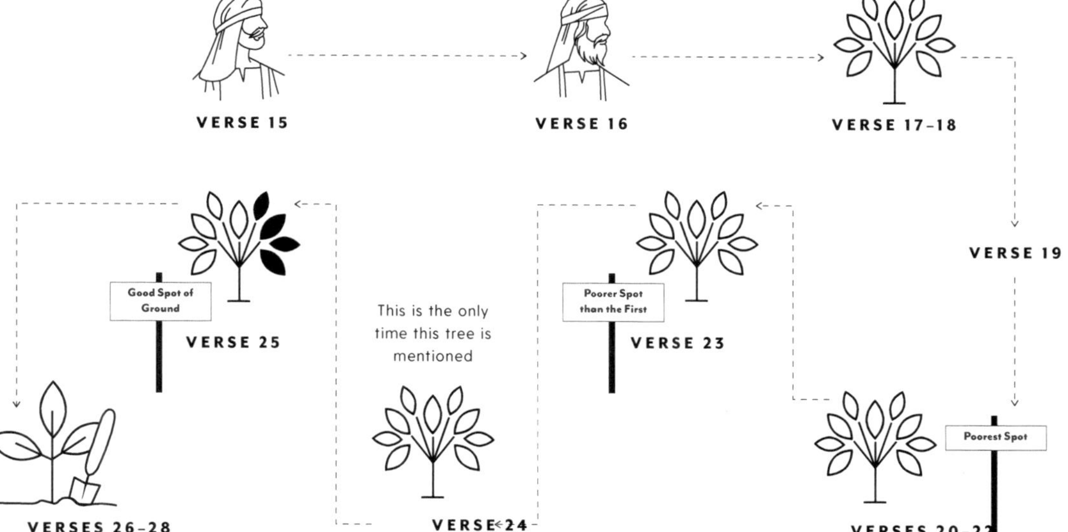

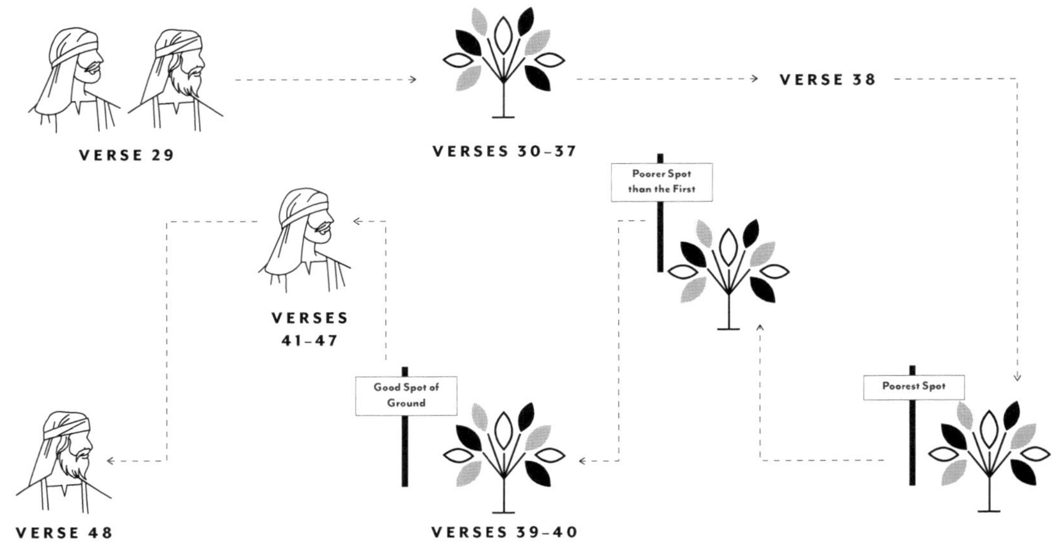

Visit **04**

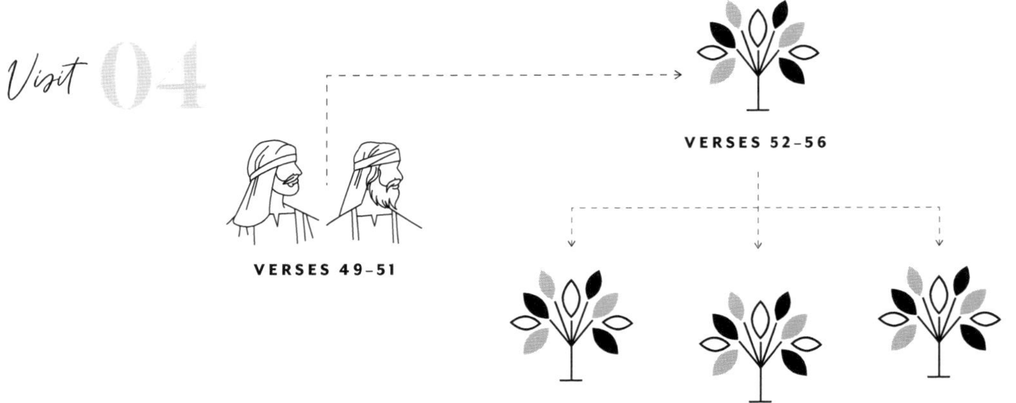

JACOB 5:57–58 *Instructions*	JACOB 5:59–60 *Goals*	JACOB 5:61–72 *The Plan*	JACOB 5:73–77 *The Results*

Jacob 6

After Jacob finished quoting Zenos' allegory, Jacob pointed out some truths he wanted to make sure the Nephites understood. In verse 1, he makes it very clear that he is prophesying and that the things in the allegory will surely come to pass.

(1) JACOB 6:1–4

Write or draw what you learn about the Lord restoring Israel in the last days.

(2) JACOB 6:5–8

Jacob was pleading for the Nephites to repent. Write or draw some of your favorite phrases and questions he uses as he tries to touch their hearts.

(3) JACOB 6:9–13

What warnings did Jacob give those who refuse to repent? Write or draw what you find here.

WHAT ARE SOME SPECIFIC TIMES (OR SPECIFIC WAYS) YOU HAVE "LABORED DILIGENTLY IN HIS VINEYARD"? (VERSE 3)

Sherem the Antichrist

JACOB 7:5

"And he had hope to shake me from the faith ... I could not be shaken."

This chapter introduces the first antichrist in the Book of Mormon. Sherem (in this chapter), Nehor (Alma 1), and Korihor (Alma 30) are the three antichrists. An antichrist is one who denies Jesus Christ or essential parts of His Gospel. The Book of Mormon reveals the subtle and deceptive tactics these antichrists use to destroy people's faith in Christ and His Gospel. What tactics can you find in this chapter?

JACOB 7:1–4 **Sherem the Antichrist // Sherem Targets Jacob**

JACOB 7:5–7
Sherem speaks to Jacob

JACOB 7:8–12
Jacob responds to Sherem

Christian Courage: The Price of Discipleship

"One of mortality's great tests comes when our beliefs are questioned or criticized."

ELDER ROBERT D. HALES
October 2008 General Conference

JACOB 7:13–15
Sherem falls to the earth

JACOB 7:16–22
Sherem speaks to the people

JACOB 7:23–27
State of the people

"Sherem with his learning, his eloquence and his flattery, sought to turn away people from the simple faith, and he died in remorse and humiliation."

PRESIDENT SPENCER W. KIMBALL
April 1955 General Conference

Sherem Denies Christ
Jacob 7 | 7:17 minutes

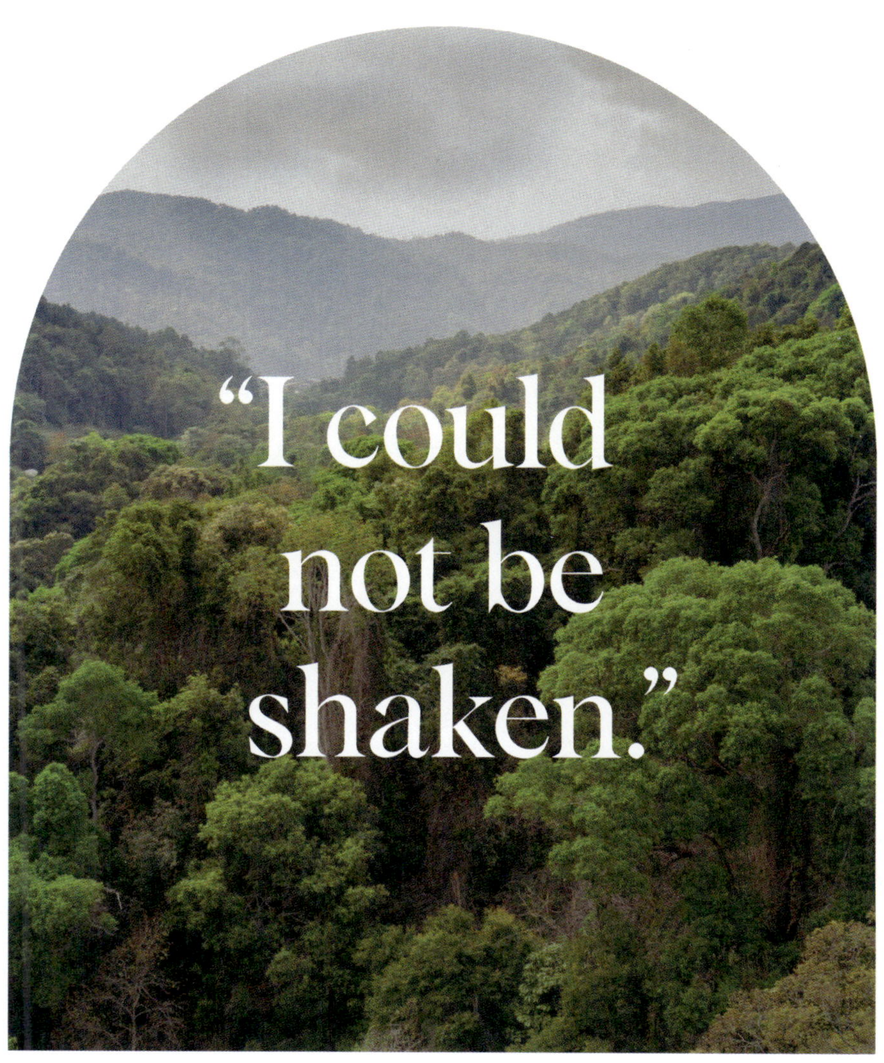

Leave Your Record

WHEN ARE SOME TIMES SHEREMS HAVE COME INTO YOUR
LIFE? WHAT DID YOU DO TO STAND STRONG?

Enos | Jarom | Omni
Words of Mormon

- Enos, the son of Jacob, wrote the book of Enos.

- Enos received the small plates of Nephi from his father Jacob.

- Before Enos' death he passed the plates to his son Jarom.

- The book of Jarom covers about 38 years of Nephite history.

- Jarom passed the plates to his son Omni.

- The book of Omni has five different writers: Omni, Amaron, Chemish, Abinadom, and Amaleki. The first four writers added small entries onto the plates; together they wrote verses 1–11. Amaleki then added verses 12–30.

- Words of Mormon was written by the prophet Mormon. Mormon interrupts the Nephite record and briefly gives an explanation of the record he was making.

And it came to pass that the people of Zarahemla,
and of Mosiah, did unite together; and Mosiah was
appointed to be their king.

Omni 1:19

Timeline

Here are these books at-a-glance. The main stories are found in the timeline below. If you ever want to find a story in your scriptures, you can look at this page for help. You can add your own notes to this page as well.

ENOS 1

- Enos prays for forgiveness for his sins
- Enos prays for the Nephites and Lamanites
- Enos prophesied to the Nephites

JAROM 1

- Jarom receives the plates from father Enos
- Jarom testifies
- Jarom mentions wars
- Jarom passes plates to his son Omni

WORDS OF MORMON

- This book is not chronologically placed
- This book was written about AD 385 - at the end of the Nephite civilization
- Mormon writes to those who will read the Book of Mormon in the future

OMNI 1

- Omni describes peace and war
- Amaron, Chemish, and Abinadom write on plates
- Nephites in state of apostasy
- Amaleki records about Mosiah and King Benjamin

EVENTS AMALEKI WROTE ABOUT

- Mosiah led people out of the land of Nephi
- Mosiah discovered the people of Zarahemla
- Mosiah made king over Nephites and people of Zarahemla
- Mosiah's son Benjamin made king
- Amaleki passed plates to King Benjamin
- Amaleki mentions group of Nephites who left to return to the land of Nephi and had not been heard of

People to Know

If you need a reminder of who is who, return to this page.

Enos

Enos was the son of Jacob, grandson to Lehi and Sariah, and wrote the book of Enos. He sought forgiveness and labored to bring salvation to others.

Jarom

Jarom was the son of Enos and wrote the book of Jarom. He did not record his own prophecies. He thought the words recorded by his fathers "revealed the plan of salvation" (Jarom 1:2).

Omni

Omni was the son of Jarom. The Book of Omni is named after him, but the book also has four other writers. He fought much with the Lamanites and considered himself wicked.

Amaron

Amaron was the son of Omni. He wrote five verses in the book of Omni and explained that "the more wicked part of the Nephites were destroyed" (Omni 1:5) as the Lord preserved the righteous from the Lamanites.

Chemish

Chemish was a brother to Amaron. He wrote one verse in the book of Omni.

Abinadom

Abinadom was the son of Chemish. He wrote two verses in the book of Omni. He witnessed much war between the Nephites and Lamanites.

Amaleki

Amaleki was the son of Abinadom. He wrote 19 verses in the book of Omni. He wrote about King Mosiah, Zarahemla, and King Benjamin. He passed the plates to King Benjamin.

Mosiah

This is Mosiah the Elder (his grandson is also Mosiah). Mosiah was a Nephite prophet who was warned to flee the land of Nephi and take all who would come with him. He discovered the people of Zarahemla and was made king there.

Zarahemla

This was the city and people discovered by Mosiah. Shortly after Lehi's family left, Mulek led a group out of Jerusalem to the promised land as they escaped the Babylonians. The descendants of the Mulekites lived in Zarahemla.

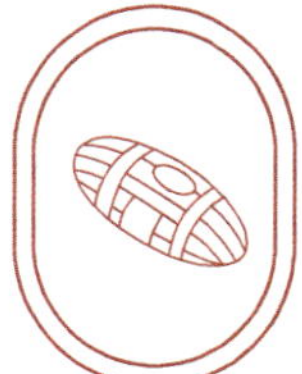

Jaredites

The Jaredites had been led to the promised land in the days of the Tower of Babel and lived in the promised land for around 1,600 years until they destroyed themselves. Coriantumr was the last surviving Jaredite. The book of Ether is a record of the Jaredites.

King Benjamin

Benjamin was the son of Mosiah the Elder. He was a righteous king in Zarahemla. He received the plates from Amaleki.

Mormon

Mormon was a prophet at the end of the Nephite civilization. He abridged (shortened) the 1,000 years of Nephite history and prophecies into a single record.

Enos, Jarom, Omni, & Words of Mormon

In these chapters

Enos prays mightily   //   Jarom testifies   //   King Mosiah I leads the Nephites out of the land of Nephi and finds Zarahemla   //   Some Nephites leave Zarahemla to return to the land of Nephi   //   King Benjamin is king of the Nephites   //   Mormon inserts some of his own words

---

Enos thru Omni will cover a time period during which the plates are passed through seven different writers.

↓

The books of Enos, Jarom, and Omni cover 290 years. Omni, alone, covers 193 years. The only two other books in the Book of Mormon that cover more time than the book of Omni are: 4 Nephi and the book of Ether.

Who were the people in Zarahemla that the Nephites found?

After Lehi and his family left Jerusalem, Jerusalem was destroyed by Babylon. All of King Zedekiah's sons were killed except his son Mulek. Mulek took many Jews with him and escaped into the wilderness, and then they, like Lehi's family, were led to the same promised land. The two civilizations (the Mulekites and Nephites/Lamanites) did not cross paths for many generations. Mulek's people established their capital of Zarahemla in a land north of the Nephites and Lamanites. Mosiah discovered this great city when he was commanded to get out of the land of his fathers (the Land of Nephi).

Enos 1

The Story of Enos

The story of Enos will resonate with many of us and those that we care about. He was a son, a grandson, and a nephew of prophets—but he wrestled with his own sins. The redemption he experiences will change the man he is and qualify him for one of his great missions, which is to have stewardship over the sacred records.

ENOS 1:1 | *Enos and his father Jacob*

ENOS 1:2-8 | *Enos prays and is forgiven*

ENOS 1:9-11
Nephi prays for Nephites and Lamanites

ENOS 1:12-19 | *Enos' desire; Enos prophesies*

ENOS 1:20-24 | *The Lamanites; The Nephites*

ENOS 1:25-27 | *Enos' last words*

"Enos recounted how his soul had hungered and that he had prayed all the day long. Prayers vary in their intensity. Even the Savior "prayed more earnestly" in His hour of agony (Luke 22:44). Some are simple expressions of appreciation and requests for a continuation of blessings on our loved ones and us. However, in times of great personal hurt or need, more may be required than mere asking. The Lord said, "You have supposed that I would give it unto you, when you took no thought save it was to ask me" (D&C 9:7). Blessings sought through prayer sometimes require work, effort, and diligence on our part.

PRESIDENT JAMES E. FAUST
April 2002 General Conference

My One Chapter

After Enos received the plates, he chose to add one chapter, which included the story of him wrestling and gaining unshaken faith.

IF YOU HAD ONE CHAPTER TO ADD TO THE SCRIPTURES, ONE STORY THAT WOULD HELP OTHERS COME UNTO CHRIST, WHAT STORY WOULD YOU INCLUDE?

Jarom

As you study the book of Jarom, try to find at least three principles that stand out to you and write about them below.

Stewardship of Records

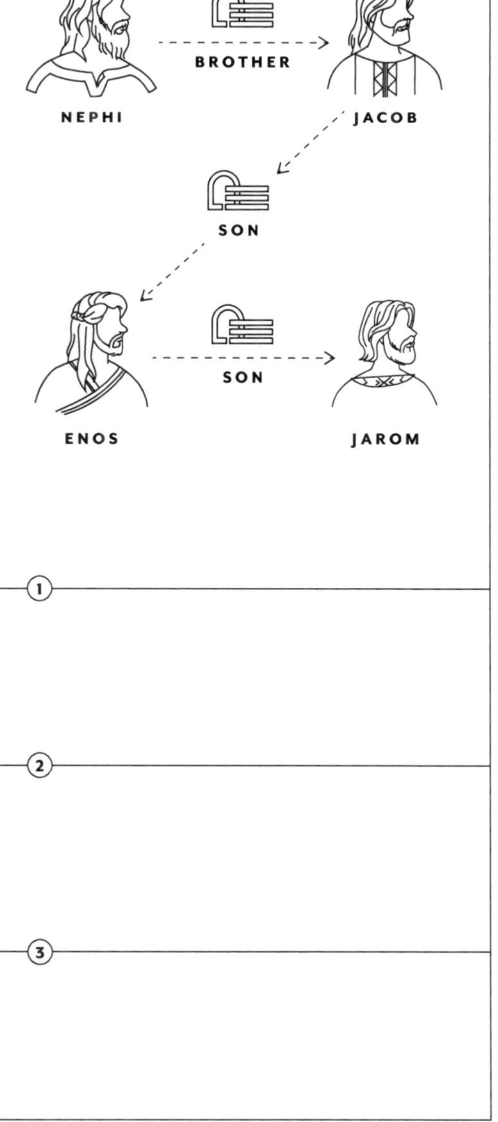

1

2

3

Omni 1:1–12

The book of Omni covers nearly 200 years and has five writers. Starting with Omni and ending with Amaleki (verses 1-12), write or draw what you learn from or about each writer.

Stewardship of Records

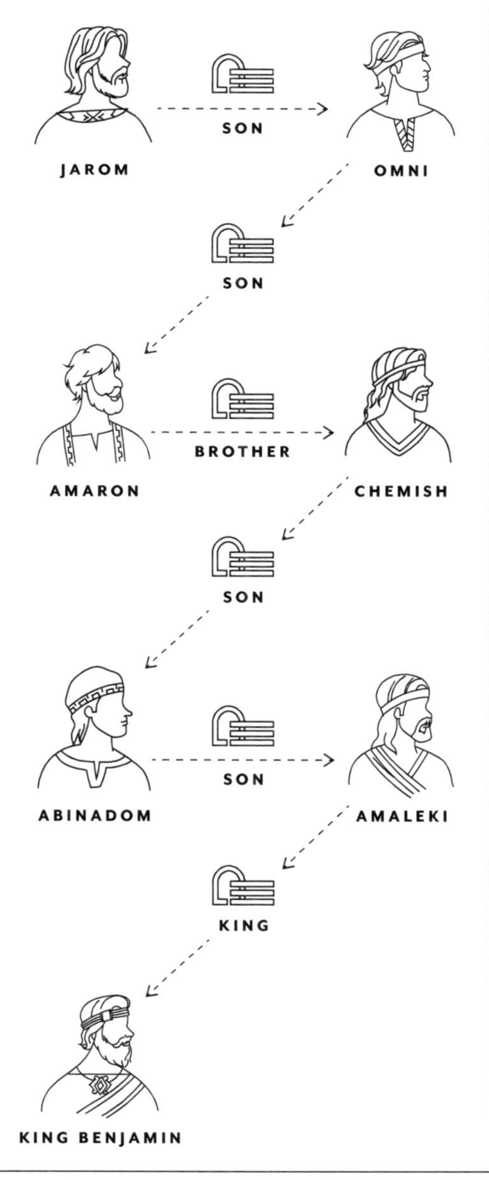

Omni 1:12-30

The writer Amaleki (in the book of Omni) covered some really important stories that happened. On the story map below, follow the numbers and write or draw what happened.

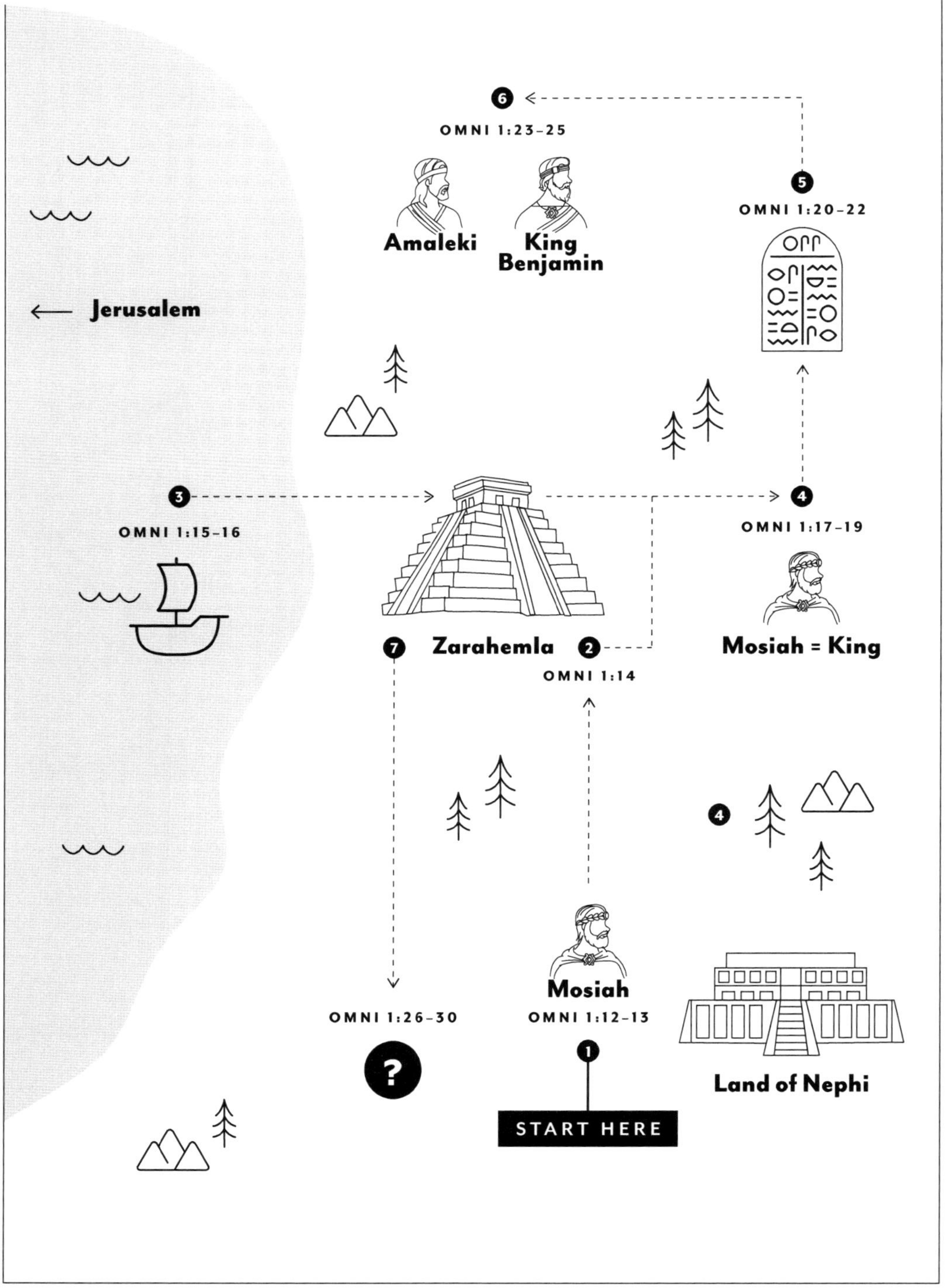

Words of Mormon

This is the first time that we hear from the prophet Mormon. Up until this point, you have been hearing directly from prophets who wrote upon the small plates, and now Mormon will continue the storyline using the large plates of Nephi.

Did You Know?

Mormon did not live during this time period; he lived 500 years later during the end of the Nephite civilization. (see verse 2). Before the Nephites were completely destroyed, his mission was to compile and abridge all of the Nephite records into one record which we now know as "The Book of Mormon."

Since Mormon was transitioning from the small plates to the large plates, he gives us an explanation and inserted this explanation in between Omni and Mosiah.

Abridge means to make shorter. So he took the records and shortened them as he wrote upon the gold plates.

"And I do this for a wise purpose; for thus it whispereth me, according to the workings of the Spirit of the Lord which is in me. And now, I do not know all things; but the Lord knoweth all things which are to come; wherefore, he worketh in me to do according to his will."

Mormon had already abridged part of the Nephite history from Lehi's time to the time of King Benjamin. Then Mormon came across the small plates of Nephi which covered the same time period. As Mormon searched these small plates of Nephi, they were full of prophecies—including many that had already been fulfilled.

Mormon then took the small plates and put them with the plates he was abridging, so there would have been a duplication in history covered. Mormon knew he was doing this for a "wise purpose" because the Spirit confirmed that to him, but he did not know exactly why.

Over 1,000 years after Mormon lived, Joseph Smith began the translation of the Book of Mormon; he first translated the book of Lehi. He had 116 pages of translated scripture when Martin Harris begged Joseph to let him take the manuscript (not the plates) and show his family. Joseph asked God three times if Martin could take the manuscript, and God finally gave him permission. Those 116 pages were then lost and it was revealed to Joseph that wicked men were in possession of them (see D&C 10).

The Lord then told Joseph not to retranslate the plates but to continue the translation with the small plates of Nephi (see D&C 10:30 and 38–45) which contained the same history. The wicked men had altered the translation (see D&C 10:42–43) so a retranslation would not match and the wicked men would then seek to discredit Joseph. But God is all-knowing and His wisdom is greater than "the cunning of the devil" (D&C 10:43), so God had planned for this all along.

"At least six times in the Book of Mormon the phrase 'for a wise purpose' is used in reference to the making, writing, and preserving of the small plates of Nephi (see 1 Nephi 9:5; Words of Mormon 1:7; Alma 37:2, 12, 14, 18). You and I know the wise purpose—the most obvious one—was to compensate for the loss of the earlier mentioned 116 pages of manuscript.

"But it strikes me that there is a wiser purpose than that. …The key to such a suggestion of a wiser purpose is in verse 45 of Doctrine and Covenants section 10. As the Lord instructs Joseph … he says, 'Behold, there are many things engraven upon the [small] plates of Nephi which do throw greater views upon my gospel'.

"So, clearly, this was not … tit for tat, this for that—you give me 116 pages of manuscript and I'll give you 142 pages of printed text. Not so. We got back more than we lost. And it was known from the beginning that it would be so. It was for a wiser purpose. We do not know exactly what we missed in the 116 pages, but we do know that what we received on the small plates was the personal declarations of three great witnesses [Nephi, Jacob, and Isaiah], three of the great doctrinal voices of the Book of Mormon, testifying that Jesus is the Christ. …"

Elder Jeffrey R. Holland

CES SYMPOSIUM, AUGUST 9, 1994

WHEN HAS THE LORD GUIDED YOU IN A WAY
THAT YOU DID NOT UNDERSTAND AT THE
MOMENT BUT LATER YOU REALIZED THAT IT
WAS "FOR A WISE PURPOSE"?

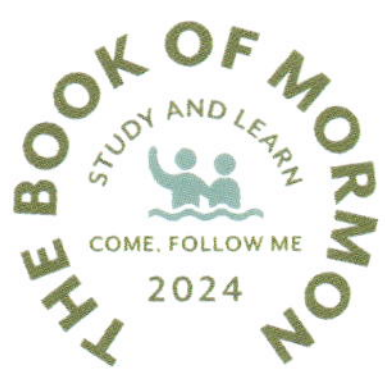

Mosiah

DID YOU KNOW?

- The book of Mosiah is an abridgment made by Mormon using the records of multiple writers.

- The events in the book of Mosiah occurred around 200 BC and 91 BC.

- The book of Mosiah is the first book in the Book of Mormon that is an abridgment from the large plates of Nephi. The previous books in the Book of Mormon came from the small plates of Nephi, and were not abridged.

- The book of Mosiah is named after the son of King Benjamin, Mosiah II.

And it came to pass that he said unto them:
Behold, here are the waters of Mormon (for thus
were they called) and now, as ye are desirous to
come into the fold of God, and to be called his
people, and are willing to bear one another's
burdens, that they may be light;

Mosiah 18:8

Timeline

Mormon used the records of several writers to make the book of Mosiah. He used Mosiah's record, Zeniff's record, and Alma's record.

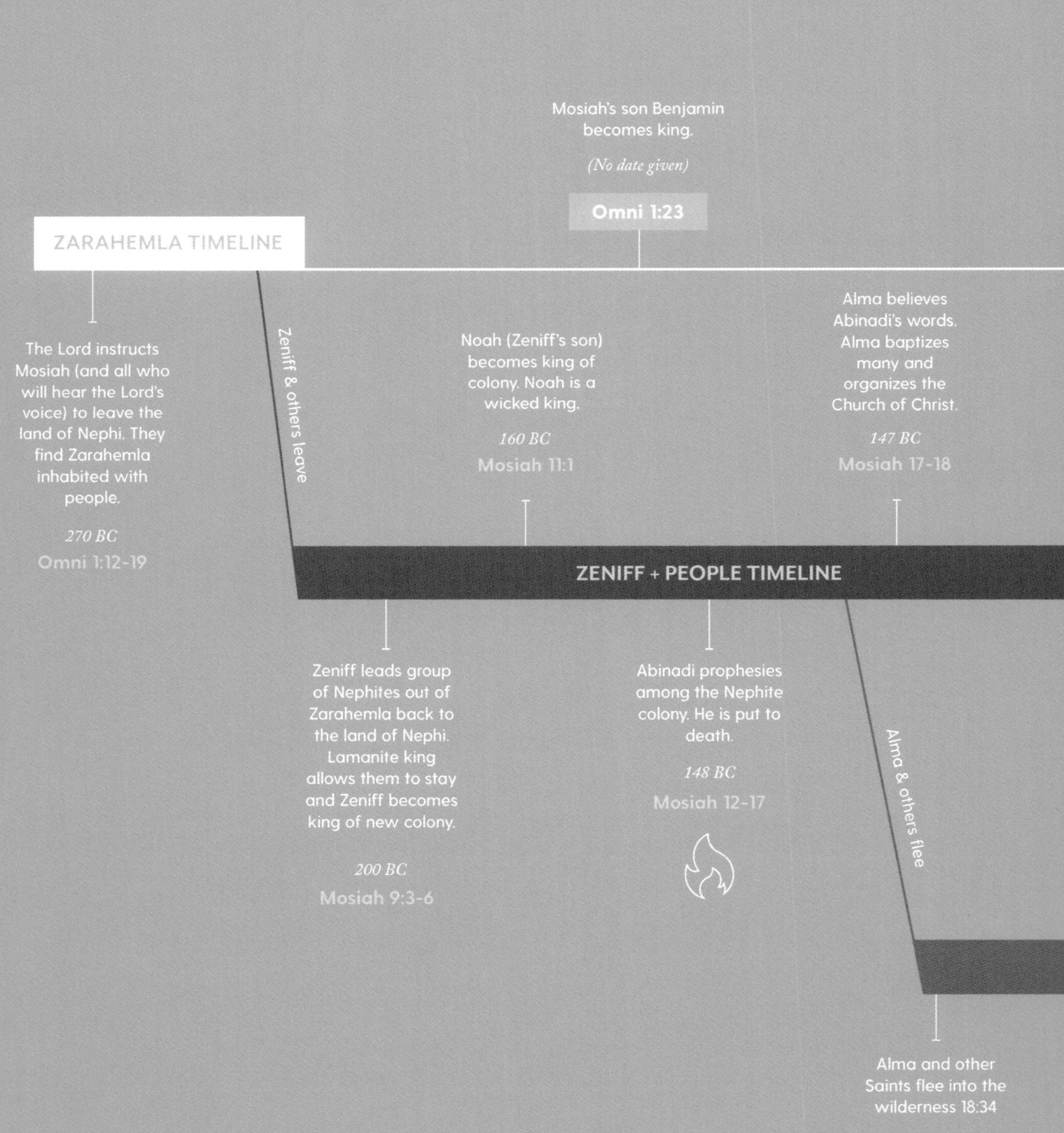

The book of Mosiah starts here and then goes back to the beginning of the darker green line.

King Mosiah II becomes king and seeks to know what happened to the Nephites who had left with Zeniff. He sends Ammon and 15 strong men to the land of Lehi-Nephi.

121 BC

Mosiah 7:1-2

Amaleki passes plates to King Benjamin.

130 BC

Omni 1:25

King Benjamin gives address.

124 BC

Mosiah 2-4

Alma the Younger and the Sons of Mosiah

Between 100–92 BC

Mosiah 27

Limhi becomes king and is in bondage to the Lamanites.

145–121 BC
Mosiah 19:26-28

Ammon leads Limhi and people to Zarahemla.

120 BC
Mosiah 22:13-14

ZENIFF + PEOPLE TIMELINE

King Noah is slain.

145–121 BC
Mosiah 19:20

Ammon finds Nephites. King Limhi (Noah's son) was king and they were living in servitude to the Lamanites.

121 BC
Mosiah 7:9-15

ALMA + PEOPLE TIMELINE

Alma and people prosper in the land of Helam.

145–121 BC
Mosiah 23:19

Alma and people are in bondage to the Lamanites in the land of Helam.

145–121 BC
Mosiah 23:25-29

Alma and people escape bondage and arrive in Zarahemla.

120 BC
Mosiah 24:25

People to Know

If you need a reminder of who is who, return to this page.

King Benjamin

Benjamin was the son of Mosiah I. He became prophet and king in Zarahemla and is known for his address to his people in Mosiah 2–4.

Ammon I

Ammon led a group of 15 other strong men from Zarahemla to the land of Nephi to find Zeniff's people who had left many years earlier.

Zeniff

Zeniff led a group of Nephites out of Zarahemla back to the land of Nephi to inherit the land of their fathers. He became king to the Nephite colony in the land of Nephi.

Abinadi

Abinadi was a prophet during the time of King Noah. He was imprisoned for prophesying about Noah's destruction. He was known for his sermon in Mosiah 12–16. Abinadi was burned to death.

Gideon

Gideon was an enemy to King Noah and counselor to King Limhi. He came up with a plan for Limhi's people to escape Lamanite bondage. Gideon was killed by Nehor.

Alma the Younger

This Alma was the son of Alma the Elder. He worked to destroy the Church of God. He was rebuked by an angel, repented, and became a righteous leader.

Mosiah II

This Mosiah was the son of King Benjamin and grandson of Mosiah the Elder. He became a righteous king after King Benjamin. He translated the 24 Jaredite plates.

Limhi

Limhi was the son of wicked King Noah, and he became the next king of the Nephites in the land of Nephi. Limhi was a righteous king and entered into a covenant to serve God.

King Noah

Noah was the son of Zeniff, and he became king after Zeniff. Noah was a wicked king, and he ordered the death of Abinadi.

Alma I

Alma was born in the land of Nephi among the people of Zeniff. He was a priest of King Noah, but he believed Abinadi's words. Alma baptized believers and fled.

Amulon

Amulon was leader to the wicked priests of king Noah. He joined Lamanites and discovered the land of Helam. Amulon brought Alma and his people under bondage.

Sons of Mosiah

There were four sons of King Mosiah: Ammon, Aaron, Omner, and Himni. With Alma the Younger, they sought to destroy the Church of God and an angel rebuked them. They became missionaries among the Lamanites.

About Zarahemla

Zarahemla was a large city.

The people of Zarahemla had originally come from Jerusalem at the time that Babylon destroyed Jerusalem and carried away captives. A group had escaped and the Lord guided them to a new land. Lehi and his family had already left Jerusalem at the time this group escaped.

Mosiah and his followers discovered the people of Zarahemla when the Lord warned him and all who would follow him to flee out of the land of Nephi (see Omni 1:13).

The Lord guided Mosiah and his people to Zarahemla where they "discovered a people, who were called the people of Zarahemla" (Omni 1:14).

Mosiah discovered that the people of Zarahemla had become numerous and had experienced many wars and contentions (Omni 1:17).

Mosiah also discovered that the inhabitants of Zarahemla now had a corrupted language, had brought no records with them, and they denied God (Omni 1:17).

Mosiah taught the people of Zarahemla his language; he and his people united with them, and Mosiah was made their king (Omni 1:19).

Zarahemla became the Nephite capital.

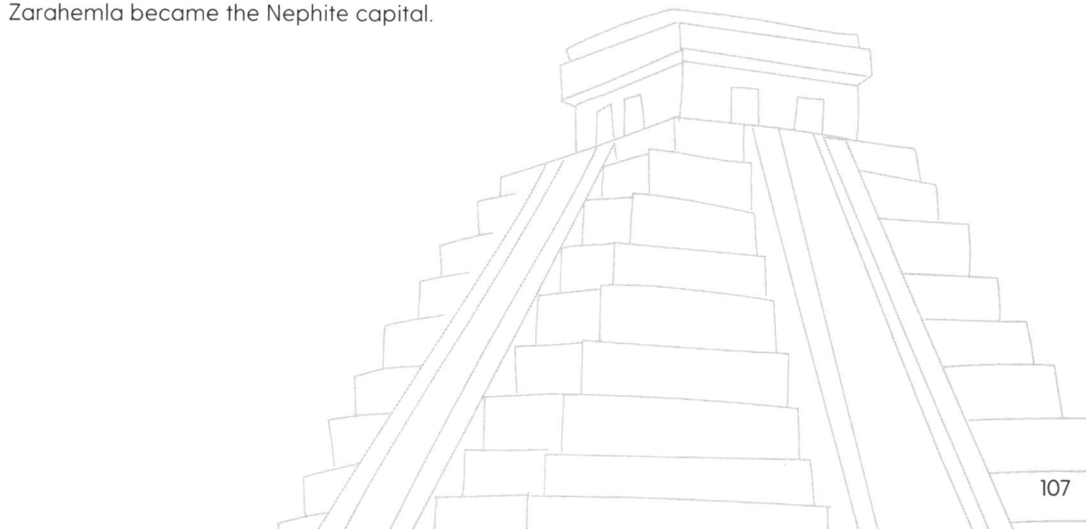

Mosiah 1–3

In these chapters

King Benjamin teaches sons // Mosiah II becomes king // King Benjamin's sermon

"...we begin to learn of Benjamin's character well before his sermon. Just as this special king labored to produce his own necessities, he personalized his leadership in other ways. As a warrior- king, he "did fight with the strength of his own arm, with the sword of Laban" in putting down unrest (Words of Mormon 1:13), to which false Christs, false prophets, and false preachers doubtless contributed (see Words of Mormon 1:16). In this challenging context he was not alone, for there were "many holy men in the land" who assisted him (Words of Mormon 1:17). Thus, well before the great sermon, King Benjamin had been involved with typical single-mindedness in his successful efforts to deal with contention and dissension. He acted, as was his pattern, "with all the might of his body and the faculty of his whole soul" and established peace in the land (Words of Mormon 1:18)."

ELDER NEAL A. MAXWELL
King Benjamin's Sermon: A Manual for Discipleship, 3–4

further learning

Read Elder Maxwell's book about King Benjamin's Sermon here

Mosiah 1

📖 Overview + Questions

King Benjamin was a great leader—the next chapters will show you how great. But his leadership first began in his own home with his own sons: Mosiah, Helorum, and Helaman.

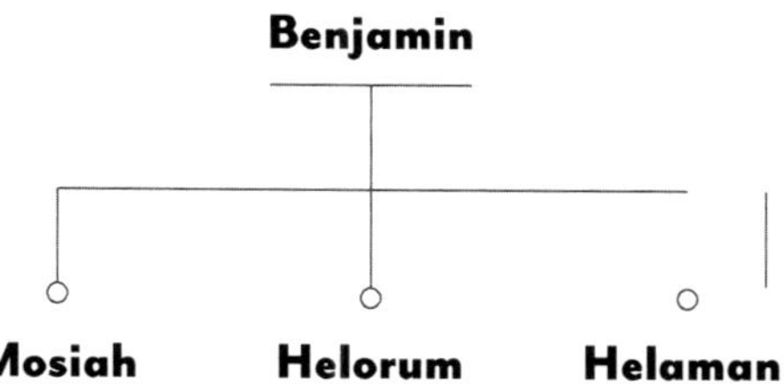

IN THIS SPACE, WRITE OR DRAW WHAT YOU LEARN IN VERSES 1–8	
	What did King Benjamin teach his sons so that they would "become men of understanding"?
	What do you think it means to become a man or woman of understanding?
	Who are some men or women of understanding in your life?
	How can you become a man or woman of understanding?

IN THIS SPACE, WRITE OR DRAW WHAT YOU LEARN IN VERSES 9–12

MOSIAH 1:13–14	MOSIAH 1:15–17	MOSIAH 1:18
What warning does King Benjamin give Mosiah about the people?	*What did King Benjamin give to Mosiah?*	*What did King Benjamin ask the people to do?*

King Benjamin's Sermon

Before King Benjamin died, he called his people together to teach them and spiritually strengthen them. This sermon, often called "King Benjamin's Sermon," is found in Mosiah 2–5.

Write or draw doctrines and principles you learn from King Benjamin's Sermon below

VERSES 1–8	VERSES 9–12	VERSES 13–15	VERSES 16–17
VERSES 18–19	**VERSES 20–21**	**VERSE 22**	**VERSES 23–24**
VERSES 25–26	**VERSES 27–28**	**VERSES 29–31**	**VERSES 32–33**
VERSES 34–35	**VERSES 36–37**	**VERSES 38–40**	**VERSE 41**

Mosiah 3

KING BENJAMIN'S SERMON CONTINUES ...

"[A natural man is] a person who chooses to be influenced by the passions, desires, appetites, and senses of the flesh rather than by the promptings of the Holy Spirit. Such a person can comprehend physical things but not spiritual things. All people are carnal, or mortal, because of the Fall of Adam and Eve. Each person must be born again through the Atonement of Jesus Christ to cease being a natural man."

GUIDE TO THE SCRIPTURES, "NATURAL MAN"

VERSE 1	VERSES 2–4	VERSE 5	VERSES 6–8
VERSES 9–11	VERSES 12–13	VERSES 14–15	VERSE 16
MESSIANIC PROPHECY			
VERSE 17	VERSE 18	VERSE 19	VERSES 20–22
VERSES 23–24	VERSE 25	VERSE 26	VERSE 27

Mosiah 4-6

In these chapters

Remainder of King Benjamin's sermon // People covenant and are called by the name of Christ // King Benjamin records names of people // Mosiah II becomes king

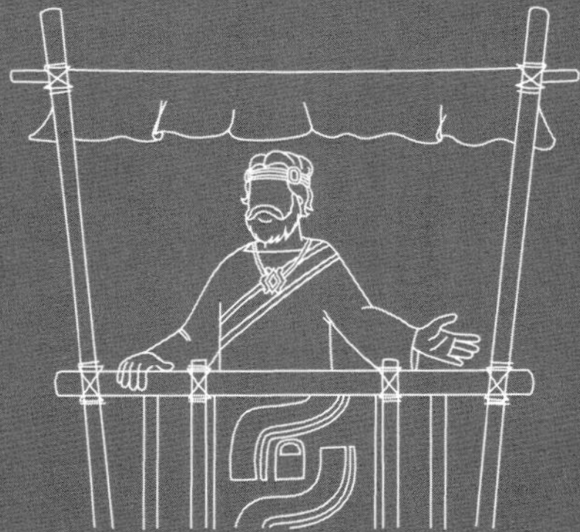

In Mosiah 1:10–11, King Benjamin had stated the two reasons he was calling his people together.

THOSE TWO REASONS WERE:

1. To name his son Mosiah II as the new king
2. To give his people a name

In Mosiah 5, the name they are given is the name of Christ (see verses 8–10).

Therefore, King Benjamin's entire sermon is about what his people must DO, BELIEVE, and BECOME in order to be worthy to take upon the name of Christ.

There is the key to leading your family to rise to that spiritual place you want for them —and for you to be there with them. As you help them grow in faith that Jesus Christ is their loving Redeemer, they will feel a desire to repent. As they do, humility will begin to replace pride. As they begin to feel what the Lord has given them, they will want to share more generously. Rivalry for prominence or recognition will diminish. Hate will be driven out by love. And finally, like it did for the people converted by King Benjamin, the desire to do good will fortify them against temptation to sin. King Benjamin's people testified that they had "no more disposition to do evil."

PRESIDENT HENRY B. EYRING
April 2019 General Conference

Mosiah 4

King Benjamin's Sermon

Write or draw doctrines and principles you learn from
King Benjamin's sermon in these boxes.

King Benjamin Addresses His People
Mosiah 1-5 | 17:52 minutes

VERSES 1–2

VERSE 3

*Where we want to be all of the time.

VERSES 4–7

VERSES 8–10

VERSE 11

VERSES 12–13

VERSES 14–16

VERSES 17–19

VERSES 20–23

VERSES 24–25

VERSE 26

VERSE 27

VERSE 28

VERSES 29–30

Taking upon the Name of Christ

King Benjamin sent people out to find out if they believed his words or not. This was important because he needed to know if they were ready for the next thing, which was to take upon themselves the name of Christ. Everything he has been teaching them is what they need to know, do, and become in order to take upon themselves Christ's name.

Write or draw about the impact the sermon had on the people.

MOSIAH 5:1–5	MOSIAH 5:6–11	MOSIAH 5:12–15

MOSIAH 6:1–2	MOSIAH 6:3	MOSIAH 6:4–7

Mottos for My Life

Look over chapters 2–5 and choose phrases that could be a personal motto for the following life scenarios. Write the the mottos you choose by each scenario.

MY FAMILY

WHO I WANT TO BE

MY DISCIPLESHIP

HOW I MINISTER TO OTHERS

MY TESTIMONY/SPIRITUAL GROWTH

MY RELATIONSHIP WITH JESUS CHRIST

Mosiah 7–10

In these chapters

Ammon finds Limhi and his people // Limhi tells of their history // Ammon teaches the people // Zeniff's record // Zeniff leads people to land of Nephi // Lamanite king allows them to live on land // Battle with Lamanites

The book of Mosiah can be confusing because it jumps back and forth to different time periods.

- Two generations before King Mosiah II's life, there was a group of Nephites who had left Zarahemla with the hopes of regaining the land of their fathers (the Land of Nephi). A man named Zeniff led them.

- Zeniff's group had not been heard of since; and King Mosiah II was concerned with their whereabouts and well-being, so he sent a search party to find them.

- Mosiah 7–8 is the journey of this group finding those lost Nephites.

- Mosiah 9–24 is the story of the lost Nephites and what had happened when they left Zarahemla all of those years before.

Mosiah 7

Study verses 1–8 and write on this story map what is happening.

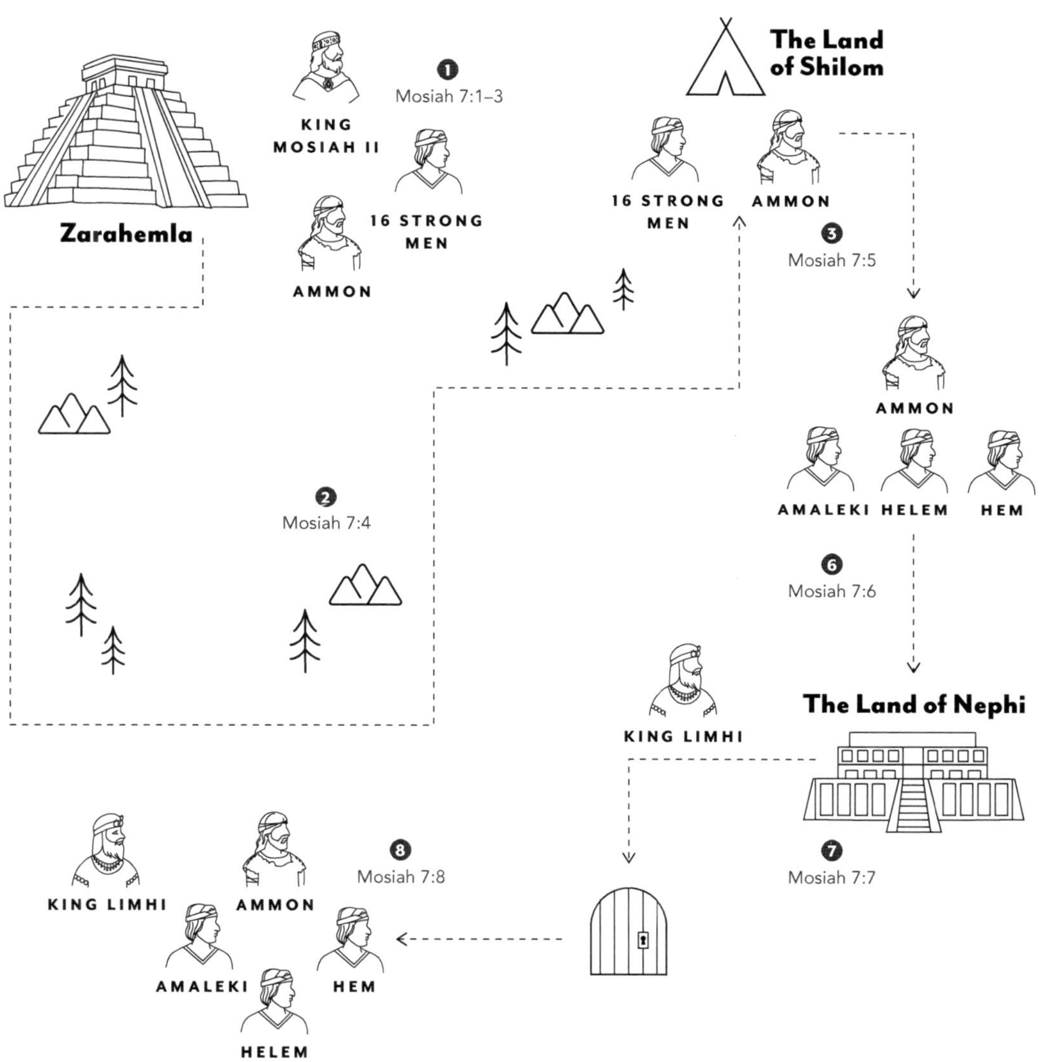

MOSIAH 7:9–33
What you learn about the Nephites Ammon and the others found

Mosiah 8

<table>
<tr><td>MOSIAH 8:1–4 What did Ammon teach Limhi's people?</td></tr>
<tr><td>MOSIAH 8:5–6 What did Limhi bring before Ammon? Why?</td></tr>
</table>

Study verses 7–11 and write on this story map what is happening.

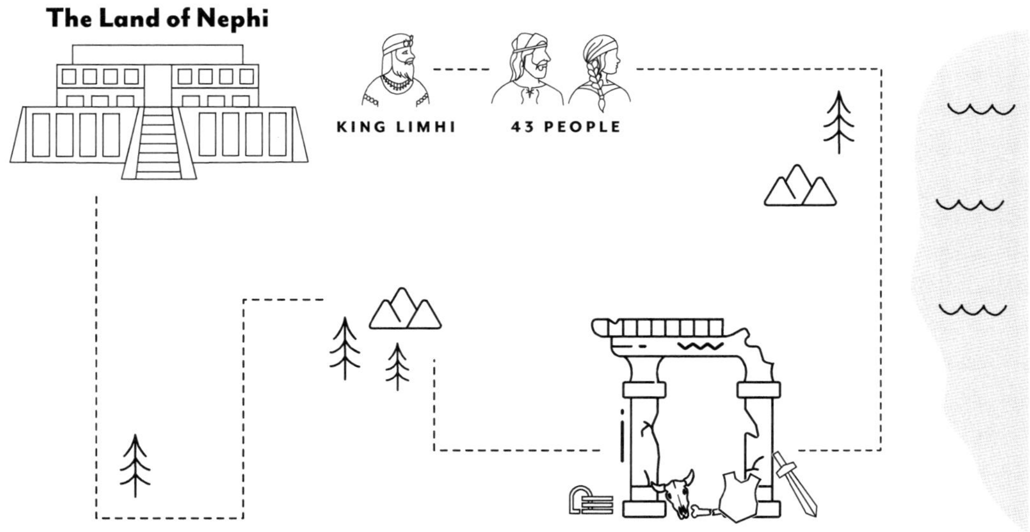

<table>
<tr><td>Re-read Mosiah 7:14. Now that you know about King Limhi sending 43 of his people off to find Zarahemla, why did he rejoice when he met Ammon and his brethren?</td></tr>
<tr><td>MOSIAH 8:12–13 Who could translate the 24 gold plates?</td></tr>
<tr><td>MOSIAH 8:14–19 What is a seer?</td></tr>
<tr><td>MOSIAH 8:20–21 What doctrines and principles can you find?
Tip: "She" is referencing "wisdom" in the line before; so the line could read "… that wisdom should rule over them!"</td></tr>
</table>

Mosiah 9

Zeniff is the grandfather of Limhi and the one who originally left Zarahemla with a group of Nephites who wanted to take back the land of their fathers (the Land of Nephi). Remember in Omni, we learned that King Mosiah I was inspired to lead the Nephites out of the Land of Nephi where they were under the constant threat of the Lamanites. Now these Nephites wanted to go back to that land where their fathers had lived. Mosiah 9 begins the record of what happened once they left, so you are jumping back in time starting in Mosiah 9 until Mosiah 21:22 as you learn about their history. This chapter begins at about 200 B.C. when Zeniff originally left Zarahemla. The chapter before, when Ammon met Limhi, was about 121 B.C., so Mosiah 9 is going back 79 years in time.

Study verses 1–2 and write what you learn about Zeniff and the beginning of his journey.

Study verses 3–9 and write and draw what is happening all over this map.

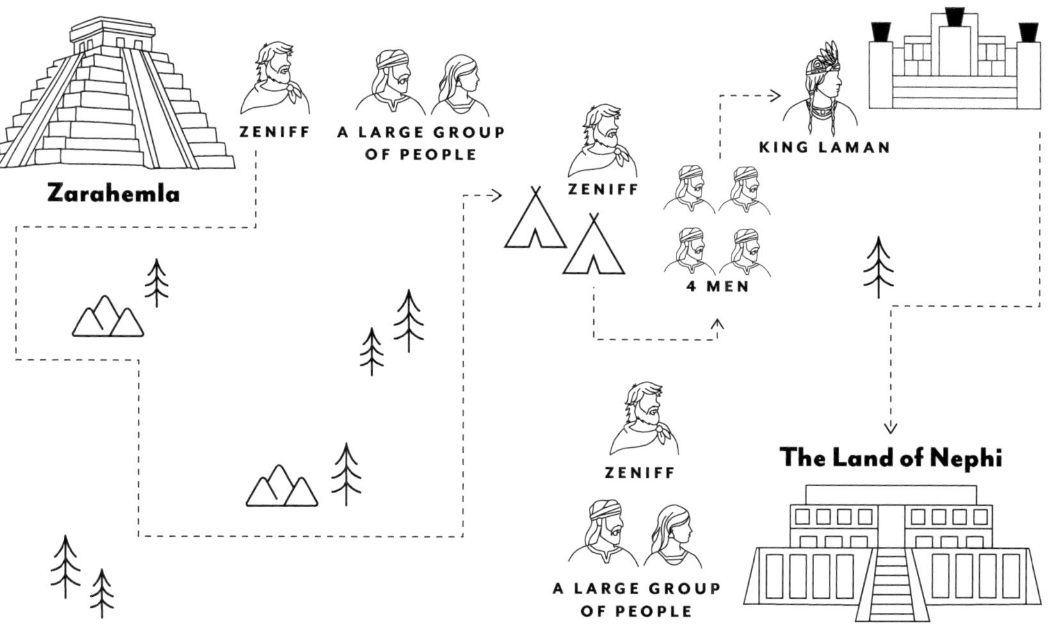

Draw or write what is happening in these verses.	
MOSIAH 9:10 *The plan of the Lamanite king*	**MOSIAH 9:11** *12 years later*
MOSIAH 9:12–13 *The Lamanites*	**MOSIAH 9:14** *Lamanites attack*
MOSIAH 9:15–17 *Zeniff's response*	**MOSIAH 9:18–19** *Nephite victory*

Mosiah 10

Study these verses and draw or write what is happening in each space. You can also add pictures or make notes on the story map down the side.

(1) MOSIAH 10:1–5
Zeniff's Leadership

(2) MOSIAH 10:6
New Lamanite King

(3) MOSIAH 10:7
Guarding Themselves

(4) MOSIAH 10:8
Lamanite Army

(5) MOSIAH 10:9
Nephite Army

(6) MOSIAH 10:10–11
How to Battle

(7) MOSIAH 10:12–18
Why the Lamanites Hated the Nephites

(8) MOSIAH 10:19–20
How to Battle

(9) MOSIAH 10:21–22
Zeniff Makes His Son King

In the Strength of the Lord

And it came to pass that we did go up to battle against the Lamanites; and I, even I, in my old age, did go up to battle against the Lamanites. And it came to pass that we did go up in the strength of the Lord to battle.

Leave Your Record

WHEN IS A TIME THAT YOU HAVE GONE FORTH "IN THE STRENGTH OF THE LORD"?

Mosiah 11–17

In these chapters

Wicked King Noah   //   Abinadi prophesies and is imprisoned   //
Abinadi teaches   //   Abinadi suffers death by fire

These chapters introduce and teach us about the wicked King Noah and
the great prophet Abinadi. One principle that can be discussed and
pondered in these chapters is how to be an Abinadi in a King Noah world.
King Noah will blind the eyes of his people through flattery, worldliness,
wickedness, and denying true doctrine, but Abinadi will stand
courageously in opposition to what King Noah was doing and teaching.
Abinadi does not become blinded because he knows truth.

Another hero in this story is Alma. Because he believed Abinadi, his scales
of blindness fell away and then he helped others become unblinded too.
As you and your family study these chapters, you can ask yourselves,
"What can we learn from Abinadi and Alma about how to live in a world
that is full of things that cause spiritual blindness?"

Mosiah 11

What do you learn about King Noah and the Nephites he reigned over?
Record what you find in each box.

Mosiah 11:1–5	Mosiah 11:6–10	Mosiah 11:11–15

Mosiah 11:16–18

*What happened when the
Lamanites came upon the Nephites?*

Mosiah 11:19

*What are some important
teachings you see in verse 19?*

Mosiah 11:20–25

*What important counsel and warnings
did Abinadi give the people?*

Mosiah 11:26–29

*What was the reaction of the king
and people to Abinadi?*

Mosiah 12

What do you learn about Abinadi's character and strength in verse 1?	List or draw specific prophecies Abinadi gave the people in verses 2–8.	How did the people react to Abinadi's prophecies? (verses 9–16) Record some of the foolish things they said.

MOSIAH 12:17-19 *Write or draw what happened next in these verses.*

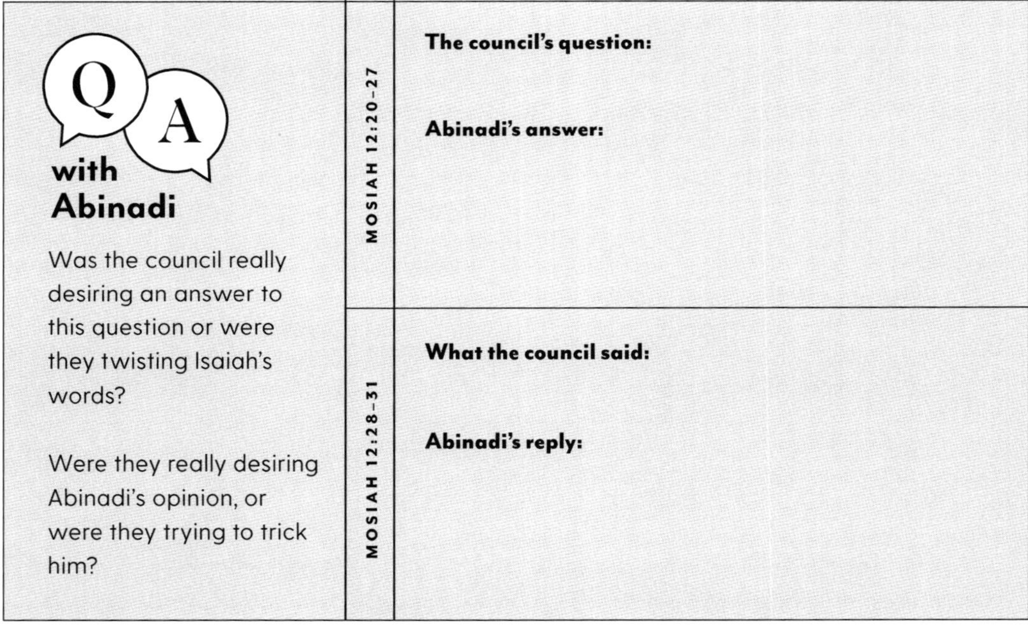

MOSIAH 12:32-37
Abinadi put the council on the spot and asked them about the commandments of God. What point do you think Abinadi was making?

Abinadi & King Noah

VERSES 1–9

Make an outline of the interaction between King Noah and Abinadi in verses 1–9. We have given you the first part of the outline.

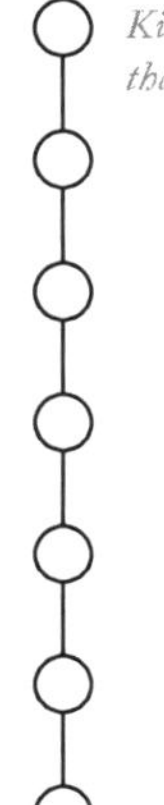

King Noah called Abinadi "mad" and said that they had to do away with him.

VERSES 10–24

What did Abinadi teach in these verses? Why?

VERSES 25–26

What do these verses teach you about the importance of the commandments?

The Law of Moses

Look up "Law of Moses" in the Bible Dictionary and try to explain what it is in a few sentences.

VERSES 27–35

Study these verses and then imagine someone asking you the questions below; use verses 27–35 to answer them.

Why did Moses give the law of Moses to the Children of Israel?	*Can someone be saved by the law of Moses?*

Mosiah 14

In the midst of Abinadi's teachings, he quoted Isaiah. This particular prophecy of Isaiah is called a "Messianic Prophecy" which means it is a prophecy that teaches about the Messiah who will come and save all men. Abinadi quoted Isaiah in Mosiah 14 and then taught about it in Mosiah 15.

HELPFUL TIPS	WHAT I LEARNED
Mosiah 14:1 Isaiah begins with a question: "Who will believe this?" The Jews want a king for a Messiah, a conquering warrior, not a Jew who will be killed. That is not the Messiah they want, but it is the one they need.	
Mosiah 14:2 Isaiah compares Christ to a tender plant in dry ground. The dry ground symbolizes the spiritual drought that He will be born into and receive no nourishment from. It will be a time of apostasy among the Jews.	
Mosiah 14:3 Imagine how inconceivable this would have been to those looking forward to the day Christ would come. When the Almighty, Alpha and Omega, the Creator of the Earth comes as a mortal, He will be rejected. He will know sorrow and grief, men will turn from Him, and He will be despised and not given value.	
Mosiah 14:4–7 Isaiah makes it clear the reason for Christ's sufferings. They are for us. They are all borne for us to help us escape punishment. He will take the whip, the thorns, and the nails so "we are healed." We are all like sheep who have wandered and gone our own way, so He will provide a way for us to return (see verse 6). And He will take it (see verse 7). He will be brought as a lamb to the slaughter. In fact, He will be "the lamb." He will willingly lay His life down as a sacrifice.	
Mosiah 14:8–9 When the Creator of the Earth came to Earth, "he was cut off out of the land of the living," which means that He was cut down like a flower. Christ will also be condemned to die with the wicked (see verse 9). This could refer to how Christ was placed between two thieves; it could also mean that He suffered death just like all mankind (we are all sinners).	
Mosiah 14:10–12 Abinadi explains what it means that Christ "shall see his seed" in the next chapter (see Mosiah 15:10-11).	

What is a phrase from this chapter that teaches you some things about Jesus Christ?

Mosiah 15

In these boxes, draw or write what you learn from Abinadi in each set of verses.

MOSIAH 15:1–2 God will become a mortal	**MOSIAH 15:3–4** The Father and The Son	**MOSIAH 15:5–9** Prophecy of Christ
MOSIAH 15:10–18 Explanation of who is Christ's seed	*"The Savior, as a member of the Godhead, knows each of us personally. Isaiah and the prophet Abinadi said that when Christ would "make his soul an offering for sin, he shall see his seed" (Isaiah 53:10; compare Mosiah 15:10). Abinadi explains that "his seed" are the righteous, those who follow the prophets (see Mosiah 15:11). In the garden and on the cross, Jesus saw each of us and not only bore our sins but also experienced our deepest feelings so He would know how to comfort and strengthen us."* **ELDER MERRIL J. BATEMAN** | April 2003 General Conference	
MOSIAH 15:19–20 Christ brings resurrection to all	**MOSIAH 15:21–25** The First Resurrection	**MOSIAH 15:26–27** Warning to those who die in sin

What is the First Resurrection?

"Those being resurrected with celestial bodies, whose destiny is to inherit a celestial kingdom, will come forth in the morning of the first resurrection. Their graves shall be opened and they shall be caught up to meet the Lord at his Second Coming. They are Christ's, the firstfruits, and they shall descend with him to reign as kings and priests during the millennial era."

ELDER BRUCE R. MCCONKIE \| Mormon Doctrine, p. 640

Prophecies

28 —————— 29 —————— 30 —————— 31

Mosiah 16

ABINADI'S LAST WORDS
Fill this box with things you learn from Abinadi's last words.

In this chapter, Abinadi is beginning to close his sermon. He warned that "the time shall come when all shall see the salvation of the Lord … and confess before God that his judgments are just" (v. 1). To the righteous, this is happy and joyous news. To the wicked, it is a reason to mourn. To these priests, it was a warning. They will not be able to slip through, use flattery, or any other method to avoid punishment. For all will see and confess that God's judgments are just.

Mosiah 17

Study verses 1-6 and write on this illustration what was happening.

Write or draw what happened to Abinadi in verses 7–20

One Among the Crowd

"There are other interesting accounts in the scriptures of one faithful person among a crowd. Alma was among the wicked priests of King Noah. These were men described as being lifted up in the pride of their hearts, lazy and idolatrous, who spoke lying and vain words to the people. They had perverted the ways of the Lord because they had not applied their hearts to understanding. When Abinadi delivered his message of repentance, they mocked him and finally put him to death. This was indeed an evil crowd. Yet as the scriptures point out, "there was one among them" who believed. Alma alone took to heart what Abinadi had taught. With courage he stepped away from the crowd to follow the Lord. The influence of this one man among the crowd on the course of Nephite history is immeasurable. ...

In reality these stories are not about crowds but individuals among those crowds. They are really about you and me. All of us are among the crowds of this world."

ELDER DENNIS B. NEUENSCHWANDER
April 2008 General Conference

WHEN HAVE YOU STEPPED AWAY FROM THE CROWD TO FOLLOW THE LORD?

Mosiah 18-24

In these chapters

Alma baptizes in the waters of Mormon // Alma and people flee // King Noah's death // Limhi becomes king // In bondage to Lamanites // Ammon arrives // Limhi's people delivered and arrive to Zarahemla // Alma and people in bondage to Lamanites // Alma and people delivered and arrive in Zarahemla

---

The Impact of One Man

King Noah

In the last chapters, you saw how much bad one wicked king can bring to pass; and in these chapters, you can see how much good a single man can cause.

Alma

Like Abinadi, Alma was willing to put his life at risk to share the message of the gospel.

Watch the amount of good Alma will do.

Alma Baptizes at the Waters of Mormon

Draw or write what you learn in each group of verses.

MOSIAH 18:1–3	MOSIAH 18:4–7	MOSIAH 18:8–11
What Alma did and what he taught	Waters of Mormon	Covenant of baptism

MOSIAH 18:12–16	MOSIAH 18:17–31	MOSIAH 18:32–35
Baptisms	Church of Christ / How they lived	They depart

My Baptismal Promises

MOSIAH 18:8
Help lighten others' burdens

MOSIAH 18:9
Stand as a witness of God

MOSIAH 18:9
Mourn with those that mourn

MOSIAH 18:10
Serve God

MOSIAH 18:9
Comfort those who stand in need of comfort

MOSIAH 18:10
Keep God's commandments

The Death of King Noah

Noah's army was unsuccessful in their attempt to find Alma and his people. Notice how Mormon refers to Alma and these other Nephites at the end of verse 1. He calls them "the people of the Lord." These people have transformed their lives and made covenants that have made them worthy to be called the Lord's people.

Draw or write what you learn in each group of verses.

1–3 | *Division among the people*	**4–5** | *Gideon*
6–8 | *Gideon vs. King Noah + Lamanites coming*	**9–10** | *Lamanites attack*
11 | *King Noah's devastating command*	**12–14** | *Those who would not leave*
15 | *The agreement*	**16–17** | *Limhi (Noah's son)*
18 | *All but the king and his priests*	**19–21** | *Death of King Noah*
MOSIAH 12:3 | *A prophecy fulfilled*	**22–24** | *The return of those who fled*
25–26 | *New king and a heavy tribute*	**27–29** | *Their new life*

Tribute: A yearly sum of money. A price of peace.

The Wicked Priests in the Wilderness

King Noah had been killed, but what happened to his wicked priests? This chapter tells us.

Draw or write what is happening in each group of verses.

① MOSIAH 20:1-5

② MOSIAH 20:6-11

③ MOSIAH 20:12-15

④ MOSIAH 20:16-22

⑤ MOSIAH 20:23-26

Ammon & Other Strong Men Arrive

This chapter reveals what happened to Limhi's people between the time they began to be in bondage to the Lamanites and the time that Ammon and the other strong men arrived- you will see the sad state they were in. You will see why it was important that Ammon and the other strong men did not give up looking for Zeniff's descendants. Imagine if they had given up because the journey was too hard or too long.

Draw or write what is happening in each group of verses.

MOSIAH 21:1-5	MOSIAH 21:6-12	MOSIAH 21:13-16
MOSIAH 21:17-22	MOSIAH 21:23-31	MOSIAH 21:32-36

The Escape

Draw or write what is happening in each box.

MOSIAH 22:1–8 **The Escape Plan**

MOSIAH 22:9–12 **The Escape**

MOSIAH 22:13–16 **Arrival in Zarahemla**

Alma & His People in the Land of Helam

Now that Mormon has told the story of Limhi and his people being delivered and reaching Zarahemla, he will now tell you what happened to Alma and his people when they left the land of Nephi. Chapters 23 and 24 tell us their story. This chapter jumps back in time to the point when Alma and his people had fled the armies of King Noah.

Draw or write what you learn in the following verses.

MOSIAH 23:1–3 *The Lord strengthened them*	**MOSIAH 23:4–13** *New land / No king*
MOSIAH 23:14–18 *Their society*	**MOSIAH 23:19–24** *They prospered, but…*
MOSIAH 23:25–29 *They hushed their fears*	**MOSIAH 23:30–39** *The Lamanites and wicked priests*

MOSIAH 24

The Lord Delivers Alma & His People

MOSIAH 24:1–7 *Amulon placed over Land of Helam*	**MOSIAH 24:8–12** *Alma's people persecuted*
MOSIAH 24:13–15 *Alma's people strengthened*	**MOSIAH 24:16–20** *The Deliverance*
MOSIAH 24:21–23 *Alma and people praise God*	**MOSIAH 24:24–25** *Arrival in Zarahemla*

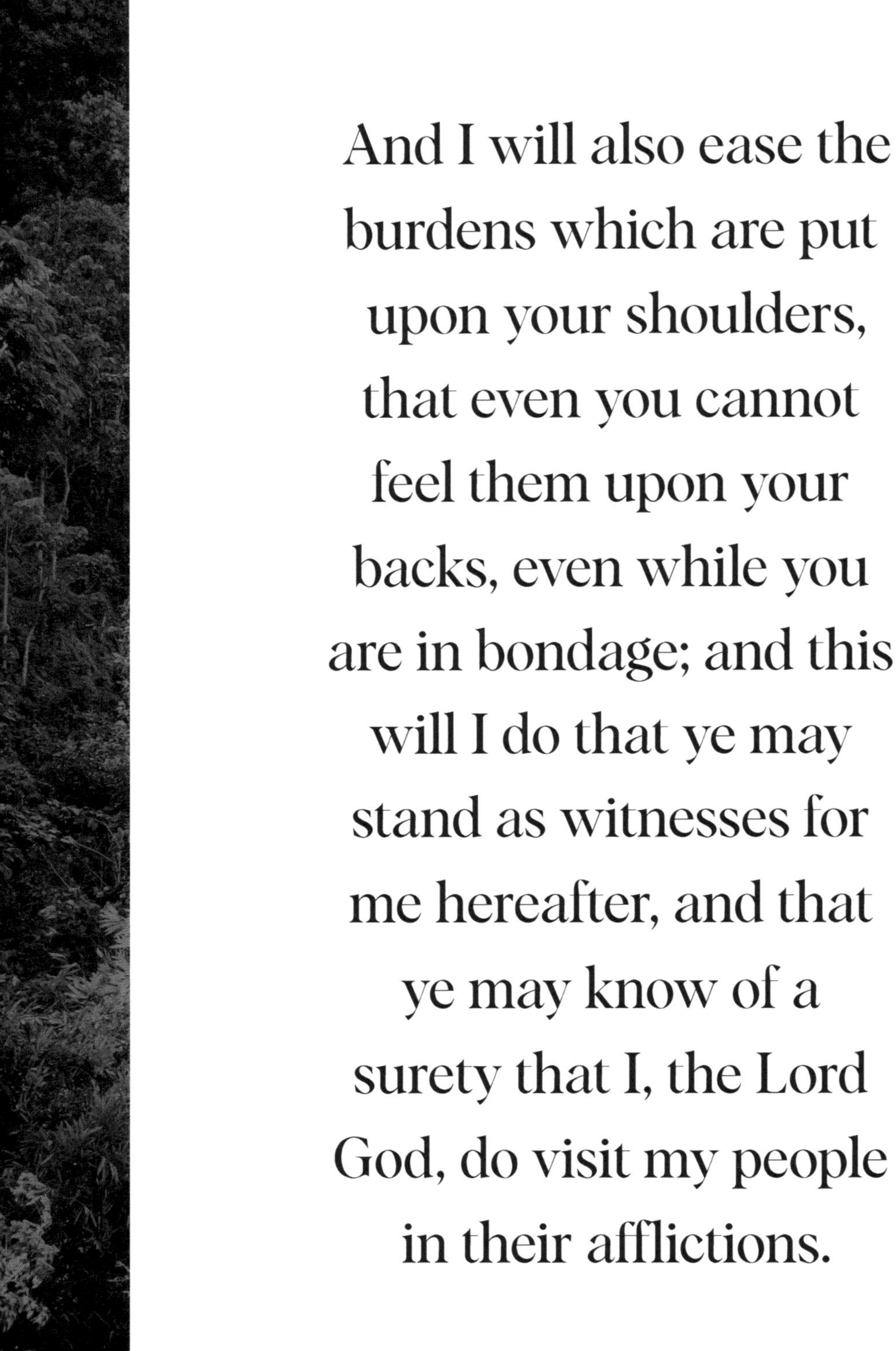

And I will also ease the
burdens which are put
upon your shoulders,
that even you cannot
feel them upon your
backs, even while you
are in bondage; and this
will I do that ye may
stand as witnesses for
me hereafter, and that
ye may know of a
surety that I, the Lord
God, do visit my people
in their afflictions.

WHEN HAS THE LORD HELPED EASE THE BURDEN UPON YOUR SHOULDERS? HOW DID THAT EXPERIENCE HELP YOU STAND AS A WITNESS OF THE LORD?

Mosiah 25–28

In these chapters

Alma organizes Church // Alma the Younger and sons of Mosiah rebel // Angel appears // Alma repents // Sons of Mosiah desire to teach the Lamanites

Now that Limhi's and Alma's people have come to Zarahemla and King Mosiah has learned their histories, he has his people gather together to learn for themselves.

King Mosiah now has the records of Zeniff and Alma, and in Mosiah 25, King Mosiah read them to the people.

The people of Zarahemla are now going to learn about King Noah, the death of Abinadi, the bondage the Nephites experienced, the Nephites fighting for freedom, and the deliverance of Limhi and Alma's people.

Consider all of the lessons the rest of the people in Zarahemla could learn from hearing these records.

Mosiah 25

Draw or write what you learn in each group of verses.

MOSIAH 25:1–4
King Mosiah gathers people

MOSIAH 25:5–6
What Mosiah read

MOSIAH 25:7–11
The people's reaction

MOSIAH 25:12
The children of the wicked priest Amulon

MOSIAH 25:13
Nephites

MOSIAH 25:14–16
Alma speaks to people

MOSIAH 25:17–18
Limhi and his people baptized

MOSIAH 25:19–24
Alma organizes Church

Mosiah 26

There were those who had not heard and witnessed King Benjamin's speech, and there were those who had not seen the difference between the world King Noah had created and the gospel that Alma introduced to them. So they did not believe. They did not remain "True to the faith that [their] parents [had] cherished. True to the truth for which martyrs [had] perished ..." *(Hymn: True to the Faith). Draw or write what you learn in each box.*

MOSIAH 26:1–7 *The rising generation*	**MOSIAH 26:8–14** *Alma is troubled*	**MOSIAH 26:15–32** *The Lord's answer*	**MOSIAH 26:33–39** *Alma did as the Lord instructed*

Mosiah 27

The Church continued to prosper and grow but so did the persecutions. King Mosiah sent a proclamation (or official notice) throughout the land declaring a "strict command" that unbelievers shall not persecute the believers.

What do you learn about this proclamation in verses 1–7?

____

____

Alma the Younger and Sons of Mosiah

You are about to learn about Alma the Younger and the sons of King Mosiah. Before you learn about them, pause and write your thoughts about the kind of influence these five young men would have had on others in Zarahemla.

MOSIAH 27:8–10	**MOSIAH 27:11–17**	**MOSIAH 27:18–19**	**MOSIAH 27:20–22**
MOSIAH 27:23–31	**MOSIAH 27:32–34**	**MOSIAH 27:35–37**	
			Alma the Younger Is Converted unto the Lord Mosiah 27; Alma 36 | 11:30 minutes

Mosiah 28

The sons of Mosiah had been going around preaching the gospel of Jesus Christ, and their hearts began to turn towards the Lamanites. Their hearts were not full of hate, or pride, or competition. But they were full of love and charity for all mankind. So then, what about the Lamanites? Imagine what the gospel of Jesus Christ could do for them and imagine the centuries-old wounds it would heal between them and the Nephites.

Draw or write what you learn in each group of verses.

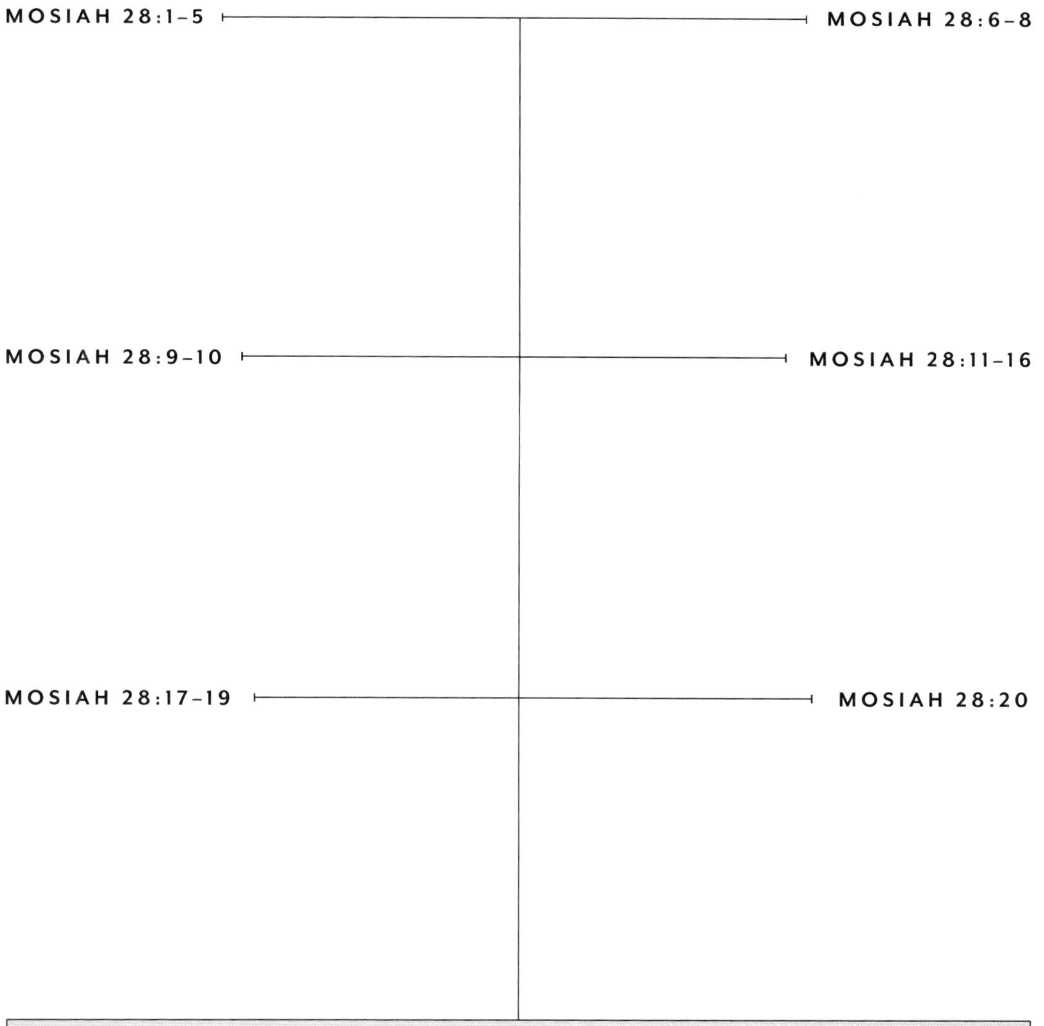

> *I pray that you will develop the bravery and love for Heavenly Father's children that led the sons of Mosiah to plead for the chance to face death and danger to take the gospel to a hardened people. Their desire and their bravery came from feeling responsible for the eternal happiness of strangers in danger of eternal misery.*
>
> **PRESIDENT HENRY B. EYRING**
> April 2009 General Conference

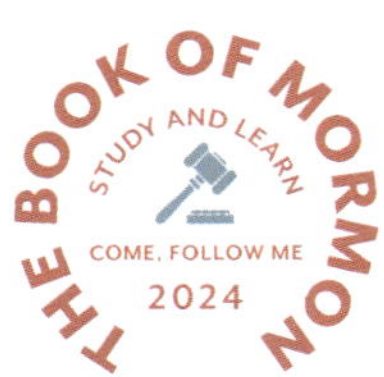

Alma

- The book of Alma is named after Alma the Younger (the son of Alma the Elder).

- King Mosiah changed the government from kings to judges. Alma the Younger was the first chief judge of the Nephites. Alma the Younger was also the high priest over the Church.

- Mormon used the following individuals' records to abridge the stories and teachings found in the book of Alma.

ALMA 1–44 . . . . *Alma the Younger's record*

ALMA 45–62 . . . . *Helaman's record*

ALMA 63 . . . . *Shiblon's record*

At the beginning of the book of Alma, it had been
over 500 years since Lehi and his family left
Jerusalem. The Lamanite and Nephite lands were
now expansive. Over 30 cities and lands are
mentioned in the book of Alma. How many more
do you think there might have been?

Think about it...

People to Know

Alma the Younger

Alma was the son of Alma the Elder. He rebelled against the Church and repented. He became the first Nephite chief judge and was a prophet and high priest.

Nephihah

When Alma chose to focus solely on his ministry, he delivered the judgment seat to Nephihah. Nephihah was the second Nephite chief judge.

Amulek

An angel visited him, and Amulek received Alma into his home in Ammonihah. He preached alongside Alma, was imprisoned, and then freed.

Ammon

Ammon was the son of King Mosiah. He preached the gospel to the Lamanites. He saved King Lamoni's flock, taught the gospel, and organized the Church among the Lamanites. His converts never fell away (Alma 23:6)

Aaron

Aaron was the son of King Mosiah. He preached the gospel among the Lamanites. He was imprisoned. He taught King Lamoni's father.

Abish

Abish was converted to the Lord due to a vision her father had. She witnessed King Lamoni and his household under the power of God. She testified to the people.

Nehor

Nehor was a wicked man that introduced priestcraft among the Nephites in Alma 1. He killed Gideon; he was executed. His followers continued his practices long after his death.

Amlici

Amlici desired to be king and change the government from judges to kings. He and his followers, the Amlicites, were defeated and joined forces with the Lamanites.

Zeezrom

Zeezrom was a lawyer in Ammonihah that argued with Alma and Amulek. He was converted, healed from a sickness, and became a missionary.

King Lamoni

Lamoni was king over a portion of the Lamanites. His father was head king (king over all the Lamanites). Lamoni was converted when Ammon taught him.

King Lamoni's Father

King Lamoni's father was king over all of the Lamanites. He converted when Aaron taught him, and granted religious freedom to his people, and allowed missionaries to preach.

Anti-Nephi-Lehies

This name was given to the Lamanites who were converted by the sons of Mosiah. They laid down their weapons of war, left Lamanite land, and were given the land of Jershon among the Nephites. They changed their name to the people of Ammon.

Helaman

Helaman was the oldest son of Alma the Younger. He was a prophet, military leader over the 2,000 stripling warriors, and was given stewardship of the plates.

Corianton

Corianton was the son of Alma the Younger. He forsook the ministry and went after a harlot. He was counseled by Alma about life after death, and was called to preach again.

Korihor

Korihor was an Antichrist who taught that there would be no Christ and that the gospel was a foolish tradition. He demanded a sign, was struck dumb, and admitted he had been deceived.

Amalickiah

Amalickiah desired to be king and he led people away from the Church. When Moroni raised the title of liberty, Amalickiah and his followers fled. He became king of the Lamanites and stirred up Lamanites to come against the Nephites.

Ammaron

Ammaron was Amalickiah's brother and became king of the Lamanites when Amalickiah died. He was a Nephite traitor and fought against the Nephites.

Shiblon

Shiblon was the son of Alma the Younger. He taught the gospel to the Zoramites, was delivered from persecution, and was given the plates.

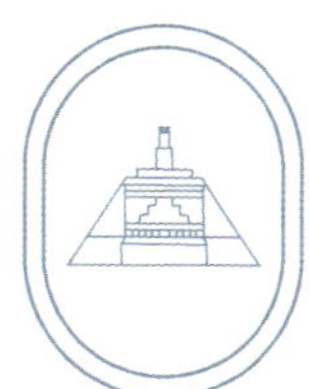

Zoramites

The Zoramites prayed upon the Rameumptom. Alma and others preached to them. The Zoramites rejected the gospel and separated themselves from the Nephites. They became chief captains among the Lamanites.

Zerahemnah

Zerahemnah was a Lamanite chief captain. Moroni commanded him to make a covenant of peace and he refused. As they were about to be destroyed, he agreed to the covenant of peace.

Captain Moroni

Captain Moroni was a righteous military commander. He was chief captain of the Nephite armies and made the title of liberty. He fortified cities and people and inspired Nephites to fight for freedom.

Pahoran

Pahoran was the third Nephite chief judge following Nephihah as chief judge. He was chief judge when the king-men took over Zarahemla.

LAND OF ZARAHEMLA = Nephite land | LAND OF NEPHI = Lamanite land

146 ***This map is not literal. The cities are placed according to descriptions in the Book of Mormon.***

*Use this page to return to and take notes as you
learn about different places and cities.*

Timeline

Here is the book of Alma at-a-glance. The main stories are found in the timeline below. At one point the book of Alma goes back in time. This timeline will help you understand what is happening.

Alma is Chief Judge. Nehor introduces priestcraft. Priestcraft spreads.
91–90 BC
Alma 1

Amlici seeks to be king. Amlicites war with Nephites and lose. Amlicites join forces with the Lamanites.
87 BC
Alma 2

Alma gives up position as chief judge to focus on ministry. Nephihah appointed new chief judge.
86–83 BC
Alma 4

Alma preaches in Zarahemla and Gideon.
83 BC
Alma 5

Alma is rejected in Ammonihah. Amulek preaches with Alma in Ammonihah.
83–81 BC
Alma 6–14

Ammonihah destroyed by Lamanites. Nephites defeat Lamanites.
81–77 BC
Alma 16

Sons of Mosiah Separate
Sons of Mosiah go different ways in Lamanite land.
Alma 17
91–77 BC

Many Lamanites converted. Ammon leads Anti-Nephi-Lehies to land of Jershon. Change name to people of Ammon.
Alma 27
90–77 BC

SONS OF MOSIAH MISSION TO LAMANITES

91–90 BC
Ammon and King Lamoni

Alma 17–21

90–77 BC
Aaron and King Lamoni's Father
Aaron imprisoned and released. Teaches King Lamoni's father. King Lamoni grants religious freedom to his people.
Alma 21–23

90–77 BC
Anti-Nephi-Lehies
Seven lands of Lamanites converted. Believers call themselves Anti-Nephi-Lehies.
Alma 23

90–77 BC
Anti-Nephi-Lehies Bury Weapons
Lamanites attack Anti-Nephi-Lehies. Anti-Nephi-Lehies bury weapons of war. They suffer death rather than fight.
Alma 24

Great battle.

77–76 BC

Alma 28

Korihor the antichrist.

74 BC

Alma 30

Zoramites and the Rameumptom.

74 BC

Alma 31–35

Alma counsels sons Helaman, Shiblon, and Corianton.

74–73 BC

Alma 36–42

Alma and sons preach. Zoramites become Lamanites. Captain Moroni arms Nephites. Nephite armies surround Lamanite army.

74–73 BC

Alma 43

Moroni fortifies land. Pahoran becomes next Nephite chief judge.

72–67 BC

Alma 50

Amalickiah becomes king of Lamanites. Amalickiah stirs up Lamanites against Nephites. Moroni fortifies people and cities.

72 BC

Alma 47–48

Amalickiah desires to be Nephite king. Moroni raises title of liberty.

73–72 BC

Alma 46

Zerahemnah refuses to make covenant of peace. Lamanite army defeated. Dissension in Church.

74–73 BC

Alma 44

King-men seek to put in a Nephite king. Amalickiah is killed.

67 BC

Alma 51

Ammoron becomes next king of Lamanites. Nephites victorious in war against Lamanites.

66–64 BC

Alma 52

Helaman and the 2,000 stripling warriors

64–63 BC

Alma 53–58

Moroni complains to Pahoran, Pahoran responds. King-men have taken Zarahemla. Moroni retakes Zarahemla.

62–57 BC

Alma 59–62

Shiblon then Helaman take possession of records. Many Nephites move northward. Hagoth sails west.

56–52 BC

Alma 63

Mosiah 29 – Alma 4

In these chapters

Nehor introduces priestcraft // Priestcraft spreads // Amlici seeks to be king // Amlicites make war and join Lamanites // Iniquity enters Church // Alma gives up judgment seat to focus on ministry

Reign of the Judges

Around 91 B.C., the Nephite government changed from kings to judges.

Here is a chart of the chief judges during the Nephite reign of the judges.

ALMA THE YOUNGER
91–83 B.C.

NEPHIHAH
83–67 B.C.

PAHORAN I
67–53 B.C.

PAHORAN II
52 B.C.

PACUMENI
52–51 B.C.

HELAMAN
50–39 B.C.

NEPHI
39–30 B.C.

CEZORAM
30–26 B.C.

SON OF CEZORAM
26 B.C.

SEEZORAM
26–20 B.C.

UNKNOWN
20 B.C. – A.D. 1

LACHONEUS I
A.D. 1–30

LACHONEUS II
A.D. 30

Mosiah 29

Overview + Question

Mosiah 29 begins with a dilemma: Who is going to be the next king? King Mosiah's sons were gone and none of them wanted the throne. What was important to them had shifted. Can you imagine four sons turning down the crown in exchange for the uncertain and inconvenient life of preaching the gospel to an "enemy"? These four sons are great examples of sacrificing something good for something greater and eternal.

HELPFUL TIPS	WHAT I LEARNED
VERSES 1–3 **Who will be the next king?**	
VERSES 4–36 **A letter to the people** Mosiah sends a letter to all of the people, and that letter will last from verse 5 to 32, and then Mormon tells you a few more things that were in that letter in verses 33–36. These generations have only known kings, but King Mosiah had just recently learned of wicked kings who brought disastrous consequences. King Mosiah will teach very wise principles in these verses.	
VERSES 37–47 **A New System: The Reign of the Judges** **Watch it Here** Alma the Younger Steps Down as Chief Judge 2:35 minutes	

The Reign of the Judges

In Alma 1, we have the new reckoning of time, "the first year of the reign of the judges." They will use this reckoning of time for 100 years (see 3 Nephi 2:5) until they start reckoning their time from the sign when Christ's birth was given (see 3 Nephi 2:8).

In Alma 1, we meet another antichrist named Nehor. Nehor's religion promised that "all mankind should be saved at the last day ... and, in the end, all men should have eternal life." How much easier this is! You can still have eternal life, but with no rules or commandments - no need to repent. Nehor knows that people will like this broader path, and if they like it, then they will support him and give him money, making him more powerful. He makes a religion they want to hear.

Draw or write what you learn in the following verses.

Alma 1:1–6
Nehor teaches false doctrines

Alma 1:7–9
Nehor kills Gideon

Alma 1:10–14
Nehor before Alma

Alma 1:15–24
Priestcraft continues to spread / persecution of righteous

Alma 1:25–31
The righteous: steadfast and immovable

Alma 1:32–33
The unrighteous

Yet another way is to think that our sins do not matter because God loves us no matter what we do. It is tempting to believe what the deceitful Nehor taught the people of Zarahemla: "That all mankind should be saved at the last day, and that they need not fear nor tremble, ... and, in the end, all men should have eternal life." (Alma 1:4). But this seductive idea is false. God does love us. However, what we do matters to Him and to us. He has given clear directives about how we should behave. We call these commandments.

ELDER DALE G. RENLUND | October 2016 General Conference

Alma 2

Write or draw what you learn in each group of verses.

Alma 2:1–2
Amlici

Alma 2:3–4
Concerns

Alma 2:5–7
The voice of the people

Alma 2:8–14
The Amlicites' next move

Alma 2:15–20
Terrible battle

Alma 2:21–25
Spies report

Alma 2:26–28
Another battle

Alma 2:29–31
Alma battles Amlici

Alma 2:32–38
Amlicites and Lamanites flee

WHO WAS AMLICI?

Amlici was a follower of Nehor. Amlici used cunning tactics to draw people to follow him. They will become the Amlicites. The Amlicites wanted to make Amlici king.

*Keep your own record side-by-side with these great prophets
testifying of these important doctrines and principles.*

WHAT MIGHT A NEHOR OR AMLICI THAT LIVES TODAY SAY OR DO TO GET PEOPLE TO FOLLOW THEM?

WHAT HAVE YOU DONE TO DETECT FALSE TEACHERS?

WHAT HAVE YOU DONE WHEN YOU HAVE ENCOUNTERED THEM?

Alma 3

The cost of war. The Amlicites
mark themselves.

*Draw or write what you learn
in the following verses.*

—— **1–3** | *The cost of war*

—— **4–12** | *The Amlicites and Lamanites*

—— **13–19** | *Amlicites mark themselves*

—— **20–24** | *War again*

—— **25–27** | *In just five years…*

Alma 4

Alma gives up position as chief
judge and devotes himself to
ministry to the people.

*Draw or write what you learn in
the following verses.*

—— **1–5** | *The Aftermath*

—— **6–10** | *Pride in the Church*

—— **11–14** | *Great inequality*

—— **15–20** | *Alma gives up the judgment
seat to bear down in pure testimony*

What is pure testimony?

As we profess truth rather than admonish, exhort, or simply share interesting experiences, we invite the Holy Ghost to confirm the verity of our words. The power of pure testimony (see Alma 4:19) does not come from sophisticated language or effective presentation; rather, it is the result of revelation conveyed by the third member of the Godhead, even the Holy Ghost.

ELDER DAVID A. BEDNAR | October 2009 General Conference

Alma 5-7

In these chapters

Alma teaches people in Zarahemla // Church in Zarahemla
is cleansed // Alma preaches in Gideon

Alma the Younger

Alma has now given up the position as chief judge, which would have been the most powerful position in Zarahemla. He gave it up so he can focus on saving souls.

In Alma 4, we learned the state of the Church. There were many who were faithful, but there were also many who were causing a lot of contention and problems (see Alma 4:9-11), even so much that "the church began to fail in its progress" (Alma 4:10).

Alma doesn't just sit back. He freed up his time by giving up his political position and will now dedicate all of his time to waking people up. And he is the perfect man for the job.

Alma started by preaching in Zarahemla. What he taught is recorded in Alma 5.

The sons of Mosiah were, at this same time, among the Lamanites introducing them to God and His plan for them. Alma was on the other end of the spectrum trying to call people back to God.

Write or draw what you learn in these verses.

<table>
<tr>
<td>Alma 5:1–2

Mormon's introduction to Alma's mission and sermon</td>
<td>Alma 5:3–12

What Alma wanted them to remember</td>
<td>Alma 5:13–14

Their fathers were changed through Christ. What about them?</td>
</tr>
<tr>
<td>Alma 5:15–18

Can you imagine these things?</td>
<td>Alma 5:19–21

Can you imagine these things as well?</td>
<td>Alma 5:22–25

What could happen if you're not ready</td>
</tr>
<tr>
<td>Alma 5:26–30

How are you right now?</td>
<td>Alma 5:31–36

Come</td>
<td>Alma 5:37–42

What fold are ye?</td>
</tr>
<tr>
<td>Alma 5:43–48

How to know truth</td>
<td>Alma 5:49–56

Speedily repent</td>
<td>Alma 5:57–62

The Good Shepherd calls to you</td>
</tr>
</table>

Alma had been in the presence of an angel while being unclean (remember he had an angel come to him and the sons of Mosiah in Mosiah 27). Alma knows a lot about standing before a heavenly being unprepared, and now he will urge the Nephites to imagine standing before God unprepared.

PICK A PHRASE OR TWO FROM ALMA 5 AND WRITE YOUR TESTIMONY AND EXPERIENCE WITH THE PHRASES YOU CHOSE.

Keep your own record side-by-side with these great prophets testifying of these important doctrines and principles.

Alma the Younger Sets
the Church in Order in
Zarahemla | Alma 5
5:07 minutes

Alma 6

Alma's message was effective and the Church began to prosper again (see verses 2 and 3). After Alma gave his message, he did not just hope things would get better. He established order in the Church. Fill this space with things you learn from this chapter.

Church Prospers

Alma 7

After Alma had completed his work in Zarahemla, he will now travel to other Nephite villages and cities—starting with Gideon. He will show up and be received by some and utterly hated by others. This will be hard, tiring, inconvenient, and risky. But Alma is not one to back down for any of those reasons.

Fill this space with things you learn from this chapter.

Alma the Younger Teaches
the People of Gideon
Alma 7 | 4:19 minutes

Alma 8-12

In these chapters

Alma in Melek   //   Alma rejected in Ammonihah   //   An angel commands him to return   //   Alma and Amulek preach together   //   Amulek silences Zeezrom   //   Alma testifies to Zeezrom

Melek

Alma had success in Zarahemla and in Gideon. Then Alma went on to Melek. Alma's ministry in Melek only gets two verses (see Alma 8:4-5). When you read those verses, imagine the unrecorded stories there.

Ammonihah

After Melek, Alma went to Ammonihah. As Mormon abridged the Book of Mormon, he chose to include a lot of detail about Alma's time in this city. Mormon gave us seven chapters (a total of 236 verses) of Alma's ministry in Ammonihah. What do you think Mormon wanted us to learn?

Write or draw what you learn in these verses.

Alma 8:1–5
Alma in Melek

Alma 8:6–9
Alma in Ammonihah

Alma 8:10
What Alma did

Alma 8:11–13
How the people responded

Alma 8:14–17
An angel's message

Alma 8:18
Alma's response

Alma & Amulek

ALMA 8:19-32

When Alma went out again to teach among the people of Ammonihah, he had a second witness at his side—Amulek, one of their own.

ELDER DIETER F. UCHTDORF | October 2016 General Conference

Alma 9

Write or draw what you learn in these verses.

Alma 9-14 comes from Alma's record. Mormon included Alma's own words upon the gold plates. Alma himself will tell you what happened in Ammonihah.

ALMA 9:1–6 *The people's response to Alma*	**ALMA 9:7–11** *Alma boldly testifes*	**ALMA 9:12–13** *Remember...*
ALMA 9:14–17 *The Lamanites*	**ALMA 9:18–20** *Warning*	**ALMA 9:21–23** *Warning*
ALMA 9:24–27 *Why they have come*	**ALMA 9:28–30** *Repent now*	**ALMA 9:31–34** *The people's response*

Alma 10

Amulek had just seen the people try to put Alma into prison, but that didn't stop him from stepping forth and being a second witness. It would have been so easy for him to slip into the crowd and escape the judgments of the people, but he didn't. Watch how perfect Amulek was for this task.

Fill this space with things that Amulek taught his own people in Ammonihah.

Alma 11

Write or draw what you learn in these verses.

VERSES 1–19

Alma explained how and what judges were paid, and as he did, he also explained Nephite money.

VERSE 20

What were the judges doing in Ammonihah in order to receive more money?

VERSE 21

A man named Zeezrom began to question Amulek. Write what you learn about Zeezrom here.

Each weight equaled a certain amount of coins.

However many weights it took to level out the scale would determine what was owed.

VERSES 22–46

Write or draw some questions Zeezrom asked and the answers Amulek gave.

Alma 12

Alma had been standing back and letting Amulek speak. Now Alma stepped forward and continued teaching.

(1) VERSES 1–6
What Alma taught

(2) VERSES 7–8
Zeezrom's questions

(3) VERSES 9–18
Doctrines Alma taught

(4) VERSES 19–21
Questions from the chief ruler

(5) VERSES 22–37
Doctrines Alma taught

Alma 13-16

In these chapters

Alma teaches in Ammonihah // Alma and Amulek imprisoned //
Believers burned by fire // Prison walls fall // Alma and Amulek go to
Sidom // Zeezrom healed // Lamanites destroy Ammonihah

Nehor

Ammonihah was after the order
of Nehor, which was priestcraft,
not after the order of the
priesthood. In chapter 13, Alma
taught the people about the
eternal nature of the priesthood.

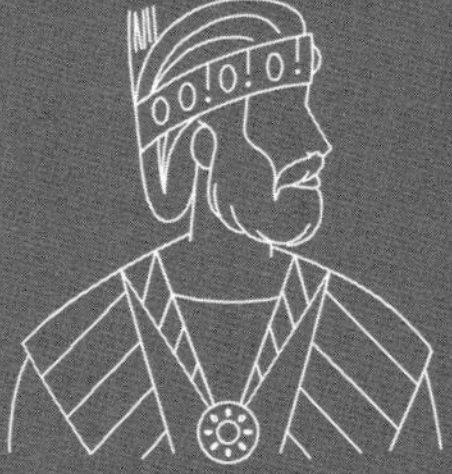

Zeezrom

As Zeezrom and the others are
listening, they can compare what
Alma is saying about the true
priesthood to their priestcraft
practices in Ammonihah.

The priesthood is also called "the order of his [God's] Son (see verse 1 and also
see D&C 107:1–4). An order is a rank, class, or division. There are serious
requirements to be a part of the ranks of those who have the priesthood and
it involves obedience in the premortal life (see Alma 13:3–4), and obedience
and sanctification in this life (see Alma 13: 10–12). This is a "holy calling."

Will the people of Ammonihah listen?

Alma 13

VERSES 1–3

When priesthood holders are called and prepared

VERSES 4–6

Who is called and what they are called to do

VERSE 7

The eternal nature of the priesthood

VERSES 8–9

How long priesthood offices are held

VERSES 10–12

Those who are called into the order of the Priesthood

VERSE 13

Those who are called into the order of the Priesthood

VERSES 14–15

Who is Melchizedek?

VERSE 16

Purpose of ordinances

VERSES 17–20

Who is Melchizedek?

VERSES 21–23

Now is the time to repent

VERSES 24–26

The Lord is coming

VERSES 27–31

Do not put off repentance

I believe they were ordained before they came here; and I believe the God of Israel has raised them up, and has watched over them from their youth, and has carried them through all the scenes of life both seen and unseen, and has prepared them as instruments in his hands to take this kingdom and bear it off. If this be so, what manner of men outght we to be? If anything under the heavens should humble men before the Lord and before one another, it should be the fact that we have been called of God."

PRESIDENT WILFORD WOODRUFF | Journal of Discourses 21:317

Alma 14

Since the people in Ammonihah were living after the order of Nehor, they believed that all would be saved. Therefore, there was no need to repent. Because of their beliefs, Alma and Amulek's testimonies were contrary to their teachings. However, after they testified, many believed "and began to repent and to search the scriptures."

Write or draw on this illustration what is happening in the verses given in the black boxes.

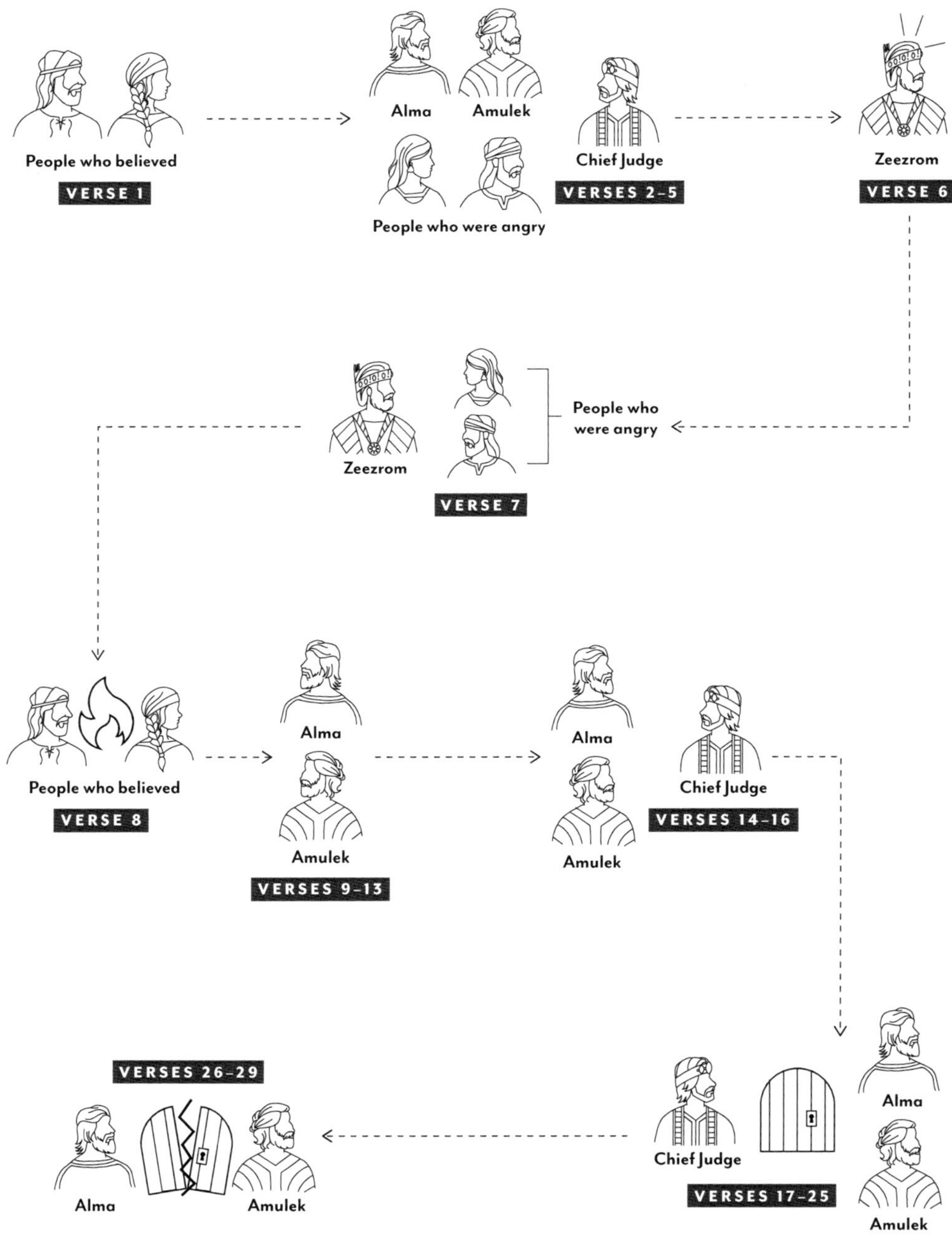

Alma 15

Alma and Amulek left Ammonihah and went to Sidom.
Sidom was full of people who were more inclined to
righteousness (see verses 13 and 14), and they received
the outcasts from Ammonihah.

*Write or draw what happens in Alma 15, along
with lessons you learn.*

Alma 16

Alma and Amulek were now in Zarahemla, and believers in Ammonihah were either killed
or in Sidom. Then the Lamanites come and attack Ammonihah.

(1) ALMA 16:1–4
Ammonihah destroyed

(2) ALMA 16:5–8
Chief captain turns to Alma

(3) ALMA 16:9–11
Total destruction of Ammonihah

(4) ALMA 16:12–17
Peace and preaching

(5) ALMA 16:18–20
Truths taught

(6) ALMA 16:21
The power of truth

Alma 17–22

In these chapters

Sons of Mosiah declare gospel to Lamanites   //   Ammon goes to land of Ishmael   //
Ammon saves king's flocks   //   Ammon teaches King Lamoni   //   Abish   //   Ammon
establishes Church there   //   Ammon and King Lamoni's father   //   Aaron and
brethren imprisoned in Middoni   //   Aaron teaches King Lamoni's father

**ALMA
THE YOUNGER**

AMMON

AARON

OMNER

HIMNI

The paragraph just before chapter 17 (that begins with "An account of the sons of Mosiah …")
was a translation from the plates. Mormon is letting us know that we have been learning
about Alma's ministry among the Nephites and now we are going to be learning about what
had happened when the sons of Mosiah left to preach to the Lamanites 14 years earlier.

Alma 17 begins with Alma journeying toward the land of Manti and along the way, he
unexpectedly crosses paths with the sons of Mosiah, who were returning home to Zarahemla.
It had been 14 years. Consider how much has changed among the Nephites. When the sons of
Mosiah left, their father was still king. Since then, they have changed the government from
kings to judges; they have had an internal war with the Amlicites; Alma had been chief judge,
captain of the Nephite army, and high priest. He had since given up all positions except high
priest, and now Alma had been all over the land preaching and strengthening the Church.

Then verse 6 could begin by saying, "14 years earlier" because at that point we will go back
and find out what had happened when they left for their mission to the Lamanites.

What do you learn about Alma and the sons of Mosiah in verses 1–5?

You will now learn what the sons of Mosiah had been doing for the past 14 years while Alma was Chief Judge, High Priest, and preaching to the people. Write on this story map what you learn in the verses given. Include your own thoughts as well.

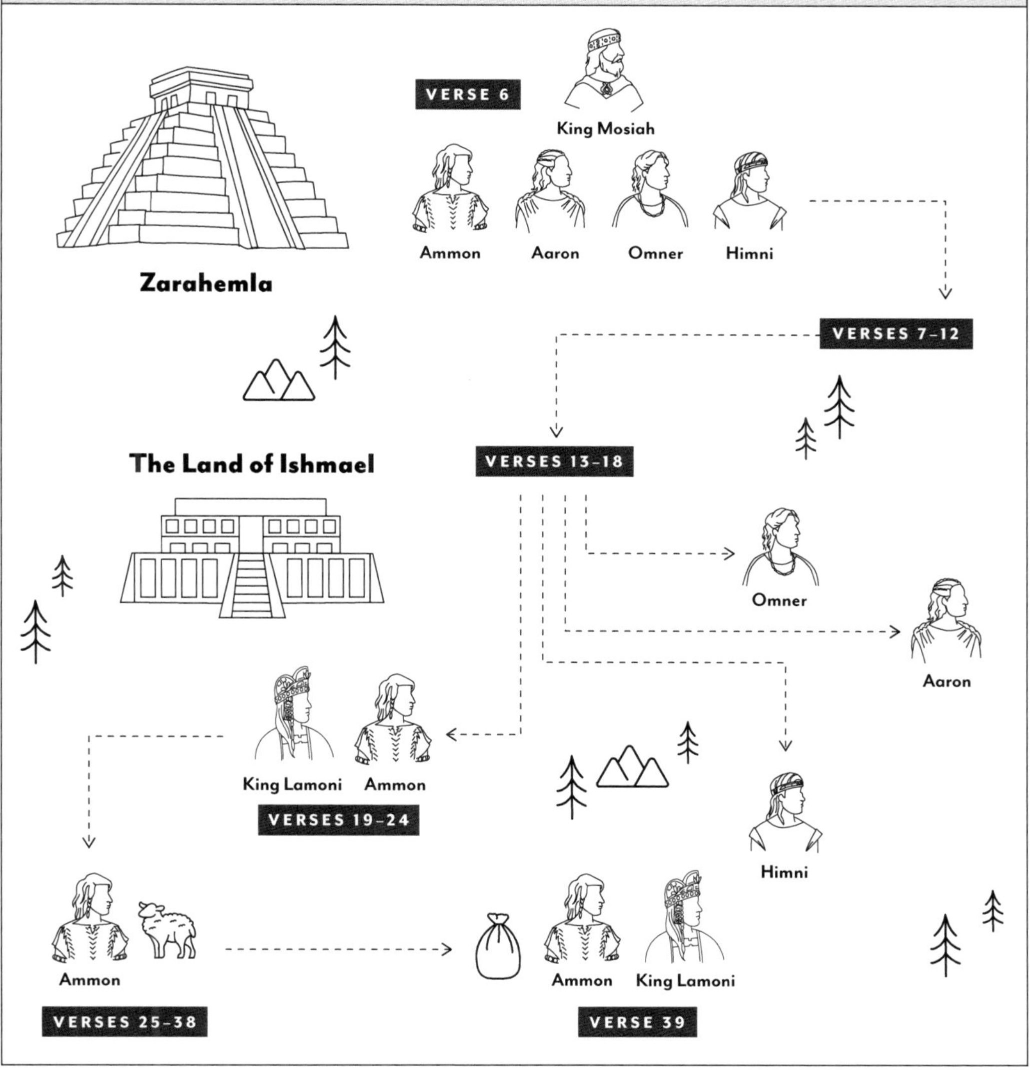

Alma Teaches King Lamoni

There was a tradition among the Lamanites that there was a Great Spirit, and King Lamoni was afraid that Ammon was this Great Spirit and that he was displeased that some of the king's servants had been killed (see v.4). King Lamoni did not have a knowledge of the true God. Ammon will take this opportunity to teach the king.

Write or draw what you learn in these verses.

1–4 | *The king thinks Ammon is the Great Spirit*	**5–7** | *King Lamoni's fear*
8–11 | *Where Ammon was*	**12–15** | *Ammon before the king*
16–19 | *Ammon is only a man*	**20–21** | *King Lamoni wants to know more*
22–39 | *Ammon teaches the king*	**40–43** | *King Lamoni believes*

Alma 19

In these boxes, draw or write what you learn from the story of Ammon and King Lamoni.

VERSES 1–7	**VERSES 8–10**	**VERSES 11–14**
The queen calls for Ammon	*The queen's faith*	*Lamoni's vision*

VERSES 15–18	**VERSES 19–21**	**VERSES 22–27**
Abish	*What Lamoni's people were saying*	*What people believed about Ammon*

VERSES 28–29	**VERSES 30–31**	**VERSES 32–36**
Abish awakens queen	*King rebukes people*	*Lamoni's people*

"*In the Book of Mormon, Abish was converted by her father's sharing with her his remarkable vision. For many years thereafter, she kept her testimony in her heart and lived righteously in a very wicked society. Then the time came when she could no longer be still, and she ran from house to house to share her testimony and the miracles she had witnessed in the king's court. The power of Abish's conversion and testimony was instrumental in changing an entire society. The people who heard her testify became a people who "were converted unto the Lord, [and] never did fall away," and their sons became the stripling warriors!*"

SISTER ELAINE S. DALTON
October 2011 General Conference

Keep your own record side-by-side with these great prophets
testifying of these important doctrines and principles.

WHAT HAVE BEEN SOME ABISH MOMENTS IN YOUR LIFE?

King Lamoni's Father

King Lamoni's father was the head king of all of the Lamanites, and then there were lesser kings set up throughout the land.

Write or draw on this story map what happened in verses 1–8.

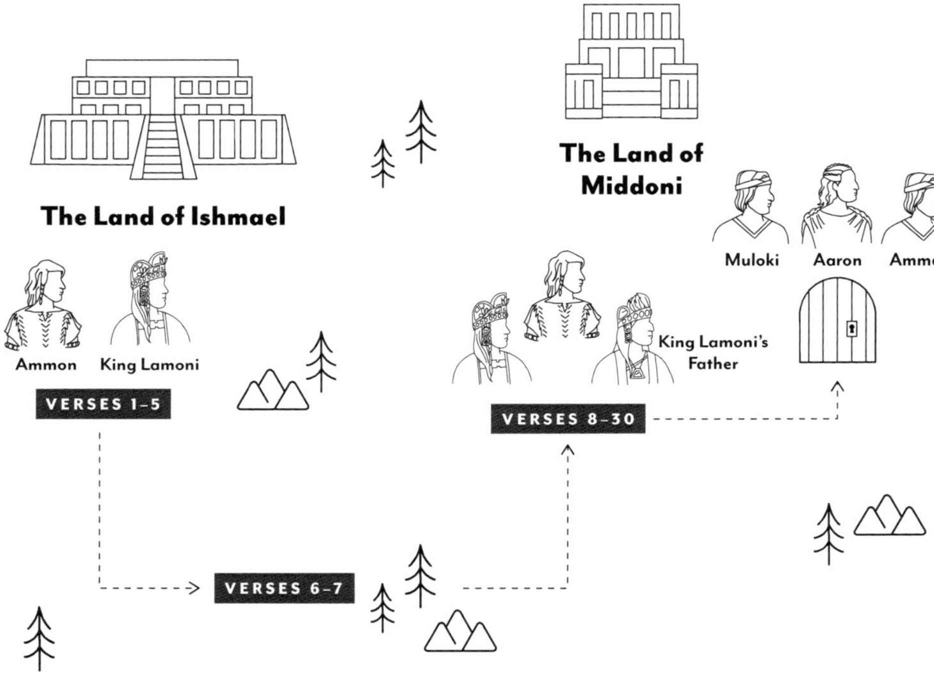

SOME THINGS I WANT TO REMEMBER FROM AMMON'S COURAGE AND EXAMPLE:

Aaron Goes to Jerusalem

This chapter is a flashback and goes back to the period of time in Alma 17:18 when all of the brethren separated from one another and went to teach in different Lamanite lands. Aaron went to a land named Jerusalem, which was named "after the land of their fathers' nativity." The population of this land was made up of Lamanites, Amalekites, and the people of Amulon. So this was a mix of Lamanites and Nephites.

Write or draw what you learn in these verses.

VERSES 1–3	VERSES 4–8	VERSES 9–10	VERSES 11–12

VERSES 13–14	VERSES 15–17	VERSES 18–22	VERSE 23

Alma 22

Aaron was led by the Spirit to the land of Nephi, which was where King Lamoni's father lived. Aaron, the son of King Mosiah was now going to teach the king of the Lamanites.

VERSES 1–26	VERSES 27–35
Write or draw what Aaron taught the king and what happened as he taught them.	*The king sent a proclamation throughout the land. In these verses, you learn about the Lamanite land. Write or draw what you learn about the land.*

Alma 23–29

In these chapters

Many Lamanites converted. They call themselves Anti-Nephi-Lehies   //   Anti-Nephi-Lehies bury their weapons of war   //   Lamanites come to battle against them   //   Anti-Nephi-Lehies choose death over fighting   //   Many more Lamanites convert   //   Ammon leads Anti-Nephi-Lehies to Nephite land   //   Anti-Nephi-Lehies given land of Jershon and change name to people of Ammon   //   Great battle

These chapters continue with the story of the sons of Mosiah among the Lamanites. Chapters 23–29 will tell a thousand stories in a few chapters.

Aaron and his companions had a rough start. Enduring rejection, imprisonment, and other sufferings, they did not retreat. Ultimately (but not initially), the main king was converted, so it is a good thing they didn't give up. Having an influential person—like the king—would open many doors.

Then "thousands were brought to the knowledge of the Lord" (verse 5). Thousands! And Mormon declared that "as many as the Lamanites as believed … and were converted unto the Lord, never did fall away" (Alma 23:6).

The gospel is taught throughout the Lamanite land and many were converted. These converted Lamanites wished for a new name, a new identity, and they chose the name "Anti-Nephi-Lehies."

What did the king tell his people in the proclamation that was sent forth? (verses 1–4)

Explain the picture at the bottom after you study verses 4–15.

What happened in verses 16–18?

What are some important lessons you can learn from this chapter?

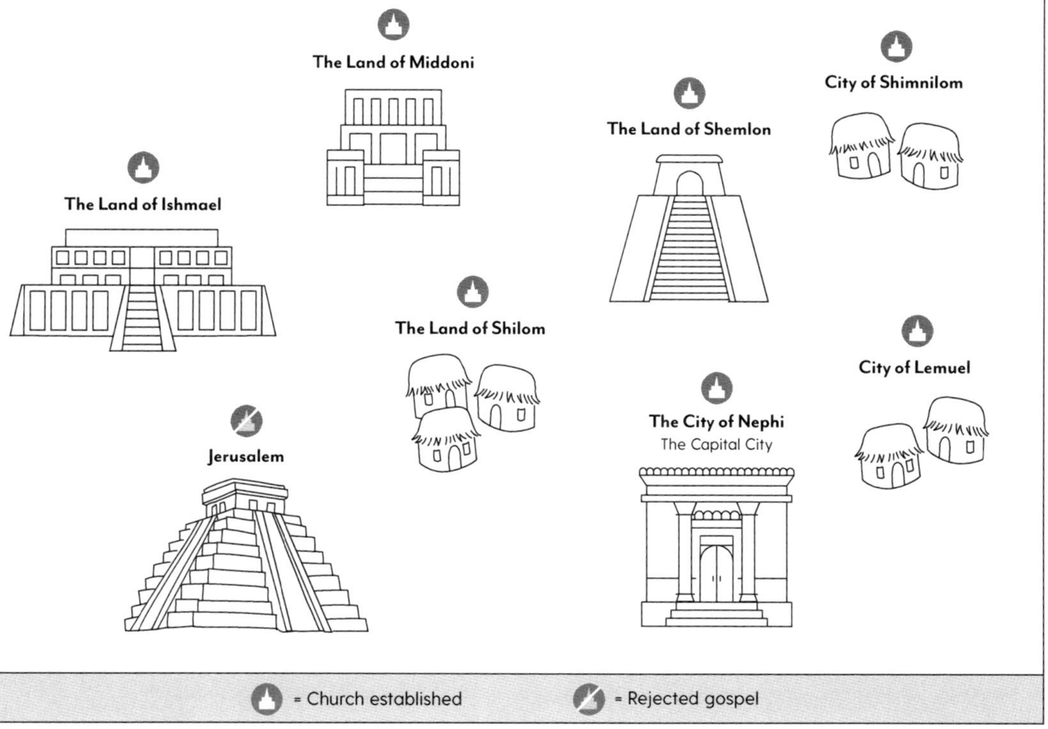

The Land of Middoni

City of Shimnilom

The Land of Shemlon

The Land of Ishmael

The Land of Shilom

City of Lemuel

Jerusalem

The City of Nephi
The Capital City

= Church established = Rejected gospel

Alma 24

In the last chapter, we have seen absolute and true conversion. Now in this chapter, we will see true ministering.

Write or draw what you learn in these verses.

1-4 | *Lamanites hatred towards the people of God*

5-6 | *People of God refuse to take up arms*

7-11 | *King Anti-Nephi-Lehi speaks to the people*

12-16 | *They will bury their swords*

17-19 | *Anti-Nephi-Lehies bury their swords*

20-22 | *Lamanites come. Anti-Nephi-Lehies do not fight.*

23-27 | *Lamanites join the people of God*

28-30 | *The Amalekites and Amulonites*

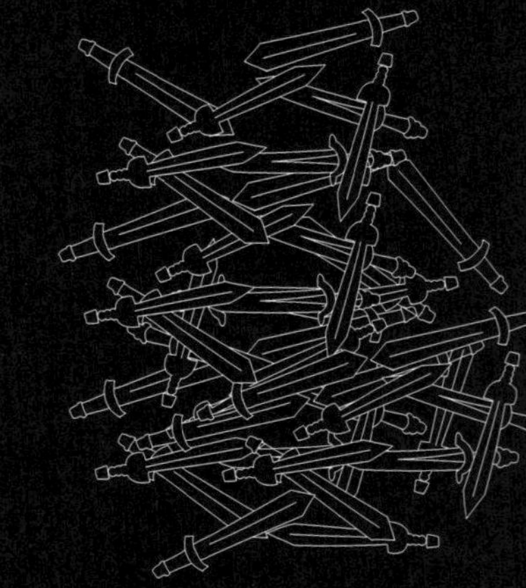

"Individuals who enter the Kinshasa Temple see an original painting entitled Congo Falls.... The waterfalls depicted in the painting call to mind a practice that was common more than a century ago among early converts to Christianity in Congo.

Before their conversion, they worshipped inanimate objects, believing that the items possessed supernatural powers. After conversion, many made a pilgrimage to one of the countless waterfalls along the Congo River, such as the Nzongo Falls. These converts threw their previously idolized objects into the waterfalls as a symbol to God and others that they had discarded their old traditions and accepted Jesus Christ. They intentionally did not throw their objects into calm, shallow waters; they threw them into the churning waters of a massive waterfall, where the items became unrecoverable. These actions were a token of a new but unwavering commitment to Jesus Christ.

People in other places and ages demonstrated their commitment to Jesus Christ in similar ways. The Book of Mormon people known as the Anti-Nephi-Lehies "laid down the weapons of their rebellion," burying them "deep in the earth" as "a testimony to God ... that they never would use [their] weapons again."...

God invites us to cast our old ways completely out of reach and begin a new life in Christ."

ELDER DALE G. RENLUND

2019 General Conference

Keep your own record side-by-side with these great prophets testifying of these important doctrines and principles.

WHAT DO YOU DO TO KEEP YOUR COMMITMENT TO JESUS CHRIST?

Alma 25

In this chapter, more Lamanites join the people of God.

1-12 | *Draw or write about what happened among the Lamanites in these verses.*	**13-16** | *More Lamanites came to believe and joined the people of God.*	**17** | *What has been the outcome of the sons of Mosiah's mission to the Lamanites?*

Alma 26

My Favorite Phrases

This chapter contains Ammon's words of rejoicing. *Fill this space with your favorite phrases.*

1	
2	
3	

Alma 27

1-5 | *Why Ammon wanted to take the Anti-Nephi-Lehies into Nephite land*	**6-13** | *The king's concern and request*	**14-19** | *Ammon and brethren meet Alma*
20-24 | *Nephites welcome the Anti-Nephi-Lehies*	**25-26** | *A new name*	**27-30** | *What the people of Ammon were like*

Alma 28

The Lamanites could not leave the people of Ammon alone. They had followed them and knew where they were and "a tremendous battle" happened, "even such an one as never had been known among all the people in the land" (v. 2). The Nephites protected them, but there was still great loss.

Verse 5 captures the aftermath of battles - the real life, terrible part of it.

Write or draw things that happened in chapter 28.

Alma 29

This chapter is commonly known as Alma's Psalm. It relates Alma's innermost desires—what he wishes at the deepest levels. It is interesting that what he wishes for himself is the very thing he once experienced—to be an angel and speak with a voice to shake the earth.

Fill this space with your favorite phrases from Alma's Psalm.

Alma 30–31

In these chapters

Korihor the anti-Christ   //   Alma testifies to Korihor   //   Alma, Ammon, Aaron, Omner, Amulek, Zeezrom, Shiblon, and Corianton go to preach to apostate Zoramites   //   The Rameumptom

Finally peace. The Nephites have just come through a tremendous battle and for almost two years, they will have peace and keep the commandments. But then a man comes who is an anti-Christ, and he will convince "many" (v.18) to rebel against God.

What is an anti-Christ?

"An anti-Christ is anyone or anything that is openly or secretly in opposition to Jesus Christ and His gospel."

Come, Follow Me - For Home and Church: Book of Mormon 2024

Who is a liar but he that denieth that Jesus is the Christ? He is antichrist, that denieth the Father and the Son (1 John 2:22).

Notice the above definition says "anyone or anything" and can be open or secret. What makes someone or something qualify as "Anti-christ" is that it opposes the true gospel plan of salvation. It is another way, another plan.

The scripture in 1 John 2:22 further explains that an anti-Christ is a liar—and they are not just denying Christ, but they are also denying Heavenly Father.

Therefore, there are all types of anti-Christs and some will be more impactful than others. Mormon tells us about Korihor, which allows us to see an anti-Christ in action and how he worked among the people. We can see what he does, what he says, and how he says it.

Korihor, the Anti-Christ

Write or draw what happened next in these verses.

VERSES 1–5 *After the war*	**VERSES 6–11** *Korihor / The law*	**VERSES 12–14** *Korihor's teachings*
VERSES 15–18 *Ye cannot know*	**VERSES 19–20** *People of Ammon's wisdom*	**VERSES 21–29** *Korihor before Giddonah*
VERSES 30–36 *Korihor before Alma*	**VERSES 37–41** *Alma questions Korihor about God*	**VERSES 42–46** *Korihor asks for a sign*
VERSES 47–51 *Alma promises sign, Korihor changes his words, sign comes*	**VERSES 52–55** *Korihor confesses he was deceived*	**VERSES 56–60** *The sad ending*

But behold they were *more wise*

ALMA 30:20

Verses 19 and 20 - two little verses. Korihor had led away the hearts of "many" (see verse 18) in Zarahemla and then he went to the land of Jershon where the people of Ammon lived. These were the converted Lamanites who had experienced their life without the gospel and had buried their weapons. Watch how they would not have anything to do with Korihor. The people of Ammon already knew the religion that Korihor was teaching and they could see right through him. All of his promises were lies. He could call them foolish all he wanted. They had finally found Christ and so Korihor's sneerings were a small thing compared to what they had now. Korihor simply had no power over them. They just bound him and took him to Ammon who kicked him out of there. Korihor only lasted there long enough to get two little verses.

A new group of Nephite dissenters arise, and they are led by a man named Zoram. They call themselves the Zoramites. They are still religious, but they have come up with their own approach. They have turned from the truth and made their own version of truth.

These people had gathered in a land near the land of Jershon, which was also close to Lamanite territory. The Nephites were nervous that these Zoramites might "enter into a correspondence with the Lamanites" which would be a great loss to the Nephites and dangerous for the nearby people of Ammon.

A power team of missionaries go to preach to this group. This missionary group was like the Navy Seals of missionaries: Ammon, Aaron, Omner, Amulek and Zeezrom. Amulek and Zeezrom both came from Ammonihah — so they know a lot about living in a wicked society. Then we are introduced to Alma's sons: Helaman, Shiblon, and Corianton. Helaman does not come on this journey, but Shiblon and Corianton do. And then we also have Alma himself.

Wouldn't you just love to see that missionary group in action?

ALMA 31

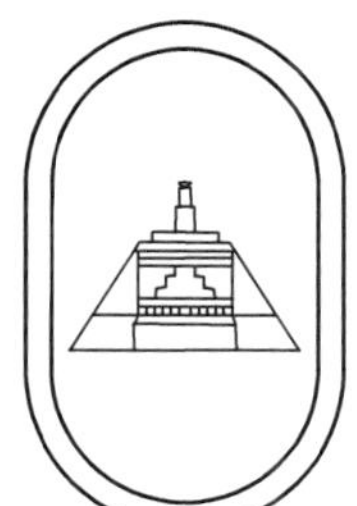

The Zoramites

What do you learn about the Zoramites in Alma 31:1–11?

What did Alma and the others find as they arrived? (verses 12–14)

Learning Activity

The Zoramites' prayer is outlined in verses 15–18. Below in the left column, record the parts of their prayer that are **true doctrines.** In the right column, record the **false doctrines.**

True Doctrine | **False Doctrine**

What was happening and what lessons can you learn in verses 19–25?

What stands out to you in Alma's prayer in verses 26–35?

As Alma and the others separated to go preach to the people, what lessons can you learn in verses 36–38?

Alma 32-35

In these chapters

Alma teaches the poor   //   Alma compares the word of God to a seed   //   Alma testifies of Christ   //   Believers forced out of Zoram and join the people of Jershon

There was a power team of men going right into the Zoramite society. Alma, Ammon, Aaron, Omner, Amulek, Zeezrom, Shiblon, and Corianton were going to "preach the word of God" (verse 1) to them.

These faithful men went all over. They went into homes, they went into synagogues, and they taught in the streets (see verse 1).

Alma's concern for this society was not just for their souls, but also what would happen if they were to join the Lamanites and fight against the Nephites - which is exactly what ultimately happens. The Zoramites will end up mixing with the Lamanites (see Alma 35:8–10) and then they end up becoming Lamanites in Alma 43. Then the Zoramites become Lamanite chief captains because they know the Nephite lands and what their strengths and weaknesses are (see Alma 48:5).

Therefore, Alma's concerns were wise. Someone could have said to Alma, "Leave them be—they aren't hurting anyone," but we will soon see that they will, in fact, hurt many.

Chapters 32–34 contain the words that Alma and Amulek spoke unto this group of people.

Verses 1–4

Who did Alma and the others begin to have success with? What do you learn about these people?

Verse 5

What concern did someone in the group express to Alma?

Verse 6

Why was Alma filled with great joy?

Verses 7–12

What are some things that Alma taught them?

Verses 13–16

What does Alma teach about choosing to be humble?

Verse 17–43

What does Alma teach about how to gain great faith? Fill this page with things that Alma teaches about growing your faith.

Tip: Alma compares developing faith to growing a seed (see verse 28). You do not have to have great faith to begin to grow faith. Something small can grow into something great. He teaches that it takes action to develop faith. Alma uses words like "exercise," "work in you," "give place," "diligence," "patience," and "long-suffering." (verses 41, 43) No one just suddenly develops great faith; it must be nurtured and developed - it is a result of effort and action.

WHAT HAS HELPED TRUTH GROW WITHIN YOU? WHAT HAS HELPED YOU DEVELOP GREAT FAITH?

Alma 33

The poor Zoramites start asking Alma specific questions about God and how to plant the seed of faith. Now Alma will address the question they originally came to ask him which was: "... we have no place to worship our God; and behold, what shall we do?" (Alma 32:5)—and watch how Alma answers it.

Write or draw what happened next in these verses.

<table>
<tr><td align="center">VERSES 1–11</td><td align="center">VERSES 12–23</td></tr>
<tr><td>What Alma teaches about worshiping God</td><td>What the scriptures teach about Christ</td></tr>
</table>

"Do you believe those scriptures?"

The prayer that the Zoramites said upon the Rameumptom included the declaration, "... but we believe ... thou has made it known unto us that there shall be no Christ" (Alma 31:16). So if they believe the scriptures, then they should be able to remove this phrase from their prayer, realizing that it conflicts with the scriptures. Also, if they would have already known the scriptures, they could have detected this apostate teaching themselves.

What are some things that are taught in the world today that you know are false because you know the scriptures?

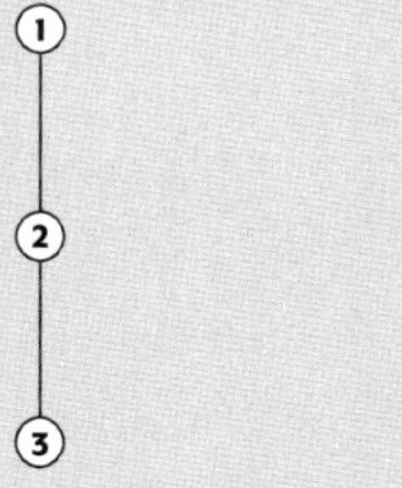

Alma 34

Amulek then stood and gave one of the greatest discourses ever given on the Atonement of Jesus Christ. He knew that the Zoramites had been taught this before they separated from the Nephites (see verse 2)—which means the seed was there, but it hadn't been nourished.

Write or draw what you learn in these verses.

1-4 | *Amulek's introduction*	**5** | *The great question all must answer*	**WHAT IS** **The Great Question?**
6-8 | *A chorus of testimonies of Jesus Christ*	**9-10** | *Why the Atonement of Jesus Christ is necessary*	**11-14** | *An infinite Atonement*
15-16 | *Our part*	**17-27** | *Pray unto Him in every possible circumstance*	**28-29** | *Importance of caring for poor and needy*
30-33 | *Start the process of faith and repentance now*	**34-36** | *Do not procrastinate repentance*	**37-41** | *A list of righteous actions we can do*

Adding to the Chorus

How can you add to the chorus of testimonies of Jesus Christ? When all is said and done, what do you want your voice to have said about Him to the world?

Alma 35

Draw or write what is happening in these verses and what the Spirit is teaching you.

VERSES 1–5	What the popular Zoramites did

VERSES 6–7	What happened to those who believed truth

VERSES 8–9	What the people of Ammon did

VERSES 10–12	What the Zoramites then did

VERSE 13	War

VERSE 14	Instruments in the hands of God

VERSE 15	State of the Nephites

VERSE 16	Alma counsels his sons (separately)

DID YOU KNOW?

As all of the missionaries finished preaching to the Zoramites, they left and went to the land of Jershon. The popular Zoramites came together and were angry because these missionaries had destroyed their craft (or priestcraft). The Zoramites had created a religion that was not for the welfare of souls, and the missionaries exposed their deceptions by using truth. Now the poor among the Zoramites started to see through it, and the elite Zoramites could not have that.

Alma and Amulek Teach about Faith in Jesus Christ
Alma 31–34 | 19:40 minutes

Alma 36-38

In these chapters

Alma teaches his son Helaman   //   Alma teaches his son Shiblon

War was now imminent...

The Zoramites have joined with the Lamanites, and you are about to study about the 14-year-long war between the Nephites and the Lamanites (starting in Alma 43). Before war begins, Alma takes this opportunity to give individual counsel to each of his sons. He will counsel Helaman in chapters 36 and 37, Shiblon in 38, and Corianton in 39–42. Then after that, it is a record of the wars.

Alma to Helaman

In Alma 36 and 37, Alma is speaking to his eldest son Helaman, whom he will trust with the sacred records.

Helaman will soon be a military commander (he will command the 2,000 stripling warriors), and Alma had also served as chief captain of the Nephite army (see Alma 2:16)—so we can only imagine the amount of wisdom that Alma could offer Helaman. Alma really wants Helaman to understand Christ's power to deliver. That is what Alma 36 is all about.

Alma to Shiblon

In Alma 38, Alma counsels his son Shiblon. In this chapter, we can see that Shiblon was a good son that brought Alma great joy (see verse 3). We also know that Shiblon had been one of the missionaries that went to teach the Zoramites—so he had worked side-by-side with his father, Amulek, Ammon, Aaron, Omner, Zeezrom, and his brother Corianton (see Alma 31:6–7).

In Alma 38:4, we learn that Shiblon had been bound and stoned "for the word's sake," and he bore it with patience. So he has already shown how valiantly he will stand.

Write or draw what you learn in each group of verses.

(1) VERSES 1–5
What Alma teaches Helaman

(2) VERSES 6–9
Alma's story: the angel

(3) VERSES 10–17
Alma racked with torment

(4) VERSES 18–23
Alma's deliverance

(5) VERSES 24–26
True joy

(6) VERSES 27–30
Christ delivers

What advice do you want to be sure to give to your children?

Alma 37

Alma now gives Helaman the charge to be entrusted with all of the sacred records, and he will also be the record keeper who adds to the records.

Write or draw what you learn in each group of verses.

1-2 | *Alma gives Helaman charge of the plates*

3-14 | *Alma speaks of the influence the plates of brass had upon their people*

15-20 | *Strict instruction concerning the records*

21-30 | *The Jaredite records*

31-47 | *Alma counsels Helaman*

Alma 38

Alma is now counseling his son Shiblon in this chapter. You will see that Shiblon was a good son that brought Alma great joy.

This chapter is only 15 verses. Read these verses and fill this space with things that stand out to you.

"By small and simple things are great things brought to pass."

A few years ago, I spoke with a young bishop who was spending hours each week counseling with members of his ward. He made a striking observation. The problems that members of his ward faced, he said, were those faced by Church members everywhere—issues such as how to establish a happy marriage; struggles with balancing work, family, and Church duties; challenges with the Word of Wisdom, with employment, or with pornography; or trouble gaining peace about a Church policy or historical question they didn't understand.

His counsel to ward members very often included getting back to simple practices of faith, such as studying the Book of Mormon... paying tithing, and serving in the Church with devotion. Frequently, however, their response to him was one of skepticism: "I don't agree with you, Bishop. We all know those are good things to do. We talk about those things all the time in the Church. But I'm not sure you're understanding me. What does doing any of those things have to do with the issues I'm facing?"

It's a fair question. Over time, that young bishop and I have observed that those who are deliberate about doing the "small and simple things" (Alma 37:6)—obeying in seemingly little ways—are blessed with faith and strength that go far beyond the actual acts of obedience themselves and, in fact, may seem totally unrelated to them. It may seem hard to draw a connection between the basic daily acts of obedience and solutions to the big, complicated problems we face. But they are related.... Small acts of faith, even when they seem insignificant or entirely disconnected from the specific problems that vex us, bless us in all we do.

ELDER WHITNEY CLAYTON | October 2016 General Conference

What small and simple things have brought to pass great things in your life?

Alma 39-42

In these chapters

Alma teaches his son Corianton

Corianton

Now Alma is going to counsel his son Corianton. Corianton had been lured away in sin and Alma is going to teach some eternal truths that will wake Corianton up. As you study these chapters, notice the truths that Alma taught and how these truths would help Corianton desire to change.

Corianton had left his mission and went over to a different land—"the land of Siron." This land was along the borders of the Lamanites, and there were harlots there. The harlot Isabel was well-known and had stolen the "hearts of many."

Corianton went to where he ought not to go. His mission was among the Zoramites, and he left and went to where harlots were. He went to a place of temptation. Had he stayed back with his missionary companions, he would have avoided Isabel—but he left and went to where she was.

Alma 39

Alma counsels his son Corianton

Write or draw what you learn in each group of verses.

ALMA 39:1–4	ALMA 39:5–8	ALMA 39:9–14	ALMA 39:15–19
Corianton's sin	The seriousness of sexual sin	Alma's counsel to his son	Why they teach about the coming of Christ, even if it is long before He comes

Alma 40

Alma teaches Corianton about the Resurrection

Alma has observed that Corianton's mind was worried about the Resurrection. Alma then teaches Corianton very clearly about the Resurrection, when it will happen, and what it is like after we die.

Write or draw what you learn in each group of verses.

VERSES 1–5	VERSES 6–11	VERSES 12–14
What must happen before people can be resurrected	*The state of the soul between death and Resurrection*	*The spirit world*
VERSES 15–17 *Some thought that spirits going to the spirit world was a resurrection, and Alma admits it could be called that.*	**VERSES 18–21** *THIS is Resurrection*	Alma Teaches Corianton About Resurrection and Judgment Alma 39–41 | 2:36 minutes

VERSES 22–26

Critical doctrines about the Resurrection

Alma Continues to Teach Corianton about the Resurrection

Write or draw what you learn in each group of verses.

VERSE 1

Many have "wrested" or distorted the doctrine of the Resurrection

VERSES 2–7

Truths about the Resurrection

Think about it: *Why do you think many want to change the doctrine of the Resurrection?*

VERSES 8–11

Sins will never lead to happiness. It is impossible. That is not the decree (law) of God.

VERSES 12–15

This is what restoration is

Wickedness never was happiness

WHAT HAS BEEN YOUR EXPERIENCE WITH THIS TRUTH?

Alma 42

"Alma 42 contains some of the most magnificent doctrine on the Atonement in all scripture. Alma helped Corianton understand that it is not an 'injustice that the sinner should be consigned to a state of misery.'"

ELDER QUENTIN L. COOK
October 2016 General Conference

Watch This
After you study these chapters, watch this video and see what additional lessons you can learn.

Alma Teaches Corianton about God's Justice and Mercy
Alma 42 | 3:25 minutes

Write or draw what you learn in each group of verses.

ALMA 42:1 | *A concern on Corianton's mind*
ALMA 42:2–10 | *Alma lays out the plan of salvation*
ALMA 42:11–12 | *The importance of the plan of redemption*
ALMA 42:13–14 | *The grasp of justice*
ALMA 42:15 | *The plan of mercy*
ALMA 42:16–26 | *Why repentance is necessary*
ALMA 42:27–31 | *Choose what you want*

Understanding Justice & Mercy

"When the Savior carried out the Atonement, He took our sins upon Himself. He was able to "answer the ends of the law" (2 Nephi 2:7) because He subjected Himself to the penalty that the law required for our sins. In doing so, He "satisfied the demands of justice" and extended mercy to everyone who repents and follows Him (see Mosiah 15:9; Alma 34:14–16). Because He has paid the price for your sins, you will not have to suffer that punishment if you repent (see D&C 19:15–20)."

TRUE TO THE FAITH

Alma 43–52

In these chapters

Zoramites become Lamanites // Captain Moroni arms Nephites // Moroni commands Lamanites to make a covenant of peace // Amalickiah desires to be Nephite king // Moroni raises title of liberty // Amalickiah and followers go to Lamanite land // Amalickiah becomes king of Lamanites // Lamanites attack Nephites // Moroni fortifies land // King-men desire to set up a king // War

Beginning of

The War Chapters

This is the beginning of a long, drawn-out battle. Starting in Alma 43:3 we will get nearly 20 chapters of war, strategy, and conflict.

From these chapters, we can learn many lessons, including:

- **PRINCIPLES FOR FIGHTING SPIRITUAL BATTLES**

- **THE IMPORTANCE OF BEING PREPARED AND FORTIFYING OURSELVES AND OUR FAMILIES**

- **HOW EVIL MEN TRY TO GAIN POWER**

- **HOW WE CAN GO FORTH TO BATTLE IN THE STRENGTH OF THE LORD**

- **THE IMPORTANCE OF KNOWING THE INTENT OF THE ENEMY**

Understanding the intent of an enemy is vital to effective preparation for possible attacks. Precisely because Captain Moroni knew the intention of the Lamanites, he was prepared to meet them at the time of their coming and was victorious. And that same principle and promise applies to each of us.

ELDER DAVID A. BEDNAR | October 2019 General Conference

Alma 43

Moroni vs. Zerahemnah

1–2 | **Alma and his sons**	3–4 | **The Zoramites**	5–8 | **Zerahemnah's purpose**
9–10 | **The Nephite's purpose**	11–14 | **The people of Ammon**	15–17 | **Captain Moroni**
18–22 | **Lamanites not prepared**	23–33 | **Moroni's plan**	34–38 | **The battle**
39–46 | **The battle**	47–53 | **The battle**	54 | **Moroni's mercy**

*What principles does this chapter teach that can help
you and your family fight evil in these last days?*

Captain Moroni Speaks to Zerahemnah

The Lamanites were in Moroni's hands. Now Moroni will speak to Zerahemnah, the leader of the Lamanite army. In your own words, explain what is happening in each group of verses. You could also look for principles that will help you fight spiritual battles today.

VERSES 1–7 *Moroni's words to Zerahemnah*	**VERSES 8–9** *Zerahemnah's response*	**VERSES 10–11** *Moroni refuses Zerahemnah's temporary solution*
VERSES 12–15 *Zerahemnah rushes towards Moroni*	**VERSES 16–18** *Battle resumes*	**VERSES 19–24** *The oath*

The Record of Helaman

Here begins the record of Helaman, the eldest son of Alma. Helaman was given the records from his father and he will also add to the records as he writes the account of the Nephites in his day. Write or draw what is happening in the following verses.

VERSE 1 *After the battle*	**VERSES 2–8** *Alma asks Helaman questions*	**VERSES 9–14** *A prophecy Helaman is to record*
VERSES 15–16 *Alma's blessing upon the promised land*	**VERSES 17–19** *Alma's "death"*	**VERSES 20–24** *Helaman goes forth*

Alma 46

In this chapter, you will see how much wickedness one man can bring to pass. You will also see the impact of a single, righteous individual.

Write or draw what is happening in these verses.

VERSES 1–2 Some gather against Helaman	**VERSES 3–5** Amalickiah desires to be king	**VERSES 6–7** Many are deceived	**THINK ABOUT IT** Why do you think this was a dangerous situation?
Tip When you see the words "and thus we see," that is prophet Mormon pointing out something he wants to make sure you notice.	**VERSES 8–10** "And thus we see"	**VERSES 11–13** Moroni raises the title of liberty	**VERSES 14–15** Christians
VERSES 16–18 A land of liberty	**VERSES 19–20** The call to come forth	**VERSES 21–22** The covenant	**VERSES 23–27** Remember who they were
VERSE 28 In all the parts of the land	**VERSE 29** Amalickiahites leave	**VERSES 30–35** Moroni pursues	**VERSES 36–41** State of the Nephites

The people came running together

What important principles are taught in this chapter? What do you want to be sure to remember?

Alma 47

While the Nephites were experiencing some peace for a bit, Amalickiah was among the Lamanites stirring them up. What do you imagine Amalickiah might have said to cause them to be stirred up enough to come battle against them?

Write or draw what is happening in these verses.

Alma 47:1 *Amalickiah stirs up Lamanites*	**Alma 47:2–3** *Some would not obey king*	**Alma 47:4** *Amalickiah's plan* 
Alma 47:5–7 *Lamanites gathered* MOUNT ANTIPAS	**Alma 47:8–9** *Amalickiah's plan* 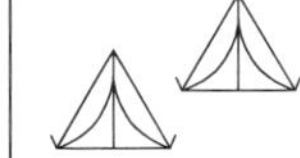 MOUNT ANTIPAS	**Alma 47:10–12** *Amalickiah's plan to get Lehonti off the mount*  MOUNT ANTIPAS
Alma 47:13–16 *The trick*	**Alma 47:17–19** *Poison by degrees*	**Alma 47:20–21** *What the king thought*
Alma 47:22–26 *The king killed*	**Alma 47:27–31** *Amalickiah gains hearts of people*	**Alma 47:32–36** *Amalickiah becomes king of the Lamanites* 

Alma 48

Amalickiah was now king, but what he really wanted was to be king over all of the land—over the Nephites and the Lamanites. Now he begins to work towards that goal.

Write or draw what is happening in these verses.

ALMA 48:1–6	*Amalickiah's plan*
ALMA 48:7–10	*What Moroni had been doing*
ALMA 48:11–13	*Moroni*
ALMA 48:14–15	*The faith of the Nephites*
ALMA 48:16–17	*Moroni*
ALMA 48:18–20	*Men of God*
ALMA 48:21–25	*Reason to fight*

Alma 48:17

"...if all men had been, and were, and ever would be, like unto Moroni, behold, the very powers of hell would have been shaken forever; yea, the devil would never have power over the hearts of the children of men."

FINISH THIS SENTENCE

I can be like Captain Moroni by...

Alma 49   *Write or draw what is happening in these verses.*

Up to this point, the Lamanite army had been in the wilderness (see Alma 48:6). But now they were approaching a Nephite city. Where will they attack first? Ammonihah. Why? Because it has been destroyed before, they thought it was easy prey. Will it be?

VERSES 1–4 *How great was their disappointment*	**VERSES 5–9** *Lamanites astonished*	**VERSES 10–17** *The wisdom of Moroni*
VERSES 18–24 *What happened at the city of Noah*	**VERSES 25–30** *Lamanites flee*	

Alma 50   *Write or draw what is happening in these verses.*

Even though the Lamanites were utterly defeated, Moroni did not sit back and think they were now sufficiently safe. He knew that the Lamanites had gained experience from this battle. They now knew exactly what they were up against and they could learn from that.

VERSES 1–6 *Moroni strengthened every city in all the land*	**VERSES 7–12** *More preparations*	**VERSES 13–19** *Nephites prosper*
VERSES 20–23 *The promise*		**VERSES 24–32** *Nephite problem - Morianton*
VERSES 33–36 *Battle*		**VERSES 37–40** *New Nephite chief judge*

Moroni strengthened every city in all the land

Moroni had the foresight to see that Morianton (a harsh leader over the land of Morianton) could be a problem since this group could become Nephite dissenters. This would be a dangerous situation because if one enemy was attacking, then the other enemy could invade from the other side. Moroni could see how this threatened their liberties.

Alma 51

The Nephites will face another problem within themselves. This will be a great issue because this will cause weakness within the Nephites, all while Amalickiah was bringing a "wonderfully great army" (v. 11) of Lamanites to attack.

Write or draw what is happening in these verses.

① **1-4** | *A contention*

② **5-8** | *King-men vs. freemen*

③ **9-13** | *Amalickiah again stirred hearts of Lamanites*

④ **14-21** | *Moroni first addresses problems within the Nephites*

⑤ **22-27** | *Meanwhile...*

⑥ **28-37** | *Teancum*

Alma 52

The Lamanites woke up to a dead king and Teancum's army ready to give them battle. They retreated to nearby Mulek - a city they had already conquered, and Amalickiah's brother, Ammoron, becomes the king of the Lamanites.

Write or draw what is happening in these verses.

① **1-6** | *Ammoron becomes king*

② **7-10** | *Moroni's instructions*

③ **11-14** | *Moroni fighting on the other side (Lamanites were attacking from different places)*

④ **15-21** | *Moroni goes to assist Teancum*

⑤ **22-28** | *Moroni's battle plans*

⑥ **29-40** | *Battle*

Alma 53-63

In these chapters

Helaman leads the two thousand stripling warriors   //   Prisoner exchanges   //
Helaman's warriors fight and none are slain   //   Helaman's warriors fight again,
all are wounded and none are slain   //   Moroni's letter to Pahoran   //
Pahoran's reply to Moroni   //   Moroni goes to Pahoran's aid   //   Lamanites
driven from land   //   Records passed to Shiblon and then Helaman

These were dangerous times and Nephites were needed to fight. The people
of Ammon wanted to help, but they had made an oath. But they had sons who
were willing to fight, and they were "exceedingly valiant for courage" (v. 20).

*"When a child reads the Book of Mormon for the first time and is enamored with Abinadi's
courage or the march of 2,000 stripling warriors, we can gently add that Jesus is the
omnipresent central figure in this marvelous chronicle, standing like a colossus over virtually
every page of it and providing the link to all of the other faith-promoting figures in it."*

ELDER JEFFREY R. HOLLAND

October 2019 General Conference

Alma 53

Draw or write what is happening in these verses.

ALMA 53:1	ALMA 53:2	ALMA 53:3–4	ALMA 53:5–6
prisoners	Lehi	prisoner orders	strongholds

ALMA 53:7	ALMA 53:8–9	ALMA 53:10–13	ALMA 53:14
fortifications	meanwhile…	people of Ammon	about to break oath

ALMA 53:15	ALMA 53:16	ALMA 53:17	ALMA 53:18
Helaman's concern	their sons	the sons' covenant	2,000 sons

ALMA 53:19	ALMA 53:20	ALMA 53:21	ALMA 53:22–23
wanted Helaman as their leader	the sons	the sons	2,000 stripling warriors

Alma 54

Ammoron asked Moroni to exchange prisoners. However, a prisoner-for-prisoner exchange was unacceptable because the Lamanites had been taking women and children as prisoners, too, and the Nephites had only been taking soldiers. So if it was prisoner-for-prisoner, the exchange would strengthen the Lamanite army more than the Nephite army. So Moroni came up with a plan.

In this space, explain what is happening in verses 1–4.

As you read the letters, record things that stand out to you.	
VERSES 5–14 **Moroni's Letter to Ammoron**	**VERSES 15–24** **Ammoron's Letter to Moroni**

Alma 55

Moroni was witnessing all of these terrible deaths on both sides, and he just saw how Ammoron was justifying it. Moroni decided to withdraw his offer to exchange prisoners because he did not want to give Ammoron any soldiers, which would give him more power. Instead, Moroni came up with another way to get the Nephite prisoners released.

1. **What was Moroni's reaction to Ammoron's letter? See verses 1–3.**

2. **Describe what Moroni did in order to take back the City of Gid from the Lamanites. See verses 4–24.**

3. **What important life lessons can you find in verses 25–35?**

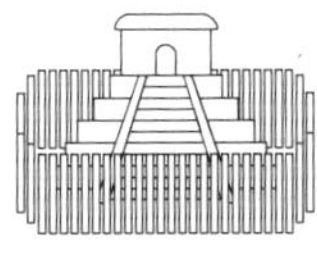

Alma 56 *Write or draw what is happening in these verses.*

At the beginning of the 30th year of the reign of the judges (around 62 B.C.), Helaman wrote a letter to Moroni. Helaman was on the western side of the nation fighting Lamanite battles there while Moroni was on the eastern side. This letter will last from Alma 56–58 and will give an account to Moroni concerning what Helaman has witnessed over the past few years.

1–2 | *Helaman reports*	**3–8** | *The people of Ammon*	**9–11** | *Helaman's 2,000 sons march to help*
12–17 | *The state of that side of the war*	**18–26** | *The situation*	**27–29** | *Lamanites try to cut off Nephite provisions*
30–38 | *The strategy*	**39–40** | *The march*	**41–44** | *The choice to be made*
45–46 | *What they chose*	**47–48** | *The stripling warriors*	**49–51** | *What they discovered*
52–54 | *Lamanites surrender*	**55–56** | *Helaman counts his warriors*	**57** | *Helaman's army grows*

Stripling
NOUN

A youth in the state of adolescence, or just passing from boyhood to manhood; a lad.

Alma 57

Due to the recent battle, Ammoron lost a lot of soldiers, and it was the most powerful Lamanite army (see Alma 56:36)—therefore, we can see that Helaman's 2,000 really made a difference. They did not just help win a battle; they impacted the whole war. And now Ammoron was in need of more soldiers.

Write or draw what is happening in each group of verses.

1–5	*Regaining the city of Antiparah*
6–12	*Regaining the city of Cumeni*
13–16	*Prisoner of war problems*
17–22	*Sudden battle*
23–27	*Stripling warriors' exceeding faith*
28–36	*What had happened to prisoners*

Alma 58

They had now successfully retaken two of the four cities that the Lamanites had captured. Cumeni and Antiparah were back in Nephite possession. Manti and Zeezrom were still held by the Lamanites. So Helaman and his army still had work to do.

Write or draw what is happening in each group of verses.

ALMA 58:1–9	ALMA 58:10–12	ALMA 58:13–24
Helaman's situation	*The Lord speaks peace to their souls*	*City of Manti regained*
ALMA 58:25–30	**ALMA 58:31–37**	**ALMA 58:38–41**
Lamanites return	*Helaman searches for answers*	*Where Helaman and his army currently were*

Alma 59

Now we are back to Moroni and he had just read the letter by Helaman. Moroni rejoiced so much in their story that he made it known to all the people in that part of the land, "that they might rejoice also."

Write or draw what is happening in these verses.

① **1–4** | *Moroni's next actions*

② **5–10** | *People of Nephihah attacked*

③ **11–13** | *Moroni doubts and gets angry*

Alma 60

Moroni wrote another letter, and he did not hold back. They were in a very fragile state and after all the years of fighting, he was feeling abandoned by the government in Zarahemla. He addressed this letter to Pahoran and all the government leaders who had been chosen to govern this war, and he was going to be as bold with them as he was in his letter to Ammoron (see Alma 54).

Moroni's letter to Pahoran

Moroni's letter is this entire chapter. In this space, write or draw things that stand out to you in the letter.

Pahoran's Letter to Moroni

Moroni received a letter back from Pahoran and Moroni learned that there had been an insurrection in Zarahemla and Pahoran had been chased out of the land. Things were really bad and if something didn't happen soon, they would lose the nation.

Pahoran's letter is this entire chapter. In this space, write or draw what you learn from Pahoran.

Alma 62   *Write or draw what is happening in these verses.*

Now Moroni understood and he mourned as he discovered what was happening in Zarahemla. And now that he knew, he gathered some men and headed to Pahoran.

1–3
Moroni's response to the letter

4–6
Moroni raises the standard of liberty again

7–11
Victory

12–17
Moroni again focuses on the war

18–29
Regaining the city of Nephihah

30–35
Regaining the city of Lehi

36–38
Teancum's death / End of war

39–41
The Nephite civilization

42–46
Moroni fortifies land; Helaman declares the word of God

47–52
Nephites prosper; Helaman dies

Alma 63

Moroni dies, but God has and will raise up others to lead his people.

Write or draw what is happening in each group of verses.

ALMA 63:1-2

Shiblon takes possession of the records

ALMA 63:3

Moroni dies

ALMA 63:4

A large group moves northward

ALMA 63:5-9

Hagoth builds ships

ALMA 63:10-13

Shiblon gives records to nephew Helaman

ALMA 63:14-17

Another battle

Life Lessons

What lessons have you learned from these war chapters about fighting spiritual battles?

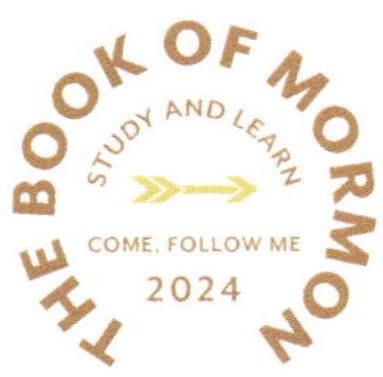

Helaman

DID YOU KNOW?

- The Book of Helaman was named after Helaman Jr., who was the son of Helaman Sr. and grandson of Alma the Younger.

- Helaman Jr. had two sons, Nephi and Lehi, who will also be an important part of this book.

- This book covers the time period among the Nephites just before the coming of Christ and is a very tumultuous time. There will be wickedness like has never been known among the Nephites, and there will also be great righteousness.

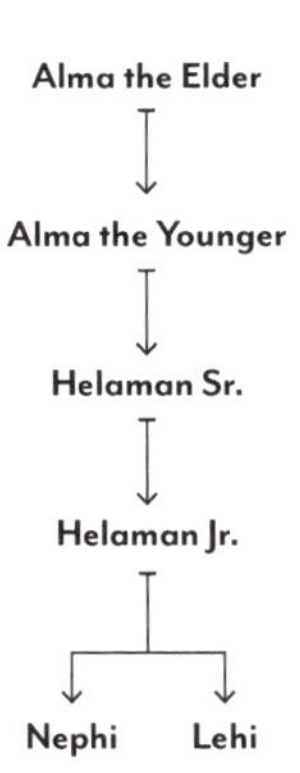

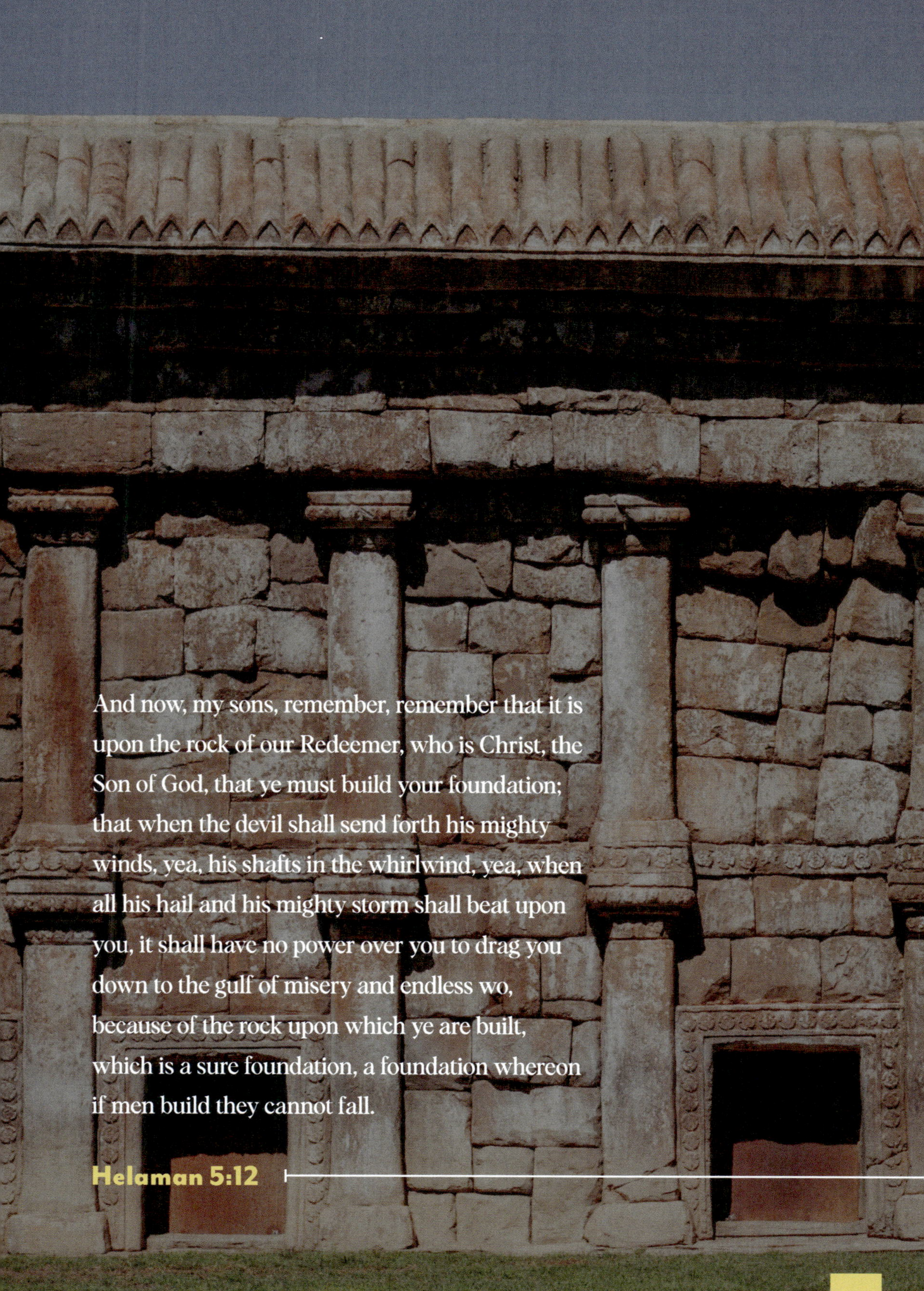

And now, my sons, remember, remember that it is
upon the rock of our Redeemer, who is Christ, the
Son of God, that ye must build your foundation;
that when the devil shall send forth his mighty
winds, yea, his shafts in the whirlwind, yea, when
all his hail and his mighty storm shall beat upon
you, it shall have no power over you to drag you
down to the gulf of misery and endless wo,
because of the rock upon which ye are built,
which is a sure foundation, a foundation whereon
if men build they cannot fall.

Helaman 5:12

HELAMAN

Timeline

Here is the Book of Helaman at-a-glance. The main stories are found in the timeline below. If you ever want to find a story in your scriptures, you can look at this page for help. You can add your own notes to this page as well.

HELAMAN 1

- Great political contention exists over next chief judge
- Pahoran becomes chief judge and is murdered by Kishkumen
- Secret combination is made to protect Kishkumen

HELAMAN 2

- Helaman Jr. becomes next chief judge
- Gadianton becomes leader of band of Kishkumen and they seek to slay Helaman
- Kishkumen is slain
- Gadianton band flees to wilderness

HELAMAN 5–6

- Nephi gives up judgment seat to Cezoram
- Nephi and his brother Lehi preach, gain many converts, are imprisoned and encircled by fire
- Righteous Lamanites preach to Nephites
- Gadianton robbers take over government

HELAMAN 3–4

- Nephi, son of Helaman, becomes chief judge
- Lamanites take Zarahemla
- Church dwindles and Nephites become weak

HELAMAN 7–9

- Nephi prays on garden tower
- Nephi announces murder of chief judge and identifies murderer

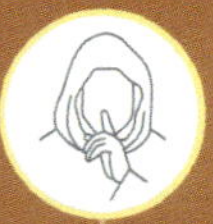

HELAMAN 10–12

- Great famine comes, many perish
- Many repent
- Gadianton robbers increase and wax strong
- Nephites again grow in pride and iniquity

HELAMAN 13–15

- Samuel the Lamanite prophesies of the destruction of the Nephites and of signs of Christ's birth and death

HELAMAN 16

- Many Nephites are baptized
- Arrows could not slay Samuel

People to Know

If you need a reminder of who is who, return to this page.

Pahoran II

Pahoran II was the son of Pahoran I. He contended for chief judge seat and became the fourth Nephite chief judge. He was murdered by Kishkumen.

Kishkumen

Kishkumen murdered Pahoran II, the Nephite chief judge. A secret combination formed to keep his identity secret. He was killed by Helaman's servant.

Moronihah

Moronihah was the son of Captain Moroni. He took over command of Nephite armies.

Helaman Jr.

Helaman Jr. was the son of Helaman Sr. and grandson of Alma the Younger. The book of Helaman is named after Helaman Jr. He received the records and was appointed chief judge.

Gadianton

Gadianton became the leader of a band of robbers. He brought much wickedness and destruction to the Nephites. He received secret oaths from the devil.

Nephi

Nephi was the son of Helaman Jr. He was appointed chief judge but gave up the judgment seat to preach with his brother Lehi. Nephi was imprisoned and was encircled with fire. He prayed on a garden tower.

Lehi

Lehi was the son of Helaman Jr. He preached with his brother Nephi and was miraculously freed from prison.

Gadianton Robbers

This was a secret criminal group that grew large. Lamanites sought to do away with the Gadianton robbers that were among them. The Nephites joined in large numbers.

Samuel the Lamanite

Samuel was a Lamanite prophet. He prophesied in Zarahemla of Nephite destruction and signs of Christ's birth and death. Arrows could not touch him.

Helaman 1-6

In these chapters

Chief judges murdered // Gadianton and secret works of murder // Gadianton's followers flee // Nephi becomes chief judge // Nephites weak like Lamanites // Nephi and Lehi preach // Nephi and Lehi imprisoned and encircled by fire // Lamanites preach to Nephites // Gadianton robbers take over government

The book of Helaman is full of war, murder, and secret combinations. This book introduces Gadianton, who worked in darkness. He was the beginning of many, many others who would be known after his name (the "Gadianton Robbers"). This group will ultimately bring about the destruction of the Nephites, and a similar group brought down the Jaredites.

The war ended in the 31st year, and in Helaman 1 it was the 40th year; and Mormon is going to tell you of "a serious difficulty" that was happening among the Nephites. Pahoran had died, and out of his many sons, three of them desire to take their father's place as chief judge. This was the most powerful political position in Zarahemla and so the people must vote wisely.

Lessons for us today:

"If we are not careful, today's secret combinations can obtain power and influence just as quickly and just as completely as they did in Book of Mormon times. Do you remember the pattern? The secret combinations began among the 'more wicked part' of society, but eventually 'seduced the more part of the righteous' until the whole society was polluted [Helaman 6:38]."

ELDER M. RUSSELL BALLARD

October 1997 General Conference

Helaman 1

Study each group of verses and write what was happening around the illustrations.

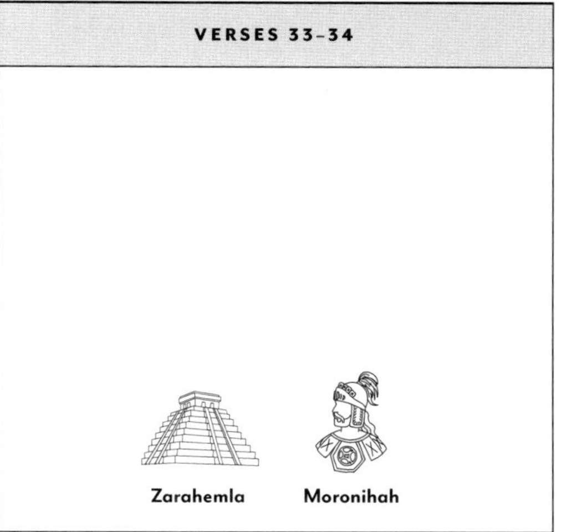

Helaman 2 *Write or draw what you learn in these verses.*

The Nephites needed a new chief judge. This was the most important position in the land. There were groups who wanted this power. Who should hold it during such a dangerous time?

1-2 | *The next chief judge*	**3-5** | *Gadianton*
6-10 | *Kishkumen tries to kill Helaman*	**11-14** | *Gadianton robbers*

Helaman 3 *Write or draw what you learn in these verses.*

Over the next several chapters, Mormon will give an overview of the problems among the Nephites and the great and small consequences that came from them.

1-12	*Many Nephites move northward*
13-16	*Many records*
17-30	*Helaman was a righteous and strong chief judge*
31-37	*Great joy/persecution among the Church*

Helaman 4 *Write or draw what you learn in these verses.*

Things begin to spiral. The Lamanites come to battle and take over every land except for Bountiful.

Verses 1–4	**Verses 5–10**	**Verses 11–14**	**Verses 15–26**
Rebellion among the Nephites	*Lamanites push Nephites to northern part of land*	*Why this was happening*	*Moronihah gains back half of lands; Nephites begin to remember*

Helaman 5

Write or draw what you learn in these verses.

With only half of their lands left, Nephi, chief judge, gave up the judgment-seat to a man named Cezoram. The majority of the Nephites were still choosing wickedness. Even with so much evidence for their need to turn back to God, they "who chose evil were more numerous than they who chose good" (verse 2). This is the first time we have heard this about the Nephites. They were now so wicked and rebellious that "they could not be governed by the law nor justice."

1-4 | *Nephi gives up judgment seat to preach with his brother Lehi*	**THE ROCK OF OUR REDEEMER** What this scripture teaches me about how Jesus Christ can strengthen me...
5-12 | *Helaman's words to his sons Nephi and Lehi*	
13-19 | *Lehi and Nephi teach with great power and authority*	
20-34 | *Nephi and Lehi preach in Lamanite land and are put in prison*	
35-42 | *Aminadab*	
43-52 | *300 souls surrounded by fire*	

Helaman 6

Now there was another Lamanite group like the people of Ammon. They were known for their firmness and steadiness and were more righteous than the Nephites. They knew what they had - they knew what life was like before they had the gospel and what it was like after. They were firm and steady.

VERSES 1-3	**VERSES 4-14**	**VERSES 15-20**
Righteous Lamanites	Lamanites preach to the Nephites	Chief judges murdered
VERSES 21-30	**VERSES 31-41**	
Gadianton robbers	State of the Nephites	

"We, too, are faced with powerful, destructive forces unleashed by the adversary. Waves of sin, wickedness, immorality, degradation, tyranny, deceitfulness, conspiracy, and dishonesty threaten all of us. They come with great power and speed and will destroy us if we are not watchful.

"But a warning is sounded for us. It behooves us to be alert and to listen and flee from the evil for our eternal lives. Without help we cannot stand against it. We must flee to high ground or cling fast to that which can keep us from being swept away. That to which we must cling for safety is the gospel of Jesus Christ. It is our protection from whatever force the evil one can muster."

PRESIDENT SPENCER W. KIMBALL | October 1978 General Conference

*Keep your own record side-by-side with these great prophets
testifying of these important doctrines and principles.*

HOW CHRIST HAS BEEN MY FOUNDATION AND
HOW THAT HAS KEPT ME SAFE...

Helaman 7–12

In these chapters

Nephi prays upon his garden tower // Nephi declares the murder of their chief judge through inspiration // Chief judge found dead // Nephi identifies murderer // Nephi given sealing power // Many people perish by famine // Gadianton robbers grow strong

At this time, Nephi was the chief judge and he gave up that position so he could preach the gospel just like his great-grandfather Alma the Younger had done. Nephi and his brother Lehi then went throughout the Nephite and Lamanite lands to preach the word of God.

The more part of the Lamanites were baptized, and they returned the captured lands to the Nephites. What followed was a time of great prosperity and rejoicing—there had never been a time like this in the land.

It was at this time that Nephi and Lehi went to the land northward to teach the gospel. There had been groups moving northward for about 30 years now (see Alma 63:4–10 and Helaman 3:3–12).

Helaman 7 opens with Nephi returning home to bad news.

Helaman 7

Draw or write what is happening and what the Spirit is teaching you.

HELAMAN 7:1–3

What happened in the land northward

HELAMAN 7:4–6

What Nephi found when he returned home

TIP: For the first time, there was a wicked chief judge and he was a member of the Gadianton robbers. In the past when the Nephites had started to fall into wickedness, at least there was a righteous chief judge who would labor to serve the people and deliver righteous judgments. But no longer. This new chief judge put aside God's commandments and did not care about justice among the Nephites.

HELAMAN 7:7–10

Nephi's prayer on the garden tower

HELAMAN 7:11–29

Nephi speaks to people

Helaman 8

There were judges in the crowd who did not like what Nephi was saying. These judges were part of the Gadianton robbers and would have received their positions because of those associations. Nephi had been the former chief judge and he knew what was going on. The only way they could get away with all of their crimes was if they were kept secret.

Write or draw what you learn in each group of verses.

HELAMAN 8:1–10	HELAMAN 8:11–26	HELAMAN 8:27–28
What the judges in the crowd did	*What Nephi continued to teach*	*The prophetic sign that Nephi gave*

Helaman 9   *Write or draw what you learn in each group of verses.*

Five people who were in the crowd ran to the judgment-seat to verify Nephi's prophecy. So they will be learning two things: 1. whether the chief judge was truly murdered, and 2. if Nephi was truly able to prophesy, which would mean that his other prophecies about their destruction were true.

1–5	*Five run to see*
6–9	*The five arrested*
10–17	*Verses 10-17 - The judges try to blame Nephi*
18–20	*Five stand up for Nephi*
21–36	*Nephi gives another sign*
37–41	*Verses 37-41 - Nephi's words were true*

WATCH & LEARN

After you study this chapter, watch these videos and see what additional lessons you can learn.

Nephi Prophesies
Death of Chief Judge
2:19 minutes

Nephi Proves His
Innocence
6:54 minutes

Helaman 10   *Write or draw what you learn in the following verses.*

Nephi was proven right, and everyone just walked away leaving Nephi alone. No one thanked him, questioned him, or took a moment to learn more from a prophet of God. They just walked away. Now he was walking home from that whole event and he was weighing things in his mind and heart.

Verses 1–10	**Verses 11–19**
As Nephi walked and pondered...	*Nephi responds immediately*

Helaman 11 *Write or draw what you learn in the following verses.*

This chapter covers 20 BC to 6 BC, which means we are really close to the coming of Jesus Christ to the earth. It is this generation that will witness the signs of His birth and many will be among those who witness the signs of His death and His coming to the Nephites. This is the generation that Nephi and all of the other prophets have been pointing to. Watch how Satan will rage in the land.

1–2
State of the Nephites

3–9
A great famine

10–18
Nephi's prayer

19–21
Peace

22–23
The power of doctrine (eternal, unchanging truths)

24–38
Large group of Gadianton robbers

Helaman 12

Mormon pauses the Nephite account and points out things he wants us to learn from these stories. Fill this space with things that you learn from Mormon in this chapter.

Helaman 13–16

In these chapters

Samuel the Lamanite prophesies // He foretells signs of Christ's birth and death //
Many believe and are baptized // Samuel cannot be slain

Samuel the Lamanite

Chapters 13–15 contain the prophecy of Samuel, who was a Lamanite prophet who lived at the same time as the prophet Nephi (son of Helaman). We have no backstory to Samuel's life—he just comes in and out of the Book of Mormon in Helaman 13–16, but we can try to imagine what his life might have looked like before and after these chapters.

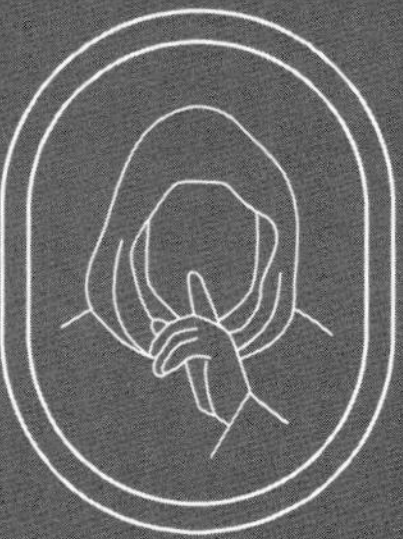

Gadianton Robbers

The Nephites and Lamanites have completely swapped places now. The Lamanites are righteous and they are strict commandment keepers, but the Nephites remain in "great wickedness" (Helaman 13:1). At the beginning of Helaman 13, it was the 86th year and we learn that in the years prior to this, the Gadianton robbers had been ruthless and they were large and powerful.

At first, the wickedness of the Gadianton robbers stirred up the people, so they remembered the Lord (see Helaman 11:34). But that did not last; in the 82nd year, the Nephites began to forget the Lord, and then it went downhill from there. Now we are in the 86th year, and Samuel has a message for the Nephites.

Write or draw what you learn in these verses.

Helaman 13:1

The state of the Nephites and Lamanites

Helaman 13:2–4

Samuel the Lamanite in Zarahemla

Helaman 13:5–39

Fill this space around the picture with things Samuel taught and prophesied.

Helaman 14

Samuel prophesies of signs that will come when Christ is born. These signs would come soon - in just five years.

Write or draw what you learn in each group of verses.

VERSES 1–8
Signs of Christ's birth

VERSES 9–13
Why Samuel has come to Zarahemla

VERSES 14–19
What Christ's death will bring to pass

VERSES 20–27
Signs of Christ's death

VERSES 28–31
Choose

Helaman 15

Samuel clearly tells the Nephites of the destruction that they will experience if they do not repent. He was saying to them, "choose to change - don't let this happen because when it does, it is going to be relentless."

Write or draw what you learn in each group of verses.

VERSES 1–3
Warning

VERSES 4–6
The Lamanites

VERSES 7–9
The power the scriptures had among the Lamanites

VERSES 10–13
The Lamanites in the last days

VERSES 14–17
Warning

Helaman 16

Many believed Samuel and they went and found Nephi and were baptized. But those who did not believe did not disagree silently. Write or draw what you learn in these verses.

HELAMAN 16:1
Those who believed

HELAMAN 16:2–3
Arrows and stones

HELAMAN 16:4–5
Believers prepare for signs that will soon come

HELAMAN 16:6–8
Nonbelievers try to capture Samuel

HELAMAN 16:9–12
The next few years

HELAMAN 16:13–14
Great signs

HELAMAN 16:15–21
What the unbelievers said

HELAMAN 16:22–25
Satan's influence upon the people

3 AND 4 Nephi

DID YOU KNOW?

- 3 Nephi is named after Nephi who was the son of Nephi (the mighty prophet in the book of Helaman).

- If you ever get confused, just remember it goes, "Alma, Alma, Helaman, Helaman, Nephi, Nephi, Nephi" (see chart below).

- Nephi (the son of Nephi) kept the records before, during, and after the Savior's appearance to the people. He was there to witness the signs of Jesus' birth; he was there when the Savior came to visit after His Resurrection; and he will become one of the Savior's chosen disciples (see 3 Nephi 19:4).

Alma the Elder
↓
Alma the Younger
↓
Helaman Sr.
↓
Helaman Jr.
↓
Nephi Sr.   Lehi
↓
Nephi Jr.
↓
Nephi III

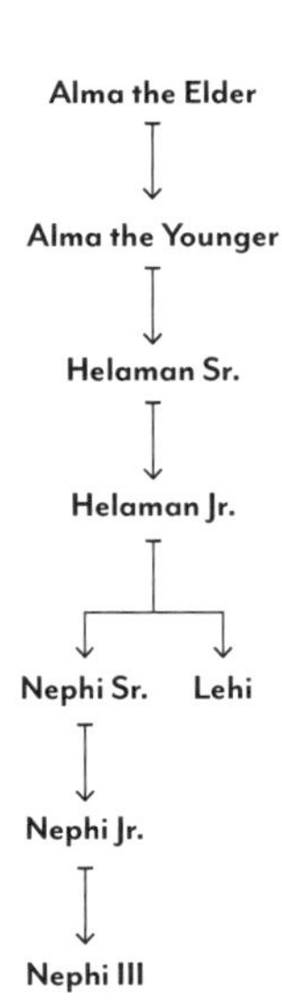

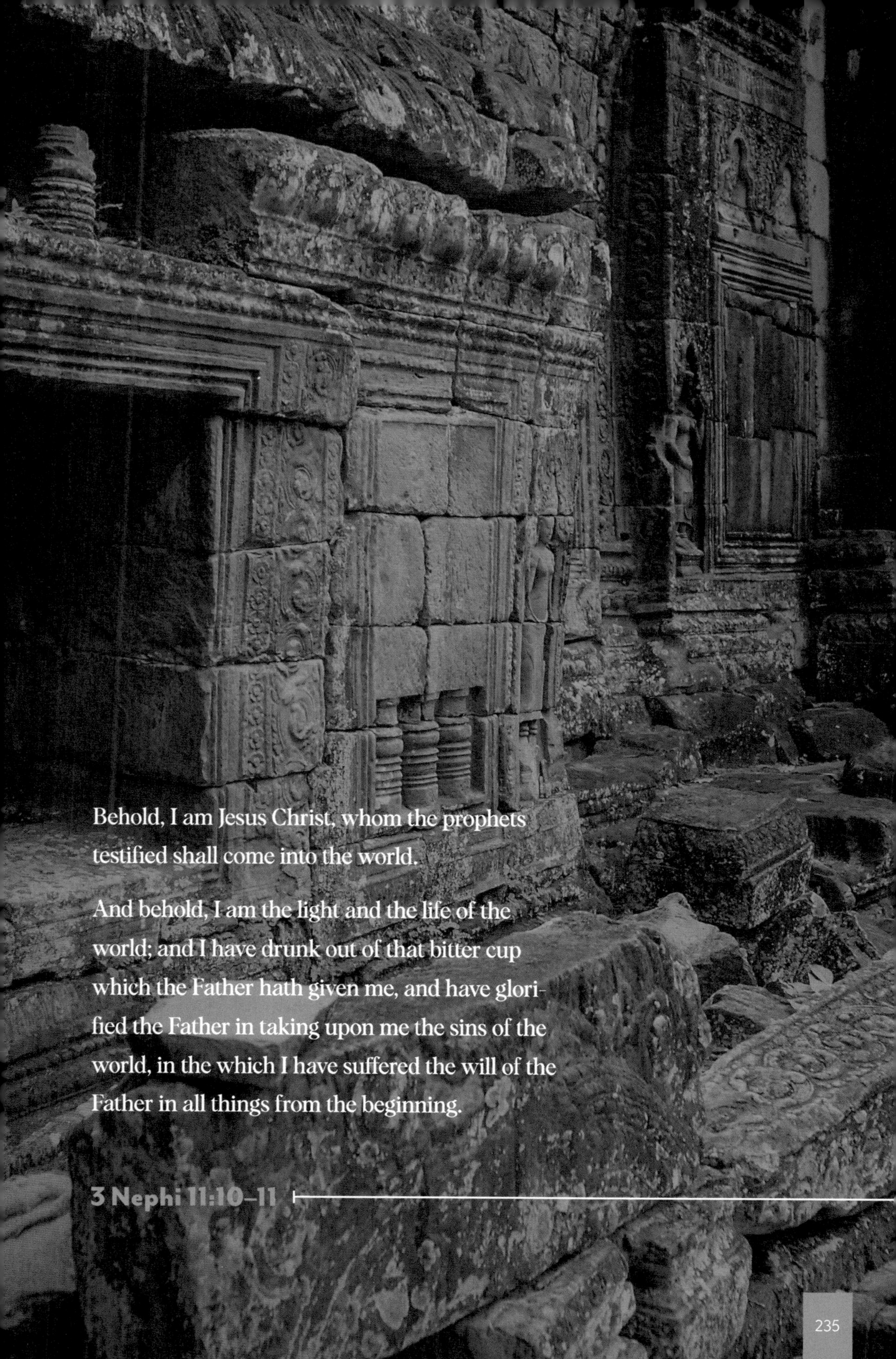

Behold, I am Jesus Christ, whom the prophets testified shall come into the world.

And behold, I am the light and the life of the world; and I have drunk out of that bitter cup which the Father hath given me, and have glorified the Father in taking upon me the sins of the world, in the which I have suffered the will of the Father in all things from the beginning.

3–4 NEPHI

Timeline

Here is 3 Nephi and 4 Nephi at-a-glance. The main stories are found in the timeline below. If you ever want to find a story in your scriptures, you can look at this page for help. You can add your own notes to this page as well.

3 NEPHI 1

- Nephi, the son of Nephi, becomes the record keeper (3 Nephi 1:2)
- Signs of Christ's birth appear
- Satan sends forth lies to harden hearts
- Gadianton robbers infest the land
- Many Lamanite children join Gadianton robbers

3 NEPHI 2

- Nephites and Lamanites come together to fight against the Gadianton robbers

3 NEPHI 6–7

- Prophets cry repentance and are killed (3 Nephi 6)
- Chief judge is murdered, people divide and separate into tribes (3 Nephi 7)
- Nephi preaches repentance (3 Nephi 7)

3 NEPHI 12–18

- Jesus calls 12 disciples (3 Nephi 12)
- Jesus teaches and introduces the sacrament (3 Nephi 12-18)

3 NEPHI 9–11

- Christ's voice speaks through the darkness (3 Nephi 9-10)
- Jesus appears to the Nephites (3 Nephi 11)

3 NEPHI 8

- Signs of Christ's death, many are destroyed (3 Nephi 8)

3 NEPHI 29–30 | 4 NEPHI 1

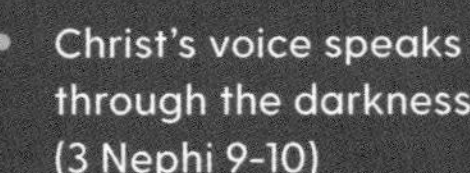

- Mormon explains the coming forth of the Book of Mormon
- Zion established among Nephites and Lamanites; they prosper and multiply
- After 200 years, some begin to be lifted up in pride
- People begin to be divided into classes and build their own churches
- People cast disciples into prison and seek to kill them
- Great division among the people
- Gadianton robbers over all the face of the land
- Ammaron hides up records

3 NEPHI 19–28

- Jesus appears again, administers sacrament, and teaches words of Isaiah and Malachi (3 Nephi 19-25)
- Three Nephites are translated (3 Nephi 28)

People and Places to Know

If you need a reminder of who is who, return to this page.

Nephi Sr.

This Nephi was the son of Helaman. He was a great missionary. He was the father to Nephi Jr.

Nephi Jr.

He received the plates from his father, Nephi. He heard the voice of the Lord say that the signs of Jesus' birth were coming. He ministered with great power. Jesus called him forward to be one of twelve Nephite disciples.

Giddianhi

Giddianhi was leader of the Gadianton robbers and demanded Nephite lands. He was slain.

Lachoneus

Lachoneus was a Nephite chief judge. He received a letter from Giddianhi to give up lands. He gathered Nephites, called Nephites to repentance, and helped establish peace.

Gidgiddoni

Gidgiddoni was commander of the Nephite armies. He had the spirit of revelation and prophecy. He defeated Gadianton robbers.

Jacob

Jacob became king of secret combination and took his people north. His city was burned.

Nephi III

Son of Nephi Jr. 4 Nephi is named after him. Kept the record until 4 Nephi 1:19.

Amos Sr.

Amos was Nephi's son. He was the record keeper after his father.

Amos Jr.

He was the son of Amos and the record keeper after his father.

Ammaron

Ammaron was the son of Amos and lived in the time when wickedness covered the land. He was the record keeper and hid the sacred records.

3 Nephi 1–7

In these chapters

The wicked plan to kill the righteous if sign of Christ's birth does not come   //   Signs of Christ's birth comes   //   Many converted   //   Gadianton robbers increase   //   Nephites and Lamanites unite to defend against the Gadianton robbers   //   Giddianhi demands the Nephites surrender lands   //   Nephites repent and prosper   //   Sin abounds   //   Prophets cry repentance   //   Prophets slain   //   Government destroyed   //   People divide into tribes   //   Jacob the antichrist   //   Nephi preaches   //   Many repent

Sometime in the 86th year, Samuel had given the prophecy that Christ would come in 5 years.

Now it was past the fifth year (on the dot), so some "began to say that the time was past for the words to be fulfilled" (3 Nephi 1:5) and the unbelievers "did make a great uproar throughout the land."

WHAT DO YOU THINK THAT UPROAR MIGHT HAVE LOOKED OR SOUNDED LIKE? WHAT MIGHT PEOPLE HAVE SAID OR DONE TO CAUSE OTHERS TO DOUBT?

Things became so bad that a day was set apart by the unbelievers to put to death the believers. They finally thought they had proof that their religion was not true—Christ was not born because there were no signs of His birth, as Samuel had declared.

The believing Nephites would really have to weigh their faith. It was all on the line now.

3 Nephi 1

Write or draw what you learn in these verses.

3 NEPHI 1:1–3
The 91st year

3 NEPHI 1:4–9
Extreme persecution

3 NEPHI 1:10–14
Nephi learns the sign will come that night

3 NEPHI 1:15–21
Signs fulfilled

3 NEPHI 1:22–30
After the signs

3 Nephi 2

Write or draw what you learn in these verses.

Three years go by and people began to forget the signs, and they became "less and less astonished." By now, Satan had three years to craft deceptions and lies, and many began to disbelieve. Give Satan enough time, and he will come up with arguments that will pull people away, even after seeing incredible signs. What can you learn from this chapter? Write or draw what you learn in these verses.

3 NEPHI 2:1–7
People began to forget the signs

3 NEPHI 2:8–10
New time reckoning

3 NEPHI 2:11–19
War with Gadianton robbers

3 Nephi 3   *Write or draw what you learn in these verses.*

The Nephites and Lamanites were able to drive the Gadianton robbers into the mountains. The leader, Giddianhi, then writes a letter to Lachoneus, the governor of the land.

VERSES 1–10	VERSES 11–16	VERSES 17–26
Giddianhi's letter to Lachoneus	*Lachoneus' response to the letter*	*The people gather and prepare*

3 Nephi 4   *Write or draw what you learn in these verses.*

The Nephites had about a year to gather and prepare to defend themselves against the robbers. Then the armies of robbers began to "sally forth from the hills." "Sally forth" means to set out in a sudden or violent manner.

VERSES 1–14	VERSES 15–23	VERSES 24–33
The Gadianton robbers come	*Robbers return*	*Gidgiddoni's plan*

3 Nephi 5   *Write or draw what you learn in these verses.*

There was now great faithfulness among the Nephites. Not a single Nephite doubted the words of the prophets now - every living soul was convinced. They had seen and witnessed enough to know that the prophecies were true, and so they also believed that Christ had been born. But Satan will not give up.

VERSES 1–6	VERSES 7–26
State of the Nephites	*Mormon's words*

3 Nephi 6

Now the people returned to their own lands. In verse 2, we learn that "they had not eaten up all their provisions" so they could use those provisions as they were rebuilding and replanting. Their physical and spiritual preparation was key to winning the war.

Write or draw what you learn in these verses.

① **1-3** | *People return to lands*

② **4-9** | *Prosperity and peace*

③ **10-14** | *Pride brings division*

④ **15-16** | *Satan's power*

⑤ **17-21** | *A state of awful wickedness*

⑥ **22-30** | *Secret combinations*

3 Nephi 7

That year, the secret combination had the son of Lachoneus murdered and the people became divided, so they separated into tribes. There was no longer a unified Nephite nation.

Write or draw what you learn in these verses.

① **1-4** | *People divide into tribes*

② **5-8** | *State of the Nephites*

③ **9-13** | *Jacob, king over the secret combination*

④ **14** | *The tribes*

⑤ **15-20** | *Nephi ministers with power*

⑥ **21-26** | *The believers*

3 Nephi 8–11

In these chapters

Signs of Christ's death   //   Many cities and people destroyed   //   Three days of darkness   //   Jesus speaks through the darkness   //   Heavenly Father testifies of His Son   //   Christ appears   //   The people feel Christ's wounds one by one

Government Destroyed

It has been 33 to 34 years since the signs of Christ's birth. The Nephites had now divided into tribes, so there was no longer a chief judge or a central government.

Waiting for Signs of Christ's Death

The believers knew that the sign of Christ's death must be coming soon, and they began to look for them (3 Nephi 8:3), but there were also "great doubtings and disputations" (3 Nephi 8:4).

What do you think that might have sounded like? A disputation is when someone reasons or argues in opposition, and this was happening as people argued against the signs the believers were waiting for. And they were "great" disputations, meaning that it was really heated.

Guidance for Us

"Meanwhile, brothers and sisters, no one ever promised us that discipleship in the last days would be a picnic in the park.

Former periods of stress can guide us. When the earlier coming of Jesus was imminent, signs abounded. Still, for some, there were "doubtings." But the faithful prevailed and were vindicated."

ELDER NEAL A. MAXWELL | April 1984 General Conference

In this chapter, the signs of the Savior's death came.

As you study this chapter, make notes on and around this map of things that happened.

The Voice of the Lord Is Heard by the People

Use this page to write or draw what the Savior taught in the darkness.

3 Nephi 11 *Write or draw what you learn in these verses.*

After the voice of the Lord spoke to them, the people gathered to the temple to marvel, wonder, and talk about what happened.

| **3 NEPHI 11:1–2** *After the voice* | **3 NEPHI 11:3–7** *God the Father* |

3 NEPHI 11:8–12
Jesus descends from Heaven

Watch This

After you study these chapters, watch this video and see what additional lessons you can learn.

Jesus Christ Appears in the Ancient Americas
3 Nephi 8–11 | 16:44 minutes

| **3 NEPHI 11:13–15** *The invitation* | **3 NEPHI 11:16–17** *After they witnessed for themselves* | **3 NEPHI 11:18–21** *The Lord speaks to Nephi* |

| **3 NEPHI 11:22–28** *Proper baptism* | **3 NEPHI 11:29–30** *The spirit of contention* | **3 NEPHI 11:31–41** *The true doctrine of baptism* |

WHAT HAS STOOD OUT TO YOU THE MOST AS YOU STUDIED THIS CHAPTER?

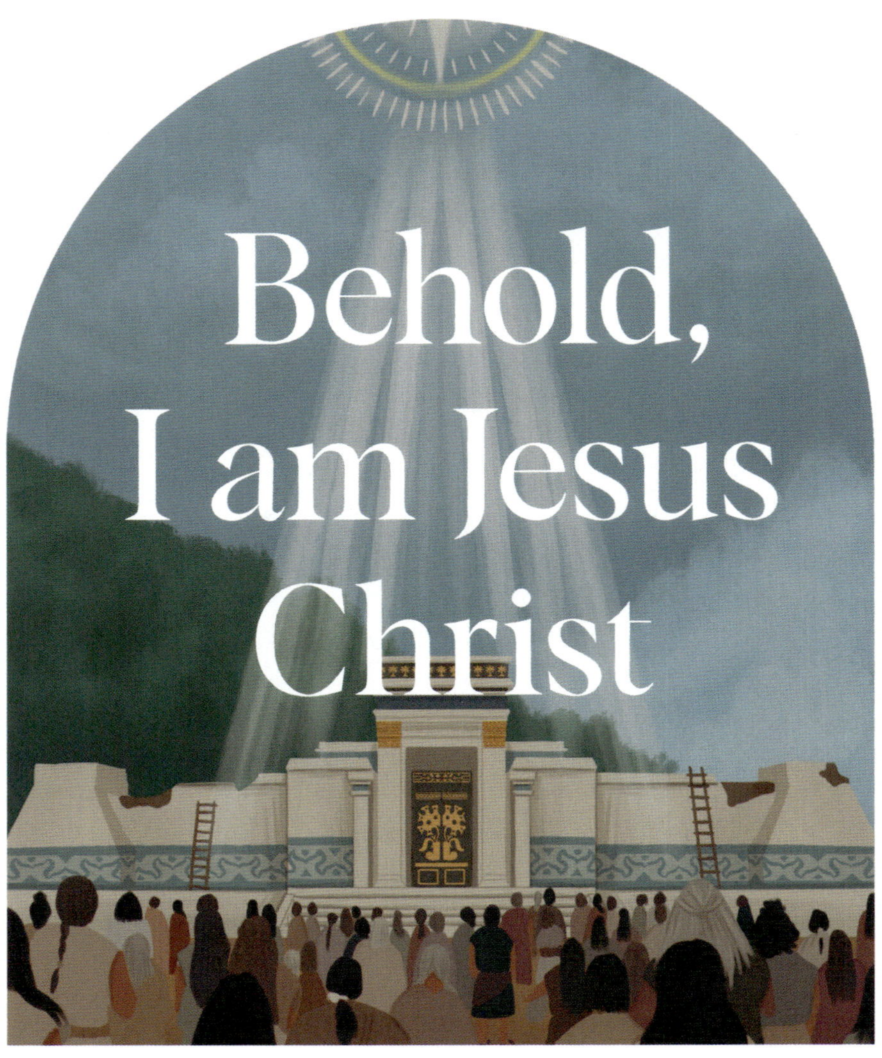

BEHOLD, I AM JESUS CHRIST, WHOM THE PROPHETS TESTIFIED SHALL COME INTO THE WORLD. AND BEHOLD, I AM THE LIGHT AND THE LIFE OF THE WORLD; AND I HAVE DRUNK OUT OF THAT BITTER CUP WHICH THE FATHER HATH GIVEN ME, AND HAVE GLORIFIED THE FATHER IN TAKING UPON ME THE SINS OF THE WORLD, IN THE WHICH I HAVE SUFFERED THE WILL OF THE FATHER IN ALL THINGS FROM THE BEGINNING.

*Keep your own record side-by-side with these great prophets
testifying of these important doctrines and principles.*

HOW JESUS HAS MINISTERED TO YOU "ONE BY ONE"...

3 Nephi 12–16

In these chapters

Twelve Nephite disciples chosen // Jesus teaches the higher law //
the Lord's Prayer // Law of Moses fulfilled in Christ // Gospel will
go forth to Gentiles in last days

Jesus Christ was organizing and setting up His Church among the Nephites.
He began by calling and giving authority to twelve disciples, and then He
taught the higher law since the law of Moses was now fulfilled.

Christ then goes into the same sermon that he gave in Matthew 5-7 that we
refer to as "The Sermon on the Mount." He was teaching the same gospel.

IN 2 NEPHI 29:8, CHRIST SAID,

> "Wherefore, I speak the same words unto one
> nation like unto another. And when the two
> nations shall run together the testimony of the
> two nations shall run together also."

This sermon is all about overcoming the natural man and becoming one
worthy of receiving eternal life. These are the qualities we must seek to
obtain in order to become as Christ is.

3 Nephi 12

Write or draw what you learn in these verses.

VERSES 1–2 *The twelve disciples*	
VERSES 3–12 *The Beatitudes*	
VERSES 13–17 *Salt and Light*	
VERSES 18–20 *Law of Moses fulfilled*	
VERSES 21–26 *No hatred in heart*	*The Higher Law…*
VERSES 27–30 *No lust*	*The Higher Law…*
VERSES 31–32 *Marriage*	*The Higher Law…*
VERSES 33–37 *Swearing oaths*	*The Higher Law…*
VERSES 38–42 *Be a peacemaker*	*The Higher Law…*
NERSES 43–47 *Love your enemies*	*The Higher Law…*
VERSE 48 *Becoming perfect*	*The Higher Law…*

1

Greater Blessings

The law of Moses was a preparatory law with a preparatory priesthood and lesser blessings. The Gospel of Jesus Christ in it's fullness is superior and requires more self-mastery and offers greater blessings (along with the Higher Priesthood).

2

Old Law vs. Higher Law

Christ will now illustrate over and over again what the old law was and what the higher law is instead. The higher law is more inward, requires more Christlike character, helps us overcome the natural man, and involves a lot of repentance as we chip away at our fallen nature.

Watch This

Jesus Christ Teaches and Gives Power to Baptize

3 Nephi 11–12
7:08 minutes

Jesus Teaches a Higher Law

In these two chapters, Jesus continued to teach the Nephites the higher law. And living this law will help them achieve Zion (see 4 Nephi 1).

Write or draw what you learn in these verses.

Watch this

After you study these chapters, watch this video and see what additional lessons you can learn.

Jesus Christ Teaches How to Live the Higher Law
3 Nephi 12–14 | 11:03 minutes

3 NEPHI 13:1–4 | *Giving alms*

3 NEPHI 13:5–8 | *Prayer*

3 NEPHI 13:9–13 | *The Lord's Prayer*

3 NEPHI 13:14–15 | *Forgiving others*

3 NEPHI 13:16–18 | *Fasting*

3 NEPHI 13:19–21 | *Treasures*

3 NEPHI 13:22–24 | *Two masters*

3 NEPHI 13:25–34 | *Trust God*

3 NEPHI 14:1–5 | *Righteous judgment*

3 NEPHI 14:6 | *Holy things*

3 NEPHI 14:7–11 | *Ask and ye shall receive*

3 NEPHI 14:12 | *The golden rule*

3 NEPHI 14:13–14 | *Strait and narrow*

3 NEPHI 14:15–20 | *How to determine false prophets*

3 NEPHI 14:21–23 | *Importance of doing God's will*

3 NEPHI 14:24–27 | *Wise man and foolish man*

3 Nephi 15   *Write or draw what you learn in these verses.*

Jesus looked around and perceived that some of the Nephites were not understanding what it meant that the law of Moses had passed away, "and that all things had become new" (verse 2). Christ is demonstrating to us an important principle of a master teacher. He was not just teaching a sermon; He was teaching individuals and when He observed that they did not fully understand, He taught them more.

1–2	*Jesus perceives*	**3–10**	*Christ is the Law*
11–13	*To the disciples*	**14–24**	*Other sheep*

3 Nephi 16   *Write or draw what you learn in these verses.*

Jesus explains that He has "other sheep, which are not of this land, neither of the land of Jerusalem." We do not have a record of these other people, but they were of the house of Israel and were considered part of Christ's fold—and He was going to still minister unto them. Write or draw what you learn in these verses.

Watch This

Jesus Christ Testifies of One Fold and One Shepherd

3 Nephi 15–16
5:56 minutes

1–3	*Other sheep*
4–6	*Write these sayings*
7–10	*In the last days*
11–15	*Israel will be gathered*
16–20	*Prophecy of Zion*

3 Nephi 17–19

In these chapters

Jesus prays // Angels encircle their little ones // Jesus introduces the sacrament // Disciples given power to confer the Holy Ghost // Disciples are baptized // Jesus prays

This was still day one of Jesus' ministry. In 3 Nephi 15:1–2, Jesus announced that it was time for Him to go, but then He perceived that they did not understand what it meant that the law of Moses was fulfilled, so He stayed and taught some more.

Now again at the beginning of chapter 17, He announced that it was time for Him to depart. And again He looked and perceived that they were weak and could not understand all that He was teaching them. So He gave them instructions to "go ye unto your homes … and prepare your minds" (3 Nephi 17:3). And then He stayed, healed the sick, and then called the children to Him and angels came and ministered to them.

Perceive means to observe, and Christ was always doing that while He was with these Nephites. He was constantly observing what they needed to learn more about and what they needed from Him. He would perceive and then respond.

Write or draw what you learn in these verses.

3 NEPHI 17:1–3	3 NEPHI 17:4	3 NEPHI 17:5–10
Instructions	Where Jesus was going	Jesus' compassion

3 NEPHI 17:11–17	3 NEPHI 17:18–22	3 NEPHI 17:23–25
Jesus calls little children to Him	Joy	Angels descend

Imagine being with the Savior

"… I found myself one evening in the dreams of the night in that sacred building, the temple. After a season of prayer and rejoicing I was informed that I should have the privilege of entering into one of those rooms, to meet a glorious personage, and, as I entered the door, I saw, seated on a raised platform, the most glorious being my eyes have ever beheld or that I ever conceived existed in all the eternal worlds.

As I approached to be introduced, He arose and stepped towards me with extended arms, and He smiled as He softly spoke my name. If I shall live to be a million years old, I shall never forget that smile. He took me into His arms and kissed me, pressed me to His bosom, and blessed me, until the marrow of my bones seemed to melt! When He had finished, I fell at His feet, and, as I bathed them with my tears and kisses, I saw the prints of the nails in the feet of the Redeemer of the world. The feeling that I had in the presence of Him who hath all things in His hands, to have His love, His affection, and His blessing was such that if I can receive that of which I had but a foretaste, I would give all that I am, all that I ever hope to be, to feel what I then felt!

… I see Jesus not now upon the cross. I do not see His brow pierced with thorns nor His hands torn with the nails, but I see Him smiling, with extended arms, saying to us all: "Come unto me!"

ELDER MELVIN J. BALLARD | Ensign, December 2014

3 Nephi 18

Christ has still not left the Nephites, despite announcing He was leaving two separate times (and He had really important things to do [see 3 Nephi 17:4]). But Jesus stayed and ministered, and now He will introduce the sacrament to them. They wanted to be with Him, and now He will show them how they can always remember Him and have the Spirit with them.

Write or draw what you learn in these verses.

Watch This

Jesus Christ Introduces the Sacrament to the People

3 Nephi 18 | 10:50 minutes

3 NEPHI 18:1–5 *Jesus gives to His disciples and then the disciples give to the multitude*	**3 NEPHI 18:6–11** *The introduction of the sacrament*
3 NEPHI 18:12–14 *How to be built upon the rock of Christ*	**3 NEPHI 18:15–21** *Pray always*
3 NEPHI 18:22–25 *Meeting together often*	**3 NEPHI 18:26–35** *Ministering to those who are not worthy*
3 NEPHI 18:36–37 *Jesus gives disciples the Holy Ghost*	**3 NEPHI 18:38–39** *Jesus ascends*

SOMETHING I WANT TO REMEMBER...

Lessons About Prayer

Everyone finally went home, and people began spreading the message that Jesus had come! Only those at the temple had seen Him and there were many others who were not there, so the message was spread abroad, even all through the night. They wanted everyone else to know, so there was no hour that was too late to share this news.

The Disciples Minister and Jesus Christ Prays for the People

3 Nephi 19 | 7:27 minutes

What does this chapter teach you about prayer?

1-3 | *The news was spread*	**4-9** | *The Nephite disciples*
10-14 | *Baptisms, Holy Ghost, and angels*	**15-18** | *Jesus returns*
19-23 | *Jesus prays*	**24-27** | *Disciples do not cease praying*
28-29 | *Jesus prays*	**30** | *Disciples continue to pray*
31-34 | *Jesus prays*	**35-36** | *"So great faith"*

3 Nephi 20–26

In these chapters

Sacrament miraculously provided // Remnant of Israel will inherit Americas // Israel will be gathered when Book of Mormon comes forth // New Jerusalem // Zion in the last days // Search Isaiah's words diligently // Jesus quotes Malachi // Jesus expounds all things

In 3 Nephi 16, Jesus started speaking of the house of Israel and His plan to redeem them in the last days. However, at the beginning of 3 Nephi 17, He perceived that they were weak and could not understand everything, so He told them to go home and ponder His words. Now here, He is going to teach them this subject again (He must because the Father commanded Him to teach these things [see 3 Nephi 17:2]).

Understanding the Gathering of Israel

An understanding of the doctrine of the gathering of Israel is essential to a sound understanding of the gospel. Of the gathering, the Prophet Joseph Smith said, "It is a principle I esteem to be of the greatest importance to those who are looking for salvation in this generation."

The doctrine of the gathering stands at the very heart of the message of the restored gospel. We do not really understand who we are as a people, the covenants God has made with us, or the destiny that is ours until we gain a meaningful understanding of this doctrine.

JOSEPH FIELDING MCCONKIE | Religious Educator 11, no. 1 (2010): 47–64

3 Nephi 20

Write or draw what you learn in these verses.

VERSES 1–9

Jesus miraculously provides bread and wine for the sacrament

VERSES 10–19

Israel will be gathered

VERSES 20–24

Israel WILL be gathered / New Jerusalem

VERSES 25–28

The Nephites are of the house of Israel

VERSES 29–36

Other members of the house of Israel will be gathered in Jerusalem

VERSES 37–46

Those who are gathered will praise those who brought them back into the covenant

3 Nephi 21

Jesus then gives a sign that will tell the world that Israel is about to be gathered. It is when the things that He was declaring unto them will be made known unto the Gentiles. "These things" are the record that would one day come forth that contains Christ's words—the Book of Mormon. The Book of Mormon is the ensign that will be raised. It will reveal to them the covenants that have been lost.

Write or draw what you learn in these verses.

1–3 | *The sign that the gathering is beginning*	**4** | *The Gentiles will be a free people in America*
5–7 | *If the Gentiles believe, they will be numbered with Israel*	**8–10** | *A great and marvelous work*
11 | *Warning to those who do not believe*	**12–13** | *The strength Israel will have*
14–21 | *Warning*	**22–29** | *New Jerusalem*

The coming forth of the Book of Mormon

is a sign to the entire world that the Lord has commenced to gather Israel and fulfill covenants He made to Abraham, Isaac, and Jacob.

PRESIDENT RUSSELL M. NELSON \| October 2006 General Conference

Christ Quotes Isaiah

Jesus has spent the last two chapters teaching about how He will gather Israel. These words would have brought comfort to the Nephites, who were one of the scattered branches.

Now in this chapter, Christ quotes Isaiah's prophecy that we can also find in Isaiah 54:1–17. He begins by saying that this prophecy will come to pass.

VERSE	HELPFUL TIP	WHAT YOU LEARN
1–3	Isaiah uses the imagery of a barren woman - one woman who has not been able to have children. But the day will come when she will have to enlarge her tent (make her home larger) because of the children she will have.	
4–8	The shame of Israel's past (her apostasy) will be erased. Israel is like the bride and Christ the husband, who will marry her. Even though she abandoned Him and hurt Him (see verse 8), He will gather her with great mercies (see verse 7).	
9–10	The Lord's promises concerning Israel are sure. Just as He promised never to flood the earth again, so will His anger towards Israel cease. And what seems more certain to us than the hills and mountains? They are solid and immovable. But these immovable things are removable, but the covenant of His peace towards Israel is not. It is certain.	
11–17	These verses express that the safest place for Israel to be is with the Lord. As Israel is gathered, the Lord promises to bless and adorn her - even after all of the tossing and tempests (verse 11) or tribulations she has gone through. She will be given great spiritual blessings and treasures.	

The Gathering of Israel

WHAT HAS THIS CHAPTER TAUGHT YOU ABOUT THE GATHERING OF ISRAEL?

Notice the name "Redeemer, the Holy One of Israel," in 3 Nephi 22:5. This chapter captures what the title of Christ "Redeemer of Israel" means. William W. Phelps wrote "Redeemer of Israel" in the 1800s.

Read through these verses and see what stands out to you.

Redeemer of Israel

BY WILLIAM W. PHELPS (1792-1872)

1. Redeemer of Israel,
Our only delight,
On whom for a blessing we call,
Our shadow by day
And our pillar by night,
Our King, our Deliv'rer, our all!

2. We know he is coming
To gather his sheep
And lead them to Zion in love,
For why in the valley
Of death should they weep
Or in the lone wilderness rove?

3. How long we have wandered
As strangers in sin
And cried in the desert for thee!
Our foes have rejoiced
When our sorrows they've seen,
But Israel will shortly be free.

4. As children of Zion,
Good tidings for us.
The tokens already appear.
Fear not, and be just,
For the kingdom is ours.
The hour of redemption is near.

5. Restore, my dear Savior,
The light of thy face;
Thy soul-cheering comfort impart;
And let the sweet longing
For thy holy place
Bring hope to my desolate heart.

6. He looks! and ten thousands
Of angels rejoice,
And myriads wait for his word;
He speaks! and eternity,
Filled with his voice,
Re-echoes the praise of the Lord

WHAT IS YOUR FAVORITE LINE IN THIS HYMN?

*Keep your own record side-by-side with these great prophets
testifying of these important doctrines and principles.*

WHAT PHRASES IN "REDEEMER OF ISRAEL" DO YOU HAVE PERSONAL EXPERIENCES WITH? WRITE ABOUT THEM HERE...

3 Nephi 23

Jesus then gave the commandment for the Nephites and Gentiles (us) to diligently search Isaiah's prophecies. He wants us to know these prophecies. Diligent means with careful and constant effort, and then steadily applied.

Write or draw what you learn in the following verses.

VERSES 1–5 | *The commandment to search Isaiah's prophecies*

VERSES 6–14 | *Jesus points out a prophecy from Samuel the Lamanite that had not yet been recorded*

3 Nephi 24

Jesus now wanted them to have some prophecies from Malachi. Malachi was the last prophet in our Old Testament record, but the Nephites never had Malachi's prophecies because Lehi left Jerusalem about 170 years before Malachi lived, and so Jesus will now quote what we know as Malachi 3 and 4.

Write or draw what you learn in these verses.

VERSES 1–4	**VERSES 5–7**
The Second Coming of Jesus Christ	*Those who will not abide the coming*
VERSES 8–12	**VERSES 13–18**
Tithing	*Book of remembrance*

3 Nephi 25

Now Christ quotes the fourth chapter of Malachi. This message is a major prophecy concerning the last days. This is also what Moroni repeated to Joseph Smith over and over again when he appeared to Joseph in his bedroom.

Write or draw what you learn in the following verses.

VERSES 1–3	VERSES 4–6
Strong warning and a promise	*Elijah will return before the Second Coming of Jesus Christ*

3 Nephi 26

Christ now expounds all things to them, "both great and small." He teaches them all things from the beginning until the Second Coming and what will happen then. He teaches about the great day of judgment and what will happen to the righteous and the evil. He teaches them so much that Mormon cannot write "even a hundredth part" (verse 6).

Write or draw what you learn in these verses.

VERSES 1–7 | *Jesus continues to teach*

VERSES 8–12 | *Mormon explains what he has written*

VERSES 13–16 | *Marvelous things*

VERSES 17–21 | *The new state of the Nephites (this is the power of true doctrine)*

3 Nephi 27 – 4 Nephi 1

In these chapters

Church to be called in Christ's name   //   Three Nephites are translated   //
Coming forth of the Book of Mormon is a sign that the gathering of Israel
has begun   //   Zion established among Nephites and Lamanites   //   After
200 years evil enters in   //   After 300 years Nephites and Lamanites are
both wicked   //   Ammaron hides up records

The disciples now have new responsibilities. They have been called by Jesus Christ and in
3 Nephi 27, they go about preaching and baptizing. Can you imagine hearing them
preach after all they saw and witnessed?

At the beginning of 4 Nephi, we see the disciples formed a Church in all of the lands. So
here we learn that the surviving Nephites were not all gathered in one place.

In 4 Nephi 1:2, we learn that within two years of the Savior's ministry, "the people were all
converted unto the Lord." All of the people who had been converted were now
converting others. The other Nephites needed to be taught and ministered to. It took time.

The result of the ministering was a people so deeply converted to the Lord that they had
peace, prosperity, unity, and the love of God dwelling in their hearts (4 Nephi 1:15).
Imagine living in a society like that.

Write or draw what you learn in these verses.

Watch this

Jesus Christ Declares
the Name of His Church
and His Doctrine

3 Nephi 27 | 8:03
minutes

VERSES 1–10

The name of the Church

VERSES 11–12

Church must be built on gospel

VERSES 13–22

What the gospel is

VERSES 23–27

Write these things

VERSES 28–33

Final teachings

The Church of Jesus Christ

What's in a name or, in this case, a nickname? When it comes to nicknames of the Church, such as the "LDS Church," the "Mormon Church," or the "Church of the Latter-day Saints," the most important thing in those names is the absence of the Savior's name. To remove the Lord's name from the Lord's Church is a major victory for Satan. When we discard the Savior's name, we are subtly disregarding all that Jesus Christ did for us—even His Atonement....

If we as a people and as individuals are to have access to the power of the Atonement of Jesus Christ—to cleanse and heal us, to strengthen and magnify us, and ultimately to exalt us—we must clearly acknowledge Him as the source of that power. We can begin by calling His Church by the name He decreed.

PRESIDENT RUSSELL M. NELSON | October 2018 General Conference

3 Nephi 28

Before Jesus left, He asked the twelve disciples what they each desired. Write or draw what you learn in these verses.

3 NEPHI 28:1–3	3 NEPHI 28:4–11
What nine desire	What three desire

3 NEPHI 28:12–17	3 NEPHI 28:18–26
What the three receive	Mormon tells what happened to the three Nephites

3 NEPHI 28:27–35	3 NEPHI 28:36–40
About these three Nephites	Doctrine of translation

The Three Nephites

"These three Nephites continue in their translated state today, just as when they went throughout the lands of Nephi. At one point Mormon was about to reveal their names to his latter-day readers, but he was forbidden by the Lord from doing so. Nevertheless, these three ministered to Mormon and Moroni, and they are yet ministering to Jew, Gentile, and the scattered tribes of Israel, even all nations, kindreds, tongues, and people.

ELDER JEFFREY R. HOLLAND

Christ and the New Covenant, p. 307

3 Nephi 29

These verses are prophecies from Mormon and he is re-emphasizing things that the Lord taught during His Nephite ministry. Mormon was a part of scattered Israel, and here he is talking to us.

Write or draw what you learn in these verses.

Verses 1–3

Important things to know

Verses 4–9

Warnings

3 Nephi 30

3 Nephi ends with words from Mormon speaking to the Gentiles in the last days.
This chapter is only two verses.

Fill the space with things that stand out to you in these verses. You can also look up the words you would like to better understand and fill the white space with definitions.

1 Hearken, O ye Gentiles, and hear the words of Jesus Christ, the Son of the living God, which he hath commanded me that I should speak concerning you, for, behold he commandeth me that I should write, saying:

2 Turn, all ye Gentiles, from your wicked ways; and repent of your evil doings, of your lyings and deceivings, and of your whoredoms, and of your secret abominations, and your idolatries, and of your murders, and your priestcrafts, and your envyings, and your strifes, and from all your wickedness and abominations, and come unto me, and be baptized in my name, that ye may receive a remission of your sins, and be filled with the Holy Ghost, that ye may be numbered with my people who are of the house of Israel.

contention, anger, contests

TIP: *The 1828 Webster's Dictionary (found online or on an app) contains meanings of words in Joseph Smith's day when he translated the plates.*

4 Nephi 1

4 Nephi is only 49 verses but will cover almost 287 years of Nephite history. About one third of the Nephite time period is covered in this single chapter.

Next to each year (these are years since the sign of Christ's birth), write or draw what happened among the Nephites during those years.

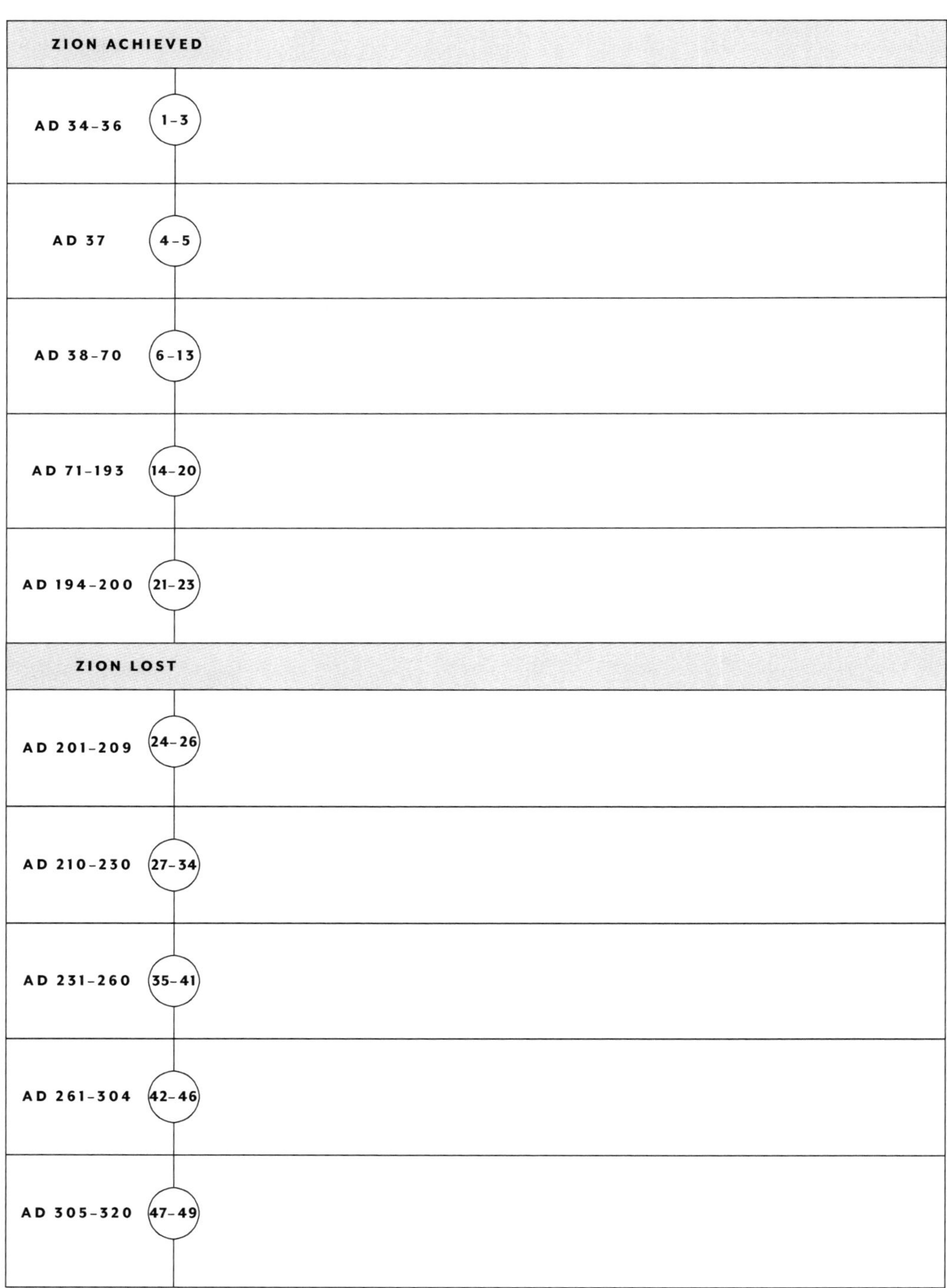

The Building Up of Zion

"We may not yet be the Zion of which our prophets foretold and toward which the poets and priests of Israel have pointed us, but we long for it and we keep working toward it. I do not know whether a full implementation of such a society can be realized until Christ comes, but I know that when He did come to the Nephites, His majestic teachings and ennobling spirit led to the happiest of all times...

The Prophet Joseph Smith had such a grand view of our possibilities, a view given him by the revelations of God. He knew that the real task was in being more Christlike —caring the way the Savior cared, loving the way he loved, "every man seeking the interest of his neighbor," the scripture says, "and doing all things with an eye single to the glory of God."

ELDER JEFFREY R. HOLLAND | April 1996 General Conference

WHAT ARE YOU DOING TO HELP BUILD ZION TODAY?

Mormon

- Mormon lived in a time when wickedness covered the land.

- Mormon wrote the first seven chapters in his book. Before he died he instructed Moroni to finish the record. Moroni then wrote the remaining two chapters.

- Mormon led the Nephites in their last battle against the Lamanites.

O ye fair ones, how could ye have departed from the ways of the Lord! O ye fair ones, how could ye have rejected that Jesus, who stood with open arms to receive you!

Mormon 6:17

MORMON

Timeline

Here is Mormon at-a-glance. The main stories are found in the timeline below. If you ever want to find a story in your scriptures, you can look at this page for help. You can add your own notes to this page as well.

MORMON 1

- Ammaron tells Mormon to retrieve records when 24 years old
- Nephite and Lamanite war begins

MORMON 2

- Mormon is leader of Nephite armies
- Terrible war
- Nephites in open rebellion against God
- Mormon obtains plates and makes record upon them

MORMON 5–6

- Mormon again leads Nephites
- Nephites gather to Cumorah for final battle
- Nephites destroyed

MORMON 3–4

- Mormon refused to be commander to the Nephites
- War and wickedness continue
- Lamanites about to overthrow the land

MORMON 8

- Moroni takes over record and announces father's death
- Moroni prophesies of when the Nephite record will come forth to the world

MORMON 7

- Mormon invites Latter-day Lamanites to believe in Christ and lay hold of the gospel

People and Places to Know

If you need a reminder of who is who, return to this page.

Ammaron

Ammaron was a record keeper and he hid all records during time of wickedness. He instructed Mormon where the plates were hidden and when to retrieve them.

Mormon

Mormon was a Nephite prophet and military commander. He retrieved all Nephite records and abridged them into a single record. He was killed in the final battle when the Nephites were destroyed.

Moroni

Moroni was the son of Mormon. He was a surviving Nephite after the final battle. He finished his father's abridged record and added the record of the Jaredites (which he abridged).

Cumorah

Cumorah was a land of many waters where the Nephites gathered for their final battle. This is where Mormon hid up the records, except for the few plates he gave to Moroni (see Mormon 6:6).

"In one of the loneliest scenes in scriptural history, a silent, war-weary soldier looked out across time and the unspeakable tragedy his family and followers faced. Mormon, the man destined before the world was formed to abridge and summarize the Nephite story—and in so doing to have his name forever immortalized with this additional testament of Jesus Christ—surveyed the casualties of a nation that had turned from the Lord. As sobering as the account is, it does not give a full account of all the sin and sadness Mormon had seen. Indeed, such an account probably would have been impossible to record."

ELDER JEFFREY R. HOLLAND | *Christ and the New Covenant, p.317*

Mormon 1-6

In these chapters

Ammaron tells young Mormon about the records   //   Great War between Nephites and Lamanites   //   Wickedness covers the land   //   15-year-old Mormon visited by the Lord   //   Mormon leads Nephite armies at age 16   //   Terrible wars   //   Mormon cries repentance   //   Mormon refuses to lead armies   //   More terrible wars   //   Lamanites begin to prevail   //   Mormon again leads armies   //   Nephites gather to Cumorah for final battle   //   Mormon hides sacred records   //   Nephites destroyed

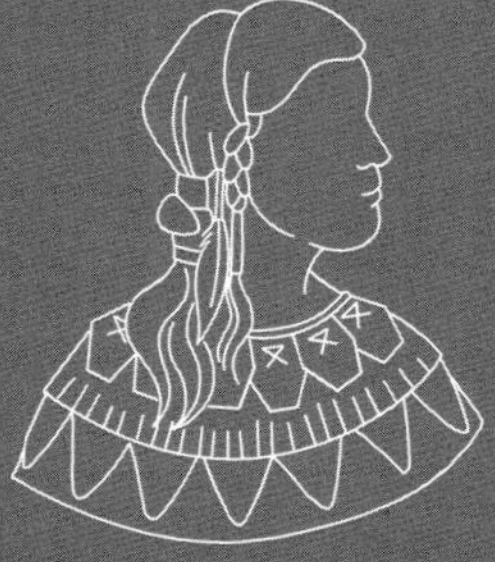

Mormon

It is now Mormon's turn to record the events in the day that he lived.

Mormon will write the first seven chapters in this book and then his son, Moroni, will add two more chapters, add an abridgment of the book of Ether, and then complete the record with his own book.

Mormon knew who he was addressing - he was not addressing his own people - for they were to be destroyed. He was addressing the future Lamanite descendants and those who would live in the last days. In verse 1, he is telling us that he will record what he has seen and heard. And the things he had witnessed were terrible things.

Mormon can now tell us how bad a civilization can become after they choose rebellion over God.

Mormon 1

Write or draw what you learn in these verses.

VERSES 1–4

Ammaron instructs Mormon

VERSES 5–14

Life during Mormon's childhood

VERSES 15–17

Mormon as a teenager

VERSES 18–19

The wickedness in Mormon's day

What do you think Mormon meant when, at 15 years old, he had "tasted and knew of the goodness of Jesus"?

When have you "tasted and knew of the goodness of Jesus"?

Mormon 2

Another war broke out between the Nephites and the Lamanites, and the people of Nephi appointed Mormon to be the leader of their armies. Mormon was only 16 years old at this time, but the people recognized his abilities, just as Ammaron had. His youth did not keep the people from looking to him, nor did it stop Mormon from leading.

Write or draw what you learn in these verses.

(1) **1-2** | *Mormon becomes leader of armies*

(2) **3-9** | *Terrible battle*

(3) **10-15** | *Nephites sorrowing*

(4) **16-19** | *Mormon retrieves plates*

(5) **20-29** | *Battles and agreements*

Mormon 3

Repentance was the Nephites' very best battle plan. So Mormon tells them to repent, but they rejected him.

Write or draw what you learn in these verses.

(1) **1-3** | *Mormon instructed to cry repentance*

(2) **4-10** | *Preparation and battle*

(3) **11-13** | *Mormon refuses to lead Nephites*

(4) **14-16** | *What will happen to the Nephites*

(5) **17-22** | *Mormon addresses us in last days (those who will read his record)*

Mormon 4

If there were ever a chapter to show that war should be avoided whenever possible – this is the chapter. Write or draw what you learn in these verses.

MORMON 4:1–6	**MORMON 4:7–9**	**MORMON 4:10–14**
Nephites attack the Lamanites	*Nephites retake city and lose many*	*Terrible war*

MORMON 4:15	**MORMON 4:16–22**	**MORMON 4:23**
The last battle the Nephites will win	*Nephites begin to be swept off*	*Mormon moves records*

Mormon 5

Mormon became the commander of the armies again. He could see all of the mistakes they were making and he loved them. They wanted him back because, with him, they had won before – so their hope was all in him. But Mormon did not have hope. He knew far more than they did. He knew the prophecies, and he knew what path they had chosen – he knew the judgments of God were upon them (see verse 2). Write or draw what you learn in these verses.

1–9	*Mormon takes command / more battles*
10–11	*Mormon speaks to us who will have the record*
12–15	*Mormon prophesies of this record*
16–21	*What has happened to the Nephites*
22–24	*Will we learn from their story?*

Mormon 6

(1) MORMON 6:1

The final story of the Nephites

(2) MORMON 6:2–5

Gathering at Cumorah

(3) MORMON 6:6

Mormon hides records

(4) MORMON 6:7–10

Final battle begins

(5) MORMON 6:11–15

Death toll

(6) MORMON 6:16–22

Mormon's cry to his people now gone

Keep your own record side-by-side with these great prophets testifying of these important doctrines and principles.

O ye fair ones

Following the tremendous battle at Cumorah, Mormon looked out over the catastrophic carnage – the destruction of a thousand years of dreams – and cried to ears that could no longer hear:

"O ye fair ones, how could ye have departed from the ways of the Lord! O ye fair ones, how could ye have rejected that Jesus, who stood with open arms to receive you!

"Behold, if ye had not done this, ye would not have fallen!...."

Elder Jeffrey R. Holland

Christ and the New Covenant, 321

WHAT DO YOU THINK MORMON HOPES WE LEARN FROM HIS RECORD?

Mormon 7–9

In these chapters

Mormon's final words   //   Moroni takes over records   //   Moroni's warnings to those who do not believe in Christ

Chapter 7 contains Mormon's last words. He knows that he has been writing to those who will one day receive the record he has put together. He has now completed his duty to abridge the Nephite history—he has read all of their records and selected the most important things for us to know. He has now witnessed the destruction of his entire people. Now, after all he has witnessed, and done, and learned—what do you think he will write to us in his final chapter?

Moroni, Mormon's son, then took over the recordkeeping in Mormon 8.

Mormon 7 has a date of 385 A.D., and Mormon 8 gives the dates of 400–421 A.D. which means that it had been at least fifteen years since the great battle at Cumorah. Mormon was now gone and his son Moroni now has the plates and he intends to finish his father's record, which his father had commanded him to do (see Mormon 8:1).

Write or draw what you learn in these verses.

Mormon's Final Words

VERSES 1–4
Mormon's message to the future

VERSES 5–7
What to know about Christ

VERSES 8–10
The power of the Book of Mormon and Bible

IF YOU COULD LEAVE A FINAL MESSAGE TO THE WORLD, WHAT MESSAGE WOULD YOU LEAVE?

Mormon 8

Mormon 8:1–3
Report on the last and final battle

Mormon 8:4–5
Moroni

Mormon 8:6–11
Lamanites at war - Three Nephite disciples

Mormon 8:12–14
The worth of the record

Mormon 8:15–16
How the record will come forth to the world

Mormon 8:17–22
Warnings

Mormon 8:23–24
A voice crying from the dust

Mormon 8:25–27
When the Book of Mormon will come forth

Mormon 8:28–33
What the world will be like when the Book of Mormon comes forth

Mormon 8:34–35
Mormon has seen our day

Mormon 8:36–37
What he saw

Mormon 8:38–41
Warnings for us

Mormon 9

Now Moroni addresses those that do not believe in Christ at all. These verses can help us know what we might say to someone who says something like, "When I die and get to the other side and find that Jesus is real, then I will follow Him." Moroni explains that it will not be that easy—this is how you will feel if you have rejected Him and His laws.

Write or draw what you learn in these verses.

1-6 | **Those who deny Christ**

7-10 | **Those who deny revelation and spiritual gifts**

11-14 | **God is a God of miracles**

15-20 | **God still works through miracles**

21-27 | **Signs follow those who believe**

28-29 | **Be wise**

30-37 | **Moroni's words**

"Seek and expect miracles."

PRESIDENT RUSSELL M. NELSON | April 2022 General Conference

WHAT MIRACLES HAVE YOU SEEN IN YOUR LIFE?

Ether

- The book of Ether is a record of an entire civilization, who like the Nephites, were guided to the promised land. Like the Nephites, they were given the gospel. Like the Nephites, they had prophets among them. And like the Nephites, secret combinations spread among them and their civilization was ultimately destroyed

Helpful Information

- The Jaredites' civilization lasted 1600 years (about 2200 B.C. to about 600 B.C).

- The Nephite civilization lasted just under 1,000 years (about 600 B.C. to about 385 A.D.)

"Wherefore, I, Moroni, am commanded to write
these things that evil may be done away, and that
the time may come that Satan may have no
power upon the hearts of the children of men, but
that they may be persuaded to do good continually, that they may come unto the fountain of all
righteousness and be saved."

Ether 8:26

ETHER

Timeline

Here is Ether at-a-glance. The main stories are found in the timeline below. If you ever want to find a story in your scriptures, you can look at this page for help. You can add your own notes to this page as well.

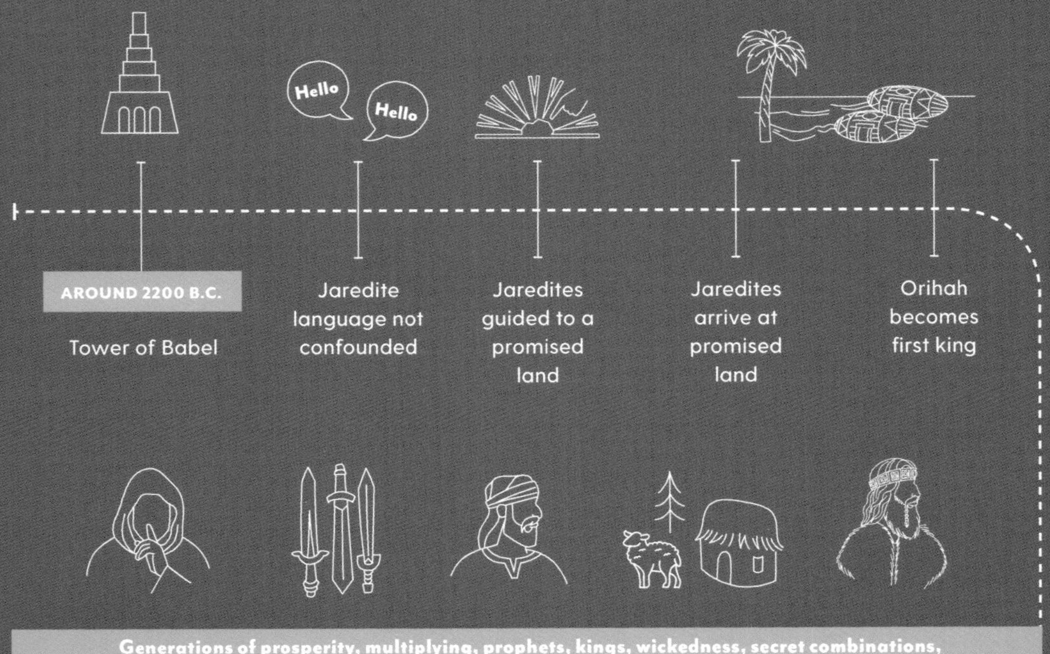

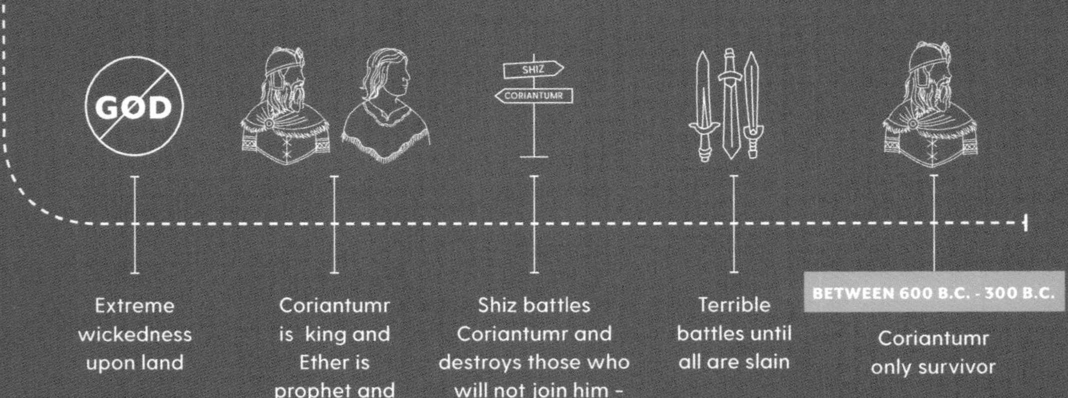

People to Know

If you need a reminder of who is who, return to this page.

Moroni

Moroni abridged the Jaredite records and added insights into the record, just like his father Mormon had done throughout the Book of Mormon.

Jared

Jared was founder of the Jaredites and lived during the Tower of Babel. His people did not have their language confounded. Jared and his people were guided to the promised land.

Brother of Jared

The brother of Jared was a large and mighty man who was highly favored of the Lord. He prayed to not have their language confounded. He saw the finger of the Lord and then saw and conversed with the Lord.

Orihah

Orihah was Jared's son and the first Jaredite king. He reigned in righteousness.

Ether

Ether was a prophet in the days of Coriantumr. He wrote the Jaredite record on 24 gold plates. Ether saw the destruction of the Jaredites.

Coriantumr

Coriantumr was a Jaredite king and the last Jaredite survivor. He had been warned by Ether. He discovered the people of Zarahemla.

Jaredite Kings

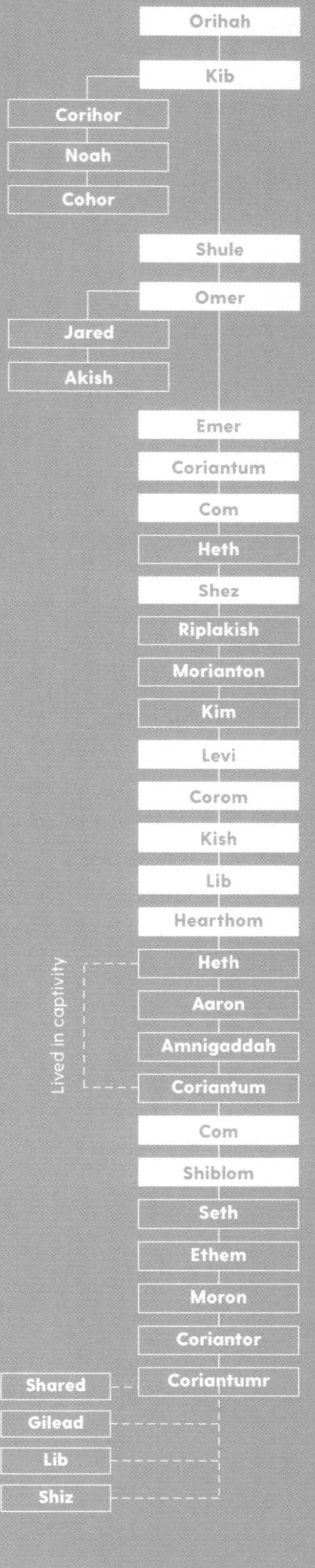

Ether 1–5

In these chapters

Jaredites' language confounded // The Jaredites will be led to a choice land // The Jaredites build barges // The sixteen stones // The brother of Jared sees the Lord // Future witnesses of the Book of Mormon

What Is the Book of Ether?

1. The book of Ether is a record of the Jaredites.

2. The Jaredites were named after their first leader whose name was Jared.

3. Jared lived during the time of the Tower of Babel (see Genesis 11). God led Jared and his group to the Americas around 2200 B.C.

4. The Jaredites lived in the Americas until sometime between 600 and 300 B.C. when they destroyed themselves through war.

5. The Jaredites lived upon the land longer than the Nephite civilization.

6. The book is named after the prophet Ether, who was the last Jaredite prophet and created a record of their history.

7. Moroni abridged Ether's record and added it to the gold plates.

8. If Moroni did not do the work of adding this record to the plates, we would have no idea these people ever existed.

9. Imagine the kinship that Moroni would have felt for Ether. They were both the last surviving prophets. They both witnessed the destruction of people they loved. They both had the task of telling future generations the history of their people.

10. Five hundred years before Moroni lived, Limhi sent a search party to find Zarahemla. Instead, they found Jaredite ruins and found 24 gold plates. Nephite record keepers then passed those plates down through the generations until Moroni received them.

11. Moroni explained that he could not include "the hundredth part" of Ether's record. So there are many details we still do not know.

12. Moroni included this record for us. It is another civilization that teaches the same truths that we learn from the Nephite civilization. When a people trust God and follow His commandments, they prosper. When they reject God, they experience all manner of suffering and ultimate destruction.

13. The Jaredites' ending is even more tragic than the Nephites'. Unlike the Lamanites, who still have descendants upon the earth today, the Jaredite civilization was brought to extinction.

Ether 1

Moroni began the history of the Jaredites with a sad introduction. Moroni had just witnessed the destruction of the Nephites, and now he had a record of another people who experienced the same fate. How might this record help us in the last days?

Write or draw what you learn in these verses.

VERSES 1-2 | *Moroni's introduction*

VERSES 3-5 | *What Moroni is and is not including*

VERSES 6-32 | *Ether's family line*

VERSE 33 | *Jared and the Tower of Babel*

VERSES 34-37 | *The brother of Jared*

VERSES 38-43 | *The Lord's plan for Jared's people*

Ether 2

They have prayed and asked for it, and now the Lord is going to lead them to the promised land, one step at a time. This journey will require a LOT of effort, planning, and faith.

Write or draw what you learn in these verses.

VERSES 1–3	**VERSES 4–7**	**VERSES 8–12**
The journey begins	*The Lord instructs the brother of Jared*	*The decrees of God concerning the land they were being guided to (the Americas)*

VERSES 13–15
Four years at the seashore

VERSES 16–17	**VERSES 18–20**	**VERSES 21–25**
The instruction to build barges	*No light and no air*	*No light*

WHAT ARE SOME "BARGES" THE LORD HAS ASKED YOU TO BUILD? WHAT PROBLEMS AROSE? HOW DID HE HELP YOU?

The Brother of Jared Goes to Mount Shelem

The brother of Jared then goes to mount Shelem in order to find a way for them to receive light. Shelem means "ladder" or "stairway," and it was an exceedingly tall mountain - so this would have taken a lot of effort—he will do all he can to ascend to the Lord.

Write or draw what you learn in these verses.

VERSE 1 | *What the brother of Jared does*

VERSES 2–5 | *The brother of Jared's prayer*

VERSES 6–9 | *The Lord touches the stones*

VERSES 10–13 | *The Lord appears to the brother of Jared*

VERSES 14–16 | *Who Jesus is*

"Christ was saying to the brother of Jared, 'Never have I showed myself unto man in this manner, without my volition, driven solely by the faith of the beholder.' As a rule, prophets are invited into the presence of the Lord, are bidden to enter his presence by him and only with his sanction. The brother of Jared, on the other hand, seems to have thrust himself through the veil, not as an unwelcome guest but perhaps technically as an uninvited one. ... Obviously the Lord himself was linking unprecedented faith with this unprecedented vision. If the vision itself was not unique, then it had to be the faith and how the vision was obtained that was so unparalleled. The only way that faith could be so remarkable was its ability to take the prophet, uninvited, where others had been able to go only with God's bidding."

ELDER JEFFREY R. HOLLAND | Christ and the New Covenant, 23

VERSES 17–20 | *What Moroni wants you to know*

VERSES 21–24 | *The brother of Jared's sealed record*

VERSES 25–26 | *The brother of Jared's vision*

VERSES 27–28 | *Instruction*

Ether 4

The Lord commanded the brother of Jared to write what he had seen (which included the history of the world—see Ether 3:25), and then those writings were forbidden to come forth until after the death of Jesus Christ.

Write or draw what you learn in these verses.

Verses 1–3

The brother of Jared's record

In verse 2, we learn that after Christ came to the Nephites and they became an incredibly righteous people, then they were able to receive Jared's record.

Verses 4–7

Moroni's words

Verses 8–10

Warning

Verses 11–12

Those who believe

Verses 13–16

The Lord's words to us in the last days

Verses 17–19

The coming forth of the Book of Mormon

The Three Witnesses

Moroni prophesied that three witnesses will "be shown [the plates] by the power of God" and "shall know of a surety that these things are true."

Write or draw about the impact the sermon had on the people.

Verses 1–6

There will be three witnesses of the plates

This was fulfilled when Joseph took Martin Harris, Oliver Cowdery, and David Whitmer into the woods near the Whitmer home in Fayette, New York. Together they knelt in prayer and as they did so, nothing happened. Martin determined that he was the reason nothing was happening, so he got up and left and the others again began to pray.

An angel then appeared and he had the plates in his hands. He showed the men the pages and the engravings. A table also appeared with the interpreters, sword, Liahona, and breastplate.

After the vision, Joseph found Martin praying in the woods and Joseph prayed with him. The angel then appeared again and displayed the plates and other objects to Martin.

Over the years, all three witnesses left the Church, and then later Martin and Oliver returned to the Church. But none of them ever denied the reality of the plates and the vision they had.

"The Three Witnesses never denied their testimony of the Book of Mormon. They could not because they knew it was true. They made sacrifices and faced difficulties beyond what most people ever know. Oliver Cowdery gave the same testimony about the divine origin of the Book of Mormon as he lay dying. …That they continued to affirm what they saw and heard in that marvelous experience, during long periods of estrangement from the Church and from Joseph, makes their testimony more powerful."

PRESIDENT HENRY B. EYRING | Oct 2003 General Conference

Ether 6–11

In these chapters

Jaredite barges sail to promised land // Arrival to promised land // Some righteous kings, some wicked kings // Contention and secret combinations corrupt the land // Prophets warn of Jaredite destruction if the people do not repent

They now had a light source. The ships that had once been dark were now filled with light. It had happened—look what faith can bring to pass. Look how the Lord can work miracles. Look how the Lord can take stones and turn them into something so much greater.

What stones do you need to be turned into light?

Ether 7 begins the story of the royal Jaredite line. Moroni will tell us in Ether 15:33 that he could not include a hundredth part of the record of Ether in his abridgment. In Moroni's condensed version, he follows this royal line and tells us what became of each king, the struggle this line experienced to keep the crown, the secret combinations upon the land, and the wars that happened until they ultimately destroyed themselves. You will learn that there were prophets, but you don't learn their names or hear their stories. Instead, Moroni shows how the promised land is lost through wickedness and secret combinations from those seeking power.

Ether 6

Write or draw what you learn in these verses.

1–3	4–11
The stones give light	The journey on the sea

12–18	19–21
Arrival to promised land	The people gathered

22–23	24–30
The dangers of a king	A king is chosen

Ether 7

Write or draw what you learn in these verses.

1–7	8–13
The rebellion of Corihor	Shule battles Corihor

14–18	19–21
Noah carries Shule away captive	A divided kingdom

22	23–27
Kingdom again united	Shule protects the prophets

Ether 8

The Jaredite civilization will show how difficult it is to have peace on the throne. Omer became the next king, and his son Jared rebelled against him and took many people with him to the land of Heth. Here Moroni gives us Jared's tactics to gain followers. He flattered and used cunning words—and he did this so successfully that he gained half the kingdom. Write or draw what you learn in these verses.

VERSES 1–2	**VERSES 3–7**	**VERSES 8–14**
How Jared convinced people to follow him	Omer in captivity	Secret combinations introduced
VERSES 15–18	**VERSES 19–22**	**VERSES 23–26**
Secret combinations	Warning against secret combinations	Moroni warns and instructs us in the last days

Ether 9

Those who had conspired together were able to overthrow Omer's kingdom (see verse 1). Just like the Lord protected Nephi and told him to leave Laman and Lemuel, so He warned Omer in a dream. Omer was able to protect his family, so they left and moved with their households to a far distant land and were out of reach of those who were bringing destruction upon their land. Write or draw what you learn in these verses.

VERSES 1–3	**VERSES 4–9**	**VERSES 10–14**
Omer is warned	Seeking power	Wicked turning on their own
VERSES 15–24	**VERSES 25–28**	**VERSES 29–35**
Peace and prosperity	More secret combinations and wickedness	Famine and poisonous serpents

Ether 10

Shez was a better king. He remembered the famine, and he remembered that the Lord had brought Jared and his brother to that land. He remembered, so he had perspective and reigned in righteousness, which was a great blessing for his people. But not all kings are like this.

Write or draw what you learn in these verses.

① **1-4** | *Shez reigns*

② **5-8** | *Riplakish reigns*

③ **9-12** | *Morianton becomes king*

④ **13-19** | *Kim, Levi, Corom, Kish, and Lib are king*

⑤ **20-28** | *Jaredite life*

⑥ **29-34** | *Hearthom and next four generations in captivity*

Ether 11

The Jaredite kingly line is in captivity at this point. We don't learn anything about the other kings who were ruling the land while the royal line was in captivity, but we do learn that there was a return of secret combinations. When Com became king, he fought against those secret combinations but he was not successful. The Jaredites were now getting closer and closer to their final days.

Write or draw what you learn in these verses.

① **1-3** | *Many prophets*

② **4-9** | *People brought to repentance*

③ **10-14** | *Such wickedness that the prophets withdraw*

④ **15-18** | *End of royal Jaredite line as king*

⑤ **19-23** | *Coriantor and Ether*

Ether 12–15

In these chapters

The prophet Ether   //   New Jerusalem to be upon the Americas   //
War over all the land   //   Coriantumr, Gilead, Lib, and Shiz engage in
war   //   Jaredites destroyed   //   Coriantumr the only survivor

Ether 12 begins a record of the final Jaredite generation.

Ether was a descendant of Jared and part of the royal line. His grandfather, Moron, had been king of the Jaredites but had been put into captivity, and the throne was now held by a man named Coriantumr.

Instead of being the Jaredite king, Ether was "a prophet of the Lord," and he was positioned to have a lot of influence because the people would have known who he was. Ether understood the situation his people were in, and even though he was not their king, he was the leader they needed him to be.

Ether "could not be restrained" and "he did cry from the morning, even until the going down of the sun" (verse 3). He gave it everything he had to save his people.

Write or draw what you learn in these verses.

ETHER 12:1–5

The Prophet Ether

Imagine the kinship that Moroni felt with Ether. Both of them witnessed the destruction of their nation who refused to repent. They both saw how there were secret combinations in their lands moving the people deeper and deeper into wickedness. Moroni understood exactly what Ether was trying to do, and Moroni now stopped telling Ether's story and spends the rest of this chapter speaking to us in the last days about faith.

6–22

Moroni's teachings about faith

23–25

Moroni's concern

26–28

The answer

29–33

The power of faith

34–37

Charity

38–41

Seek this Jesus

AND IF MEN COME UNTO ME I WILL SHOW UNTO THEM THEIR WEAKNESS. I GIVE UNTO MEN WEAKNESS THAT THEY MAY BE HUMBLE; AND MY GRACE IS SUFFICIENT FOR ALL MEN THAT HUMBLE THEMSELVES BEFORE ME; FOR IF THEY HUMBLE THEMSELVES BEFORE ME, AND HAVE FAITH IN ME, THEN WILL I MAKE WEAK THINGS BECOME STRONG UNTO THEM.

Leave a Record

Keep your own record side-by-side with these great prophets
testifying of these important doctrines and principles.

WEAKNESSES THE LORD HELPED BECOME STRENGTHS IN MY LIFE...

Ether 13

Moroni now returns to the story of the Jaredites and how they rejected all of the words of Ether. In verse 2, look how hard Ether tried to save his people—"he truly told them all things." He explained the truth, but they rejected it. And notice the specific truth that Moroni mentioned in verse 2—Ether had taught that the land they had been given had been chosen from the very beginning. When Christ created the earth, He designated this land as "a choice land above all other lands, a chosen land of the Lord." So those who are upon this land must serve the Lord—and the people in Ether's day were not. Write or draw what you learn in these verses.

VERSES 1–2	VERSES 3–13	VERSES 14–19
What Ether taught	The future of the land	Ether cast out / State of the people

VERSES 20–22	VERSES 23–31
Ether to go to Coriantumr	The state of the people

Ether 14

From here on, there will be no peace among the Jaredites. The previous kings had not been able to overpower the secret combinations, so they were now going to be destroyed by them. Coriantumr will spend the rest of his days trying to keep his throne and will either be in battle or be in between battles, and the people will be in the middle of it all. Write or draw what you learn in these verses.

VERSES 1–2	VERSES 3–9	VERSES 10–16
State of the Jaredites	Coriantumr vs. Gilead	Coriantumr vs. Lib

VERSES 17–20	VERSES 21–23	VERSES 24–31
Coriantumr vs. Shiz	The effects of war	Terrible destruction

Coriantumr Remembers the Words of the Prophets

Coriantumr had just escaped death and the words that he once rejected from Ether were now coming to pass. Two million of his mighty men, their wives, and their children had already been killed. So he began to remember the words of the prophets, "and he saw them that they were fulfilled thus far, every whit" (Ether 15:3). Ether had warned him and other prophets had prophesied of this, and now the evidence of their prophecies were before him. Write or draw what you learn in these verses.

VERSES 1–5	VERSES 6–10	VERSES 11–14
Coriantumr remembers and repents	*Relentless battles*	*Gathering for the final battle*

The Final Battle

Verses 15–16 **DAY 1**	Verses 17–19 **DAY 2**	Verse 20 **DAY 3**	Verses 21–22 **DAY 4**
Verses 23–24 **DAY 5**	Verses 25–26 **DAY 6**	Verses 27–28 **DAY 7**	Verses 29–34 **DAY 8**

WHY DO YOU THINK THE LORD WANTED MORONI TO INCLUDE THE BOOK OF ETHER IN THE BOOK OF MORMON RECORD?

Moroni

- The Book of Moroni contains the teachings of three people:

  1. Moroni's own teachings
  2. The words of Christ to His Nephite disciples (see Moroni 2)
  3. Things Mormon taught in the synagogue or in epistles to Moroni (Moroni 7–9)

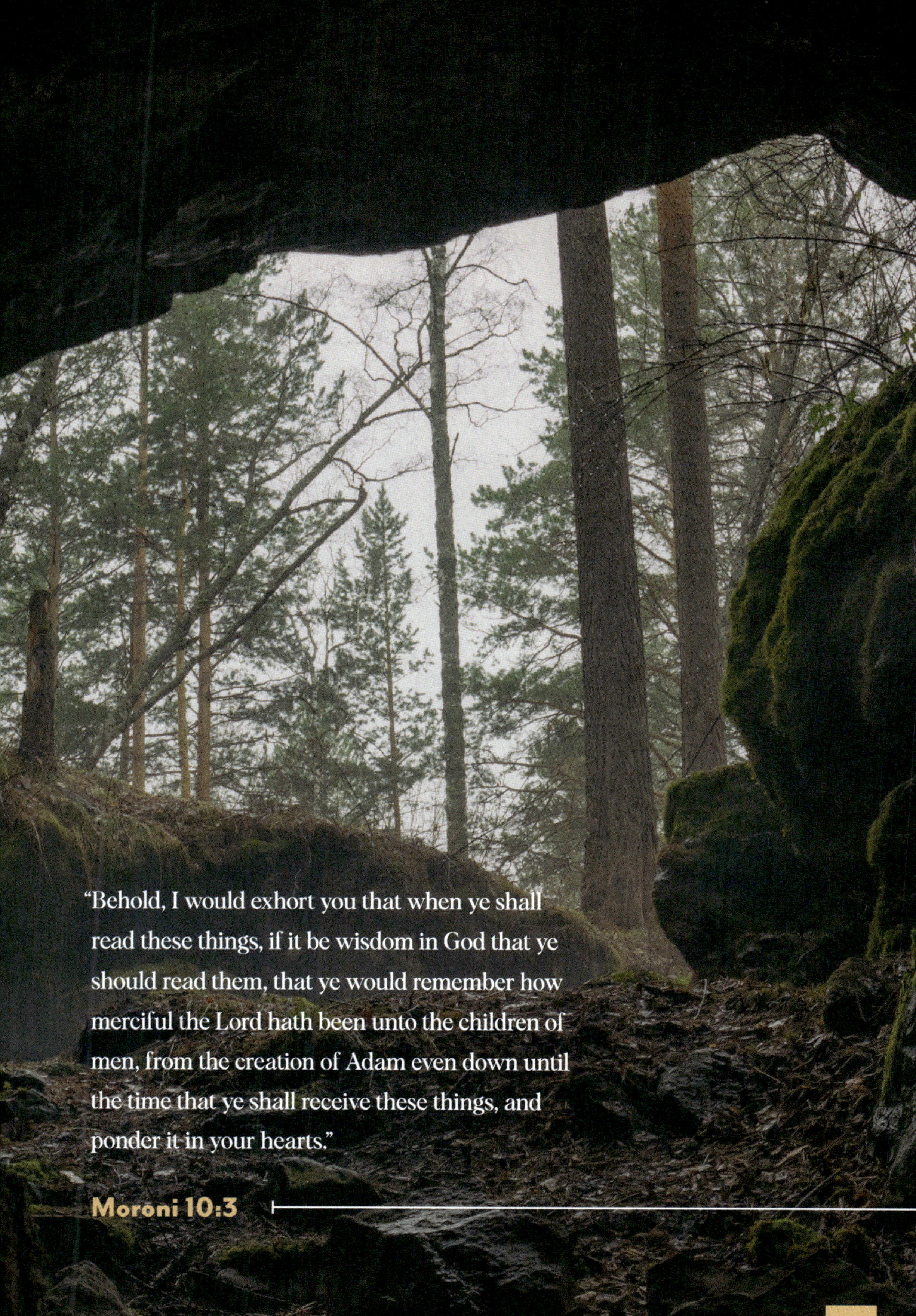

"Behold, I would exhort you that when ye shall read these things, if it be wisdom in God that ye should read them, that ye would remember how merciful the Lord hath been unto the children of men, from the creation of Adam even down until the time that ye shall receive these things, and ponder it in your hearts."

Moroni 10:3

Things to Know

Outline of Book

MORONI 1–6	Moroni includes important details about ordinances, purposes of Church meetings, and more.
MORONI 7	Moroni added to the plates a sermon by his father Mormon, including righteous judgment and teachings about charity.
MORONI 8–9	Moroni includes two epistles (or letters) by his father Mormon.
MORONI 10	Moroni completes his record by inviting all who read the Book of Mormon to pray to know for themselves that it is true.

The dates for this book are around 401–421 A.D. The great war occurred around 385 A.D. which means Moroni wrote this book 16 to 36 years after the Nephites were wiped off the land.

Who is Moroni?

MORONI WAS ALONE AND WANDERING FOR THE SAFETY OF HIS LIFE WHEN HE WROTE THIS BOOK.

Imagining Moroni's Life...

Moroni 1–6

In these chapters

Moroni will not deny the Christ // Moroni wanders for safety // Moroni teaches the words that Christ spoke to His disciples // Moroni teaches about ordinations // Moroni teaches about the administration of the sacrament // Moroni teaches about baptism and Church meetings

Moroni

Moroni thought he was done writing upon the plates. His father had commanded him to finish the record of the Nephites, which he did in Mormon 8 and 9. The Nephites were now destroyed – so there was nothing left to write about them. But he was still alive, still alone, and now we will get the ten chapters in the book of Moroni which are rich and very valuable.

Moroni explained that he was going to add to the plates things that were "of worth … in some future day" (Moroni 1:4). For example, in Moroni 2 he added details about what Christ instructed the Nephite apostles concerning the ordinance of bestowing the gift of the Holy Ghost (or confirmation). This is a saving ordinance, which means that it is essential to our exaltation.

As you read each chapter, ask yourself, "How has this chapter been of great worth for my day—the day in which the gospel was restored?" Remember that Moroni was the messenger of the Restoration, and he was already fulfilling that role before he ever instructed Joseph Smith.

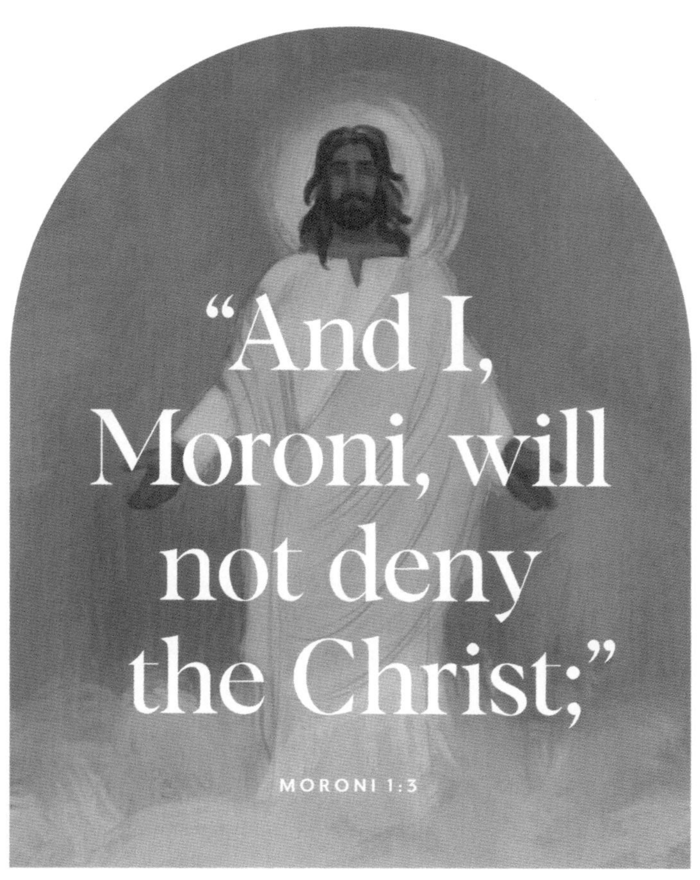

Moroni thought he was done writing upon the plates. His father had commanded him to finish the record of the Nephites, which he did in Mormon 8 and 9. The Nephites were now destroyed—so there was nothing left to write about them. But he was still alive, still alone, and now we will get these ten chapters in Moroni, which are rich and very valuable.

WRITE WHAT YOU LEARN IN MORONI 1

Moroni 2

Write or draw what you learn in Moroni 2.

Moroni 3

Write or draw what you learn in Moroni 3.

Moroni 4 & 5

When the Book of Mormon would come forth to the world, the ordinance of the sacrament would need to be restored, and here Moroni included instruction and the very prayers needed to restore this sacred ordinance.

ADMINISTERING THE BREAD	ADMINISTERING THE WINE
Write or draw what you learn in Moroni 4.	*Write or draw what you learn in Moroni 5.*

Moroni 6

These chapters are similar to the Church handbook. Moroni has clarifiied how to perform ordinances correctly and now he will teach about how an individual qualifies for baptism, how Church members should be nourished, and how Church meetings should be conducted.

Write or draw what you learn in these verses.

VERSES 1–3	VERSES 4–8	VERSE 9
Requirements for an individual to be baptized	How to nourish members	How meetings should be conducted

Nourished by the good word of God...

"Most people don't come to church looking merely for a few new gospel facts or to see old friends, though all of that is important. They come seeking a spiritual experience. They want peace. They want their faith fortified and their hope renewed. They want, in short, to be nourished by the good word of God, to be strengthened by the powers of heaven. Those of us who are called upon to speak or teach or lead have an obligation to help provide that, as best we possibly can."

ELDER JEFFREY R. HOLLAND | April 1998 General Conference

WHEN ARE TIMES YOU HAVE BEEN NOURISHED BY THE GOOD WORD OF GOD AT CHURCH?

Moroni 7–9

In these chapters

Moroni writes about righteous judgment by the Spirit, faith, miracles, charity   //   Mormon's two letters to his son Moroni

Moroni 7

In chapter 7, Moroni adds a sermon his father had given many years earlier. This sermon was about faith, hope, and charity and was given to faithful members of the Nephite Church.

Chapter 7 is packed with principles that are relevant to anyone seeking to be a disciple of Jesus Christ.

WHAT WISDOM CAN YOU GAIN FROM THIS CHAPTER?

Moroni 8–9

Moroni also includes two epistles (or letters) that his father had sent him. Moroni 8 is one epistle, and Moroni 9 is another.

Moroni 7

Write or draw what you learn in these verses.

VERSES 1–4	**VERSES 5–9**	**VERSES 10–13**
Peaceable followers of Christ	Real intent	Things of God

VERSES 14–19	**VERSES 20–28**	**VERSES 29–31**
How to judge righteously	How to lay hold of good things	Angels

VERSES 32–39	**VERSES 40–44**	**VERSES 45–48**
The power of faith	Hope and charity	Charity and how to obtain it

Mormon's Epistle to Moroni

Here in Moroni 8, we learn some new things about Moroni. Before now, we knew that Moroni was a commander in the Nephite army and was charged with stewardship of the sacred records. But here, we learn that Moroni was called to the ministry, and Mormon wrote his son and gave him guidance.

Write or draw what you learn in these verses.

VERSES 1–3 | *A father's letter*

VERSES 4–11 | *Doctrinal question: Do little children need to be baptized?*

VERSES 12–15 | *The doctrine*

VERSES 16–17 | *Why Mormon does not fear if this doctrine upsets some people*

VERSES 18–21 | *More doctrine*

VERSES 22–24 | *More doctrine*

VERSES 25–26 | *The power of baptism*

VERSES 27–30 | *Nephite wickedness*

How can you declare boldly like Mormon did?

(SEE VERSES 16 AND 17)

Mormon's Second Epistle to Moroni

Mormon did not go into much detail in his own book about how wicked the Nephites had become and what specific things they were doing. But in this letter to Moroni, we will learn of a few things - and it is truly terrible. All Mormon told us were things like, "And it is impossible for the tongue to describe, or for man to write a perfect description of the horrible scene of the blood and carnage which was among the people, both of the Nephites and of the Lamanites; and every heart was hardened, so that they delighted in the shedding of blood continually" (Mormon 4:11). And now here we will see more of what he meant.

Write or draw what you learn in these verses.

VERSES 1–5	*The state of the Nephites*
VERSE 6	*Mormon's call to labor more*
VERSES 7–10	*The state of the Nephites*
VERSES 11–15	*So much abomination*
VERSES 16–21	*The state of the Nephites*
VERSES 22–26	*Mormon's words to his son*

Moroni 10

In this chapter

A testimony of the Book of Mormon comes through the power of the Holy Ghost // Gifts of the Spirit // Come unto Christ

THIS IS MORONI'S LAST CHAPTER, THE FINAL PAGES UPON THE PLATES. THIS WAS WRITTEN OVER 30 YEARS AFTER THE FINAL BATTLE AND MORONI HAS HAD A LOT OF TIME TO PONDER AND GAIN GREAT WISDOM. THESE LAST WORDS OF HIS ARE OVERFLOWING WITH RICHNESS, AND THEY HAVE IMPACTED MILLIONS OF LIVES AND WILL YET IMPACT MILLIONS MORE.

Moroni 10

Write or draw what you learn in these verses.

(1) MORONI 10:1–7

Moroni's invitation

(2) MORONI 10:8–19

The gifts of the Spirit

(3) MORONI 10:20–23

Faith, hope, and charity

(4) MORONI 10:24–29

Remember this

(5) MORONI 10:30–34

Come unto Christ; farewell

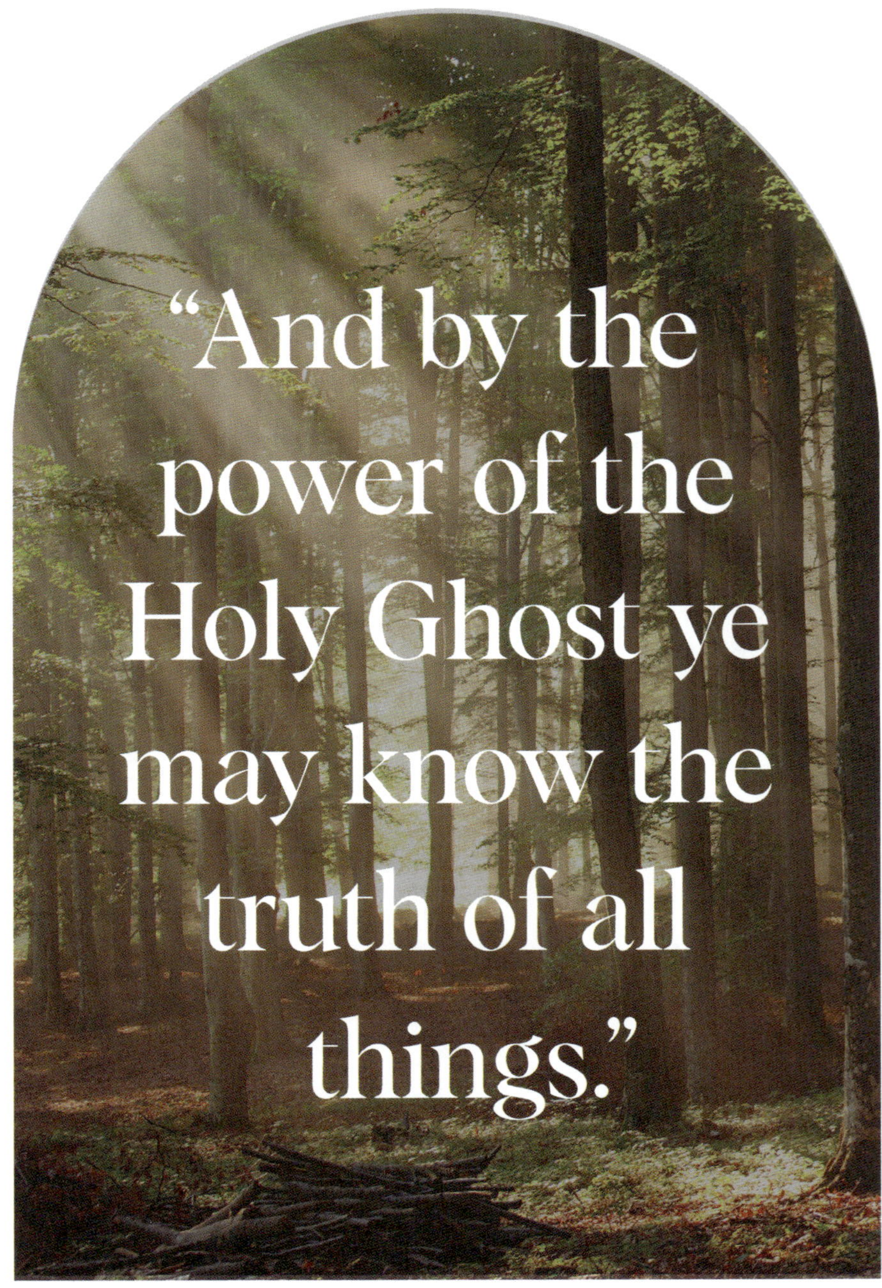

"And by the power of the Holy Ghost ye may know the truth of all things."

WHAT ARE SOME LESSONS, STORIES, AND TEACHINGS FROM THE
BOOK OF MORMON THAT YOU NEVER WANT TO FORGET?